DATE DUE

REAL GRASS, REAL HEROES

REAL GRASS, REAL HEROES

Baseball's Historic 1941 Season
By Dom DiMaggio
with
Bill Gilbert
Introduction by Ted Williams

ZEBRA BOOKS
KENSINGTON PUBLISHING CORP.

To Baseball

America's game, then, now and always—

To those who came before us and gave birth to our sport and nurtured it.

To those who came after us and strengthened its appeal while preserving its integrity.

To those players and others in our time who made personal and financial sacrifices to advance our sport toward today's enduring success and popularity.

To the stars, the colorful characters and all those who played major league baseball in 1941, and

To My Family

My wonderful wife, Emily, and our three children, who have blessed our years—Paul, Peter, and Emily,

Who will learn in these pages what a blessing it was for me to be able to play major league baseball.

Just now baseball is enjoying what may turn out to be the most amazing year of its long history.

——Baseball columnist Dan Daniel, 1941

CONTENTS

A SPECIAL NOTE

This book has been a delight to write, as we relived the special season that was 1941. The whole experience was made even more enjoyable by the help of so many people.

We spoke to the baseball players themselves who together made 1941 what it was then and remains today. With their help, and especially that of the man who was my teammate and remains my friend, Ted Williams, this has become more than the story of one baseball player. Instead, it is the story of all those who were good enough and fortunate enough to be able to play baseball in the major leagues in 1941.

For their time and insights, and for the pleasure of their company, in alphabetical order we thank:

Bobby Doerr	Mickey Owen
Bob Feller	Johnny Pesky
Tom Ferrick	Pee Wee Reese
Tommy Henrich	Enos Slaughter
Charlie Keller	Johnny Vander Meer
Ken Keltner	Mickey Vernon

Eddie Lopat   Charlie Wagner
Walt Masterson   Ted Williams
Johnny Mize

We also are grateful to two of the most respected members of the baseball media from that era, broadcaster Red Barber, who was the play-by-play radio announcer for the Brooklyn Dodgers in 1941, and Shirley Povich of the *Washington Post,* who covered the baseball beat and wrote a daily sports column in those years.

Bill Deane, senior research associate of the National Baseball Library at the Hall of Fame, research assistant Sean Rooney, and Pat Kelly, the library's photo collection manager, were valuable sources of information and verification. The staff of the Library of Congress was also helpful. So was Elizabeth Dooley, the beloved eighty-six-year-old fan of the Boston Red Sox, who has been a season ticket holder since the 1930s and still never misses a game at Fenway Park.

We are also pleased to thank our editor at Zebra Books, Wallace Exman, and our agent, Russell Galen, a vice president of the Scott Meredith Literary Agency.

Special thanks are also due to Dave Gilbert and Lillian Gilbert for their editing, and to our mutual good friend Ed Liberatore, who is known and respected by so many people in baseball, for making this account possible in the first place.

Dom DiMaggio and Bill Gilbert
April 1990

INTRODUCTION

by Ted Williams

Asking me to write about the 1941 baseball season is doing me a favor, especially for a book by my friend Dom DiMaggio.

Dom and I shared that season. We played next to each other in the outfield of the Boston Red Sox, and we hit first and third in the batting order. No two teammates ever had more respect or friendship for each other, then and now.

That was a year full of magic for both of us. I was able to hit .406 and break up the All-Star game with a home run in the bottom half of the ninth inning, which remains one of the great thrills of my life. But I wasn't the only one having a good year. Dom was having an all-star season himself.

He started rallies for us all year long as the best leadoff man in the American League. I was able to drive in 120 runs, and Dom scored 117, so you can see how big a part he was in our team's performance and in my own numbers.

In the outfield, with all due respect to Sam Chapman of the Philadelphia A's, who led the league's center fielders in putouts and assists in 1941, the best center fielders in the American League that year played in Boston and New York.

Dom was second in putouts, with one more than his brother

Joe, and he tied Joe for second in throwing out base runners. We found out in Dom's first two seasons with the Red Sox in 1940 and '41 that Joe and their brother Vince in the National League weren't the only DiMaggios who could excel in the major leagues. It was my pleasure and privilege to play with and against all three of them, and I have admired all of them as athletes and as quality people.

I don't take a backseat to anybody in my respect and fondness for Dom. There is no finer person on earth. And as for his performance as an athlete, I can tell you he was the easiest outfielder I ever played with. When he yelled "Mine!" you didn't have to worry about the rest of that play.

I used to wish I had his size. Now, that may sound strange coming from a guy six foot three talking about a teammate who was five nine, but it's true. He was built lower to the ground than I was, and he could charge in on low line drives and pick them off before they dropped in. It was a longer reach for me. Dom was a player who looked like a center fielder when he went back on a ball and an infielder when he came in for one. Only a great outfielder can do both, and that's what Dom was.

We have our memories of each other in 1941. Dom says he remembers my .400 season and the home run in the All-Star game. I remember his speed in the outfield and on the bases and that rifle he had for a throwing arm.

I remember something else about Dom, and it involves that All-Star game. He played in eight All-Star games, and 1941 was his first. He did what you'd expect any baseball player named DiMaggio to do. He singled in his first All-Star at bat, and drove in his brother Joe.

Dom has done something good in writing this book. He has preserved for the future a clear and specific history of baseball's most exciting season, and he has painted a vivid and accurate picture of what major league baseball was like for both the players and the fans in those times.

Even over the span of half a century, everything comes back to me when Dom talks about playing every game on real grass, traveling by train, suffering without air-conditioning, and playing baseball because we loved it. Oh, how we loved it! As Dom says, even the approach of another world war, one that we knew was going to have a critical effect on all of us, couldn't dim our enthusiasm for our sport in 1941.

It tells you something about baseball in those years that Zebra Books decided to publish this story. And it tells you something about Dom DiMaggio that he is the player who was selected to tell it. I'm proud to have played a part in the 1941 season, and to be a part of this historical account. I'm also proud of Dom for preserving this story in a way that can be told only by one who lived it.

Dom did. He went on to a long and successful career in the major leagues as my teammate and next to me in the outfield. He could have decided to write his autobiography. Players with careers a lot less successful than his have written their life stories, but Dom chose instead to write about this unique season.

That shows you what a special person Dom DiMaggio is, and what a special year 1941 was.

3

— 1 —

BROTHERS AND BASEBALL

Even now, almost fifty years later, I can still hear the paper boy hollering outside my bedroom window—

"EXTRA! EXTRA! JAPANESE BOMB PEARL
HARBOR! READ ALL ABOUT IT!"

Like a lot of Americans, I didn't know a whole lot about Pearl Harbor. Many of us were in the same position as Zero Mostel, the comedian who was appearing in his one-man comedy show on Broadway. The next day he told his audience, "What I want to know is what the hell was Pearl Harbor doing in the Pacific in the first place?"

But as I lay there in bed in our family home on Beach Street in the Marina District of San Francisco, I didn't need to know a whole lot about Pearl or the war threat to know that something big —really big—had happened. I knew it from my own experience as a newsboy, when my brother Joe and I used to sell the *San Francisco Call* downtown on the corner of Sutter and Sansome streets.

With radio not that long out of its infancy, newspaper extras were the most dramatic form of getting bulletins to the people in those days, and they included all the details. Whether the King of England abdicated, the *Hindenberg* exploded or Hitler invaded Poland, people grabbed those extras at three cents each so they could read all about it.

The DiMaggio brothers—Joe and me and our brother Vince—were all in the major leagues, three center fielders named DiMaggio. Joe had played six seasons with the New York Yankees, Vince had just finished his first year with the Pittsburgh Pirates after two seasons each with the Boston Braves and the Cincinnati Reds, and I had just completed my second year with the Boston Red Sox.

You didn't have to be a genius to know that the headlines that kid was screaming out there on the sidewalk on Beach Street would change everybody's life at least for "the duration." What we didn't know was that the war would change baseball itself, and not just for the duration. Our sport—our profession—would never be the same again.

It was ironic. Here we were coming off what many people were calling the most dramatic baseball season in major league history. My brother Joe hit in 56 straight games, which nobody has come close to doing since. My friend and teammate, Ted Williams, hit over .400, and nobody has done that either. Teddy also hit what is still the most exciting home run in All-Star history. Lou Gehrig died that year. The Yankees beat the Dodgers in the World Series after Tommy Henrich and Mickey Owen both missed a third strike from Hugh Casey. Lefty Grove, my teammate on the Red Sox, won his three hundredth game.

We knew it would have to be years, if ever, before major league baseball would pack that much news—both triumph and tragedy—into one season again. But the events that occurred that Sunday morning halfway around the world would spawn instant changes in baseball, and the years that followed would produce still more, spurred by a galloping technology born out of the war. Baseball may be better now, or it may be worse, but it has never been the way it was.

Everything about that time seems so special now. Kids collected bubble gum baseball cards and traded them with one another with an innocence unknown today in what is now a growth industry. Magazine ads showed which baseball stars smoked Chesterfield because "they satisfy" or Lucky Strikes because "Lucky Strike means fine tobacco." Or they told us which ones liked Camels so much they'd walk a mile for one. Nobody talked about drugs.

If your town had a major league or minor league team, you could walk down your neighborhood street and hear the home team's game being broadcast over the radio, with the crowd noise and the announcer's play-by-play description coming through the screen doors and open windows. Inside, the people who lived there were trying to stay cool in the summer heat.

In those days before air-conditioning became commonplace, people paced themselves as much as they could on hot summer days and nights, and listening to the ball game kept them entertained while they tried to stay cool. They sat in their living rooms because family rooms were unheard of and recreation rooms were for the rich folks. Most of us were just beginning to see the light at the end of a tunnel called the Great Depression. Or they sat in their kitchens, under the sticky yellow flypaper hanging from the ceiling to catch the flies and other insects that flew into the house when someone kept the screen door open too long.

Enough houses had the baseball game on the radio that you could walk down the street to the corner store and keep up with the game almost as well as you could sitting at home. They used to say that in Brooklyn you could walk almost anywhere you wanted to go without missing a single pitch.

If you heard the fans cheering but missed the play, you could stop on the sidewalk outside the house and holler, "What happened?"

Somebody would answer from the front porch or a voice without a face would call back from behind the window screen, "Greenberg just doubled to drive in two runs. The Tigers are winning, three to one, in the sixth."

You'd wave and call out your thanks and keep on walking, knowing you'd pick up the broadcast after just another door or two.

●

There was a wonderful sameness about baseball when I was growing up. The game had been played the same way in the major leagues from the time the American League was formed in 1901 as the second major league. All through those years nobody ever dreamed that a team could move from one city to another, or that players would someday be able to declare themselves "free agents" and play for another team. In 1941, for the fans and players, too, there was a reassuring quality, a dependability, about baseball. We knew that all the players on our team would be back next year unless they were traded to another team or drafted for the war. We knew the season would last 154 games—eight games fewer than today—and that as soon as it ended there would be the World Series—no playoffs first. The home team always wore white, and the visitors were in gray. It was a game that was in many ways unrecognizable by today's standards:

- Barely half the major league teams had stadiums equipped with lights for night games, and no team played more than a few.
- There were no games on television.
- Teams traveled by train, creating a closeness among players not allowed by today's air travel.
- No team had moved to another city since 1903.
- Only twelve American cities had major league teams, with St. Louis the farthest west. There were no major league teams in Canada or California or Texas.
- There were no black players.
- There was no indoor baseball played on fake grass.
- There were no agents, million-dollar salaries, multiyear contracts, or players deciding for themselves where they will play next year.
- There were no player strikes or owner lockouts.
- Drugs had not surfaced as a serious problem, although alcohol was always a concern. Smoking and chewing tobacco were commonplace.

- There were no padded fences or warning tracks to protect exuberant outfielders like Pete Reiser.

If one word described the future for every major league player as we headed for spring training in 1941, it was "uncertain." The military draft had started the summer before. Hitler was storming across Europe, and relations between the United States and Japan were at the crisis stage. Many people, including government officials, were openly predicting another world war.

Still, Eddie Joost, Joe Orengo, and I couldn't worry about what was being called "the international situation." We had our jobs to worry about, and on a February morning we piled into my new Packard in San Francisco and headed east for our spring training camps in Florida. Eddie was an infielder starting his fifth year with the Cincinnati Reds, and Joe was an infielder with the New York Giants who was beginning his third season in the majors after being sold to the Giants by the St. Louis Cardinals.

Ball players had winter jobs in those days, especially the younger players, who didn't make what the established ones did. Orengo had an off-season job. He was a cable car conductor in San Francisco, the man who collected fares and made change from a silver change holder hooked onto his belt. On the way east he was telling us about the woman who kept hitting him up for change every morning so she could drop a nickel into the fare box. She never had anything less than a dollar bill. One morning Joe decided to cure her of her habit.

When she got on the cable car and handed him the usual dollar bill, Joe asked, "Lady, have you ever seen a herd of buffalo?"

She said, "Why, no."

Joe said, "Well, you have now." Then he handed her twenty buffalo nickels.

Driving across the United States is a long ordeal at any time, especially going diagonally from northern California to southern Florida, but if you think it's tiring now, you should have tried it then. The fact that Packards were my favorite cars made the trip easier for me. People could have all those other brands, including some that aren't with us anymore either, like the Nash, the Hudson Terraplane, and the Willys. Packard was the car for me.

About the only divided highway in the country was the Pennsylvania Turnpike, which had opened the year before. The rest of the country was two-lane roads, a single lane in each direction, and if you got caught behind a truck going up a hill, too bad. Automobile air-conditioning was unheard of, which made for a lot of noisy driving as well as hot temperatures as we sped along, trying to hear one another talk. In fact, air-conditioning itself was unheard of except in restaurants and movie theaters. That's where we went on a hot day.

Undivided windshields were as far off into the future as undivided highways. We saw the U.S.A. through a windshield with a metal strip down the middle, and the back window was the same way. Some of the manufacturers were beginning to "streamline" their cars by doing away with the running boards that people used for standing outside the car's doors. Gearshifts were just then being put on the steering wheel instead of on the floor, and Oldsmobile was even coming out with something revolutionary called "hydramatic drive" that actually shifted the gears for you. A newspaper ad said it "saves 419 driving motions per hour" and was safer too. The ad said the old way was "astonishing when you think of it— 179 times within an hour the right hand must be taken from the wheel!"

Eddie, Joe, and I didn't have automatic transmission to make our life easier, but we had what was even more of a luxury in a car in those days—a radio. In the 1930s or '40s, if you told your friends you'd just bought a new car, you were bursting with pride. We were still fighting our way out of the Depression, and most Americans couldn't afford a car of any kind, much less a new one. When you added that it had a radio and heater, your friends knew you were living deep in the lap of luxury.

That's how we headed east in February 1941, reading the Burma-Shave signs by the side of the road. Those signs were a big part of any "motor trip." Eddie, Joe, and I not only enjoyed the roadside jingles, but we were as grateful as everyone else to the folks at Burma-Shave for taking a little of the monotony and fatigue out of the long trip to spring training.

You don't see Burma-Shave signs anymore. They went the way of so many other things when America started driving on super highways at speeds so fast you barely had time to read a huge billboard much less a smaller sign. They were sets of four or five rectangular signs on posts strung along the side of the road fifty paces apart, white lettering against a red background, extolling the virtues of a new development in shaving—a cream in a jar. Men didn't have to whip up a lather with a brush in a cup anymore. They were lighthearted messages, telling passing motorists about their product in a low-keyed and humorous jingle:

DOES YOUR HUSBAND MISBEHAVE
GRUNT AND GRUMBLE
RANT AND RAVE?
SHOOT THE BRUTE
SOME BURMA-SHAVE

Sometimes there was a public service message:

PAST SCHOOLHOUSES
TAKE IT SLOW
LET THE LITTLE SHAVERS
GROW
BURMA-SHAVE

Invariably somebody in the car would read the roadside rhymes out loud for the benefit of the rest of us. They even became conversation pieces when you got back from your trip, with people telling one another about the latest signs.

MANY A FOREST
USED TO STAND
WHERE A LIGHTED MATCH
GOT OUT OF HAND
BURMA-SHAVE

11

DOM DIMAGGIO

WITHIN THIS VALE
OF TOIL
AND SIN
YOUR HEAD GROWS BALD
BUT NOT YOUR SKIN
BURMA-SHAVE

As we drove across country talking baseball, listening to the radio, and reading Burma-Shave signs, we took turns behind the wheel. When it was my turn to stretch out in the backseat, I was able to appreciate the good life of a major league baseball player in 1941 and how I got there.

My brother Vince started it all. He was two years older than Joe and started sneaking out to play baseball when he was junior high school age. My parents were from the old country, born and raised in a village in the suburbs of Palermo. They didn't take too well to this American game of baseball, especially Dad.

Dad was a fisherman, a man who worked hard because he had to and because he believed you're supposed to. He labored on the waters of San Francisco Bay for forty years as a crab fisherman and made himself a success. For years, until his sons became successful in baseball, he and Mom spoke very little English. He had emigrated from Sicily five years before my mother so he could save money and send for his Rosalie.

That's the way Guiseppe DiMaggio was—a determined and independent man who never let anything interfere with him as he worked to reach his goals. That same attitude helped all of his baseball-playing sons more than he ever knew. There were eleven of us at home at 2047 Taylor Street in the North Beach-Telegraph Hill section of San Francisco, Mom and Dad and nine little DiMaggios.

We grew up in that house and lived there until Joe bought the house on Beach Street in the Marina District. (The house survived extensive damage in the 1989 earthquake, and Joe still lives there when he's in San Francisco.) By the time we were entering our teens, my older brothers Mike and Tom were working on the boats

12

with Dad, and our sisters—Marie, Mae, Nelly, and Frances—were helping our mother and going to school.

Baseball violated Dad's code of life which emphasized the work ethic. But Mom would stick up for us and calm him down eventually. Later she'd even cover for us if we weren't around. But we had to be careful about coming home with torn pants or a cut or a sprain that would be a dead giveaway as to where we had been. When those things happened, we tried to slip into the house and touch up the evidence, or get rid of it altogether, before running into Dad.

Vince wasn't playing baseball only for the fun of it. He wanted to be an opera singer and his plan was to have baseball pay for his musical education. I wanted to be a chemical engineer. I'm not sure what Joe wanted to be, but he knew what he *didn't* want to be—a fisherman. Fish and water both made him sick, especially after he quit high school at sixteen and worked in a cannery for three dollars a day picking over crab meat.

Vince tried out for the San Francisco Seals at the start of the 1932 season. The Seals were a minor league team, but one of the best, in the Pacific Coast League. When Vince made the team, he quit his job in a vegetable market.

Vince's biggest problem throughout his baseball career was strikeouts. He was a legitimate threat to hit the long ball, and like most home run hitters, he had a big swing that also made him vulnerable to striking out. In ten years as a major leaguer, he led the National League in strikeouts six times.

When he was playing for the Boston Braves in the late 1930s, his manager was Casey Stengel. Stengel once told a reporter about Vince's tendency to strike out but also about his ability to keep it from upsetting him. "Vince is the only player I ever saw," Casey said, "who would strike out three times in one game and not be embarrassed. He'd fan three times and walk into the clubhouse whistling. Everybody would be feeling sorry for Vince. But he never let it bother him."

Other National Leaguers told about the time in 1937 when the Braves were playing the St. Louis Cardinals in Boston. Johnny Perkins, a big, heavyset St. Louis nightclub entertainer, bet Dizzy

13

Dean he couldn't strike Vince out four times in one game. Diz got Vince on strikeouts his first three times up and knew he had a good shot at winning that bet.

On his fourth trip to the plate, Vince fouled off the first two pitches. Diz was only one strike away from collecting—but Vince messed him up by popping up the next pitch behind the plate.

Dean's catcher, Brusie Ogrodowski, circled under the ball but Diz came running in from the mound, screaming, "Drop it! Drop it! I gotta fan him! I got a bet!"

The story goes that Ogrodowski let the ball drop. Dean struck Vince out on the next pitch and collected on his bet too—eighty cents, twenty cents for each strikeout.

But Stengel was right. Vince never let those strikeouts get him down. Some of the players in the National League even told Joe and me that Vince would stand in center field and sing operatic arias between batters.

Vince paved the way for Joe, and Joe paved the way for me. My brother Vince told Mr. Graham that his younger brother could capably fill in for Augie Galan the last two days of the season.

The gods were smiling on Joe. The Seals' shortstop, Augie Galan, wanted to leave for a trip to Hawaii, so arrangements were made for Joe to play in his spot. Joe was playing shortstop at that time anyhow, which I did a few years later, so he felt right at home. He got a triple and a double in nine trips to the plate and hit the ball hard several other times. The next year he got off to a slow start but then caught fire and finished with a .340 batting average and a hitting streak in mid-season of sixty-one straight games. That fifty-six-game streak with the Yankees in 1941 wasn't Joe's first long streak, and in fact it wasn't even his longest.

By the time I came along, Joe had hit .398 for the Seals in 1935 and was sold over the winter to the New York Yankees for $25,000, the biggest steal in Manhattan since the Indians sold it for $24 and a few trinkets. The Pacific Coast League was such a rich source of outstanding young players that its teams were selling their stars to the major league teams for anywhere from $75,000 to $125,000, so the price that Joe brought was unusually low, especially after being such a great player in the league and winning its

Most Valuable Player award the year before. He would have gone for a much higher price, but he wrenched his knee getting out of a car and there were some doubters who were suggesting his knee might not hold up.

Then it was my turn, and Spike Hennessey entered my life. Spike was a big man in a blue baseball cap and a heavy overcoat, and nobody knew exactly what he did for a living or even where he lived. He had no official connection with the Seals or any other baseball organization, but he was always around our sandlots, offering advice and bringing promising young prospects to the attention of the Seals.

They listened to him, too, especially after Joe became such a star. The first time Spike spotted me, I was a second baseman. My arm, which became one of my strongest assets later, still hadn't developed, so I was playing second, where the throw is the shortest on the diamond.

By the time I was a senior at Galileo High School in 1934, my arm had grown so much stronger that I was a pitcher and shortstop. I hit .400 even though I was the number nine hitter in the batting order because my coach wanted some scoring punch throughout his lineup. Hitting at the bottom of the order wasn't my biggest disappointment in high school, though. That came when we lost the championship in the final game of the season. I came in as a relief pitcher in the eighth inning with the bases loaded. We lost the championship on a sacrifice fly. That kind of crushing disappointment can make a baseball player grow up in a hurry.

They were calling me "Bunky," the name of a popular comic strip character in those years, when Spike Hennessey started showing up on the sandlots where I was playing ball. He wasn't discouraged by the sight of a young player wearing glasses, which was a turnoff to many baseball people. Spike even had me umpire some of our games so I could develop leadership qualities. And he didn't try to talk me out of it when he saw me move to the outfield and start playing center field "sideways." Spike and Bunky were getting along just fine.

I played center field at a right angle to the plate, with my left

15

foot facing the plate and my right foot parallel to the center field fence. It was something I thought of myself. I don't think anybody else has ever played the position that way.

My feeling was that I got a better jump on the ball that way. I always faced the left field foul line before the pitch was released, and it didn't make any difference if the batter was right-handed or left-handed. I felt I could get a quicker start on fly balls over my head, could come in faster on line drives to short center, and could charge ground balls better. I sometimes tried the conventional position of facing the hitter, or tried turning around the other way if the batter was left-handed, but nothing felt as comfortable as standing there, facing the left field line with the left side of my body facing home plate.

When I was nineteen I was playing shortstop for the North Beach Merchants sandlot team and the Seals began to scout me. By that time, any baseball player in San Francisco named DiMaggio was going to get a good long look from the scouts. But I wanted to make sure of it.

The Cincinnati Reds and the Seals held a joint baseball camp and combined tryouts every year and then took turns on who got to make the first pick from the players trying out. I wanted to see if I had a future in baseball, so I told my boss, a man named Mike at the Simmons Bed Factory, that I was quitting my job.

That took some guts because we were still in the Depression, and you just didn't quit your job without a strong reason because you might not find another one. I told Mike I was giving him my two weeks notice so he would have time to break in a new employee.

Mike declined and said he'd hold my job for me until I saw whether I got an offer from the Seals or the Reds. Not every boss would have taken that position, so I went to the camp with slightly more peace of mind.

In that camp there were 143 kids trying out so the odds were always stacked high against you. But I had a good camp, playing in both the infield and the outfield, and the Seals liked what they saw. So they called me in from the outfield at Seals Stadium and told me they were going to sign me to a contract.

16

Spike made sure the Seals knew what they were getting. He told them I was ready to play for them and carry on the tradition of Seals center fielders named DiMaggio. His baseball knowledge ran so deep he was also able to make a prediction: "I'll tell you where he'll really shine," he told the reporters when I joined the Seals, "and that's coming in on ground ball hits and getting runners at third when they try to go from first on a single. He won't wait for the ball to roll to him the way some outfielders do. He'll come in like a sprinter, scoop up the ball, and rifle it. His infield training will help him."

And that's exactly what happened over the next three years while I played center field for the San Francisco Seals.

I was called into the Seals' offices from the field, where I had been trying out, to sign my contract, along with my brother Tom who had been Joe's business adviser and was about to become mine.

I had been shagging fly balls in center field when the Seals' public relations man, Walter Mails, hollered out for me to come to the front office. In front of a flock of reporters assembled by Mails, I went through the motions of signing a blank contract, still in my baseball uniform, with Tom standing behind me. The paper the next day said: "Dominic never opened his mouth or cracked a smile. He acted like a bewildered little schoolboy. . . ." Another paper said: "Young Dominic was visibly shaken by his first important step in the business world."

Rookies never had any doubt about where they stood in those days. Immediately after the staged signing, Mails told the reporters, "C'mon now—we'll have some beer."

I followed the crowd into the Seals' dining room. What the heck, it was my signing that everybody was celebrating. But Mails saw me and said, "You can go down and chase some more fly balls now. We're all through with you."

17

2

COAST-TO-COAST DIMAGGIOS

The three DiMaggio center fielders, and the rest of the family, too, were having fun in the late 1930s. Joe made it to the Yankees in '36, a rookie the same year that Bob Feller broke in, and Vince made good the next season with the Braves. Vince got into 132 games in his first year and 150 in '38 and hit a total of 27 home runs. Those strikeouts were still getting him, though. He led the league both years.

Joe was tearing up the American League. Ben Chapman was the New York center fielder when Joe arrived, so Joe McCarthy put him in left. But Joe was too good to be kept out of center field, so he became the Yankees' starting center fielder on July 31st of his first season. He hit .323 as a twenty-one-year-old rookie and raised it to .346 in his second year, while also leading the league with 46 home runs and 151 runs scored. He would have led the league in runs batted in, too, with 167—but Hank Greenberg had 183.

Joe kept right on rolling. In '38 he hit .324 with 32 homers and 140 RBIs, and he followed that in 1939 by leading the league in hitting. He hit .381 with 30 home runs and 126 runs batted in. Joe achieved something else that year—he was voted the American League's Most Valuable Player. He went on to become one of only five players who won the award three times. When he won it that first time, he was only twenty-four years old.

While all this was going on, I was getting started in the Pacific Coast League with the Seals—and running into a problem right away. Most of the writers covering the Seals were doing an accurate, unbiased job of reporting, like Jack McDonald, who is now ninety years old and still remembers the DiMaggios. But one of the town's most prominent sports writers, Tom Laird of the *San Francisco Daily News,* got on my back. He wrote a column called "Looking 'Em Over," and he kept telling his readers that the only reason the Seals signed me was as a gate attraction because I was Joe's brother.

He was so negative in everything he wrote about me that he even guaranteed his readers I'd never be able to make the plays in center because of my unusual fielding position. "Anybody who plays center field facing left field," he wrote, "will never be able to catch a ball hit behind him in right center."

Not long after that appeared, we were playing in Portland. We had Ted Norbert in left field, and Johnny Gill in right. Norbert was slow, and Gill was even slower. On back-to-back plays, the Portland hitters sent fly balls, one behind Norbert, the other behind Gill. I caught both of the balls, covering several miles in the process.

The next day Laird did a complete about-face. "Anybody who says this kid can't play," he wrote, "is out of his mind."

He saw Joe at the World Series one year while I was with the Seals and told him I looked like an excellent prospect. After I had made it to the Red Sox, I reminded him of his constant criticisms of me and the way he ridiculed the Seals for signing me because he was sure they wanted me only as a drawing card.

Laird denied ever writing anything like that, but I told him flatly, "Tom, I know you did. I have the clippings." Then I said, "But I want to thank you for writing that stuff. You just made me that much more determined to become a success."

After I joined the Seals and Joe and Vince were in the big leagues, the San Francisco papers ran a "DiMaggio digest" every day showing what Joe, Vince, and I were doing. The DiMaggios were playing well from one coast to the other. The "digest" had a picture of each of us, plus a report on what each did the day before and a table showing our batting averages, number of games, runs, hits, doubles, triples, home runs, runs batted in, putouts, assists, and errors.

At home the success that all three of us were having was becoming apparent. We were still living on Taylor Street then, a seven-room house where we had lived for eighteen years, and pictures of three baseball players now shared the wall space which previously had been reserved only for Christian saints.

I hit .306 in my first year with the Seals, turning down a chance to sit out the last day of the season to keep my average above .300. I wanted to hit for that coveted .300 average in my first year in the minors in the worst way, but I didn't want to back into it. I wanted to earn it, so I played, got some hits, and raised my average four points. When Ted Williams made the same kind of decision for much higher stakes on the last day of 1941, I was his biggest admirer. In my second season I raised my average two points. As the 1939 season began I was twenty-one years old and twenty pounds heavier, at 171, but my weight wasn't necessarily the main reason for my continued improvement. That was due to Lefty O'Doul, the Seals' manager.

When Joe was playing for the Seals, Lefty helped Joe raise his average 57 points in one season, to .398. I had exactly the same experience with him. He worked on my hitting techniques and philosophy, and my average jumped to .360 in 1939.

O'Doul had valid credentials on the subject of hitting. He won the National League batting championship twice, missing .400 by two points in 1929 with the Phillies and hitting .368 for the Brooklyn Dodgers in 1932. He was far and away the finest hitting instructor that ever put on a baseball uniform. He could spot anything you were doing wrong in a minute and show you how to correct it.

Lefty's primary emphasis in teaching hitting was to encourage the player to develop strong wrists so he could wait on the pitch better, something Ted Williams has been preaching all his life. The longer you can wait on a pitch, the better you'll be able to tell if it's a good pitch to hit, which brings you to another keystone of hitting preached by Ted—get a good pitch to hit.

Another one of O'Doul's basics was to look for the fast ball on every pitch, a practice now adhered to by most hitters and hitting instructors. If you're ready for the fast ball, you can always adjust your swing and wait a split second longer if you see it's a curve, but the reverse doesn't work. If you're thinking curve ball and it's a fast ball, there's no way in the world you'll be able to get around quickly enough to handle the pitch.

In fact, Lefty tried to get Teddy for the Seals. He was in San Diego watching the then minor league Padres take batting practice one day in 1936 and he liked the way the man in the batting cage was hitting the ball. Lefty was an excellent judge of young talent, and everyone in baseball knew it, so he asked the San Diego owner, Bill "Hard Rock" Lane, "Who's the kid?"

"Williams. Lives here. We picked him up off the sandlots."

As they talked, Teddy kept rapping the ball, and Lefty kept getting more interested. He asked Lane, "Why isn't he playing?"

"Can't hit."

"What'll you take for him?"

Lane gave Lefty a hard stare and said, "I wouldn't sell him to *you.*"

If Hard Rock Lane hadn't respected Lefty O'Doul's reputation as a talent scout, the Seals might have been able to buy Ted Williams. We could have been playing next to each other three years sooner than we did.

People were beginning to find out that we DiMaggios stick together. After each of us had a good year in '38, all three of us held out for more money in '39. After all of us came to terms, and while Joe went on to lead the American League in hitting and win the Most Valuable Player award, I finished second in hitting in the Pacific Coast League and won the MVP award too.

My batting average of .360 was second only to Dom Dallessandro, who was bought by the Cubs. I finished first in hits, second in triples, second in stolen bases, and first in runs scored. My contract was bought by the Red Sox on the approval of their manager, another San Franciscan, Joe Cronin.

But not everybody was a member of the Dominic DiMaggio fan club. Bill Terry, who was managing the New York Giants, said he wasn't interested in me after he supposedly heard I'd never be able to hit big league pitching. And Prescott Sullivan, a columnist for the *San Francisco Examiner,* wrote: "You can have him, dirt cheap, glove and all, for $25,000. . . . We have never regarded young Dom as an expert batsman. . . ."

But there was no doubt in Lefty O'Doul's mind. The Sox paid between $75,000 and $100,000 for me plus one of our younger pitchers, Larry Powell, who was included because he struck out Joe Cronin three times in one of our exhibition games. But Powell was to stay with the Seals for another year of seasoning. I was to report to Sarasota, Florida, for spring training with what the players call "the big club."

Lefty told the reporters in San Francisco: "He'll be a sensation up there—a positive sensation. He can't miss. I'm glad he's going to Boston because Boston is one town where the fans know and appreciate all-around good ball players. Boston is going to idolize Dom."

While Cronin was adding me to his Red Sox roster, he was getting rid of another player. He sold the shortstop on Boston's minor league team at Louisville, and that's how Pee Wee Reese became a member of the Brooklyn Dodgers.

The year 1939 was an eventful one, and a sad one too. Lou Gehrig told Joe McCarthy in May that he was taking himself out of the Yankees' starting lineup, ending his streak of playing in 2,130 straight games. That's one of two baseball records that may never be broken, and the other is my brother Joe's 56-game hitting streak in 1941.

Gehrig's achievement becomes even more monumental when compared to the streak of Cal Ripken of the Baltimore Orioles, who has the third longest streak ever. He started it in 1982 and has extended it to this day, yet he'll have to play in every game until 1995 to break Lou's record.

23

It took a terminal disease to stop Gehrig—amyotrophic lateral sclerosis—ALS, known ever since as "Lou Gehrig's disease." All of us in baseball in 1939 were deeply moved by what was happening to Gehrig, and not just because of his immortal career and his achievement of playing in all those games and winning the nickname of the "Iron Horse." Our sadness was doubled by the fact that he was one of the all-time nice guys, enormously popular all over America. When the Yankees honored him with "Lou Gehrig Day" during their doubleheader with the Washington Senators on July Fourth, the story went out all over the nation.

Joe was there with his Yankee teammates in their pinstripe uniforms as Lou said good-bye to baseball and his many friends in it. Shirley Povich, the respected columnist for the *Washington Post,* whose name now graces the halls of Cooperstown after winning the J. G. Taylor Spink Award as one of the greatest baseball writers in history, captured the moment for all America when he wrote in the paper the next morning:

NEW YORK, July 4—I saw strong men weep this afternoon, expressionless umpires swallow hard, and emotion pump the hearts and glaze the eyes of 60,000 baseball fans in Yankee Stadium. Yes, and hard-boiled news photographers clicked their shutters with fingers that trembled a bit.

It was Lou Gehrig Day at the stadium, and the first 100 years of baseball saw nothing quite like it.

They had Lou at home plate between games of the doubleheader, with the 60,000 massed in the triple tiers that rimmed the field, microphones and cameras trained on him, and he couldn't take it that way. Tears streamed down his face, circuiting the most famous pair of dimples in baseball, and he looked chiefly at the ground.

Seventy-year-old Ed Barrow, president of the Yankees, who had said to newspapermen, "Boys, I have bad news for you," when Gehrig's ailment was diagnosed as lateral sclerosis two weeks before, stepped out of the background halfway through the presentation ceremonies, and draped his arm across Gehrig's shoulder. But he was doing more than that. He was holding Gehrig up, for big Lou needed support.

As he leaned on Barrow, Gehrig said, "Thanks, Ed." He bit his lip hard, was grateful for the supporting arm, as the Yankees of 1927 stepped to the microphone after being introduced. Babe Ruth, Bob Meusel, Waite Hoyt, Herb Pennock, Benny Bengough, Bob Shawkey, Mark Koenig, Tony Lazzeri, all of the class of '27 were there. And Gehrig had been one of them too. He had been the only one among them to bestride both eras. . . .

There was a smile through his tears, but he wasn't up to words. He could only shake the hands of the small army of officials who made the presentations. He stood there twisting his doffed baseball cap into a braid in his fingers as Manager Joe McCarthy followed Mayor LaGuardia and Postmaster General Farley in tribute to "the finest example of ball player, sportsman and citizen that baseball has ever known."

. . . But Joe McCarthy couldn't take it that way, either. The man who has driven the highest-salaried prima donnas of baseball into action, who has baited a thousand umpires, broke down. McCarthy really sobbed as he stood in front of the microphone. . . .

Now it was Gehrig's turn to talk into the microphone, to acknowledge his gifts. . . . But Master of Ceremonies Sid Mercer was anticipating Gehrig. He saw the big fellow choked up. Infinitesimally, Gehrig shook his head, and Mercer announced: "I shall not ask Lou Gehrig to make a speech. I do not believe that I should."

They started to haul away the microphones. Gehrig half turned toward the dugout, with the ceremonies apparently at an end. And then he wheeled suddenly, strode back to the loud-speaking apparatus, held up his hand for attention, gulped, managed a smile and then spoke.

"For weeks," said Gehrig, "I have been reading in the newspapers that I am a fellow who got a tough break. I don't believe it. I have been a lucky guy. For sixteen years, into every ball park in which I have ever walked, I have received

25

nothing but kindness and encouragement. Mine has been a full life."

He went on fidgeting with his cap, pawing the ground with his spikes as he spoke, choking back emotions that threatened to silence him, summoning courage from somewhere. He thanked everybody. He didn't forget the ball park help, he told of his gratitude to newspapermen who had publicized him. He didn't forget the late Miller Huggins, or his six years with him, or Manager Joe McCarthy, or the late Colonel Ruppert, or Babe Ruth, or "my roommate, Bill Dickey."

And then he thanked the Giants—"The fellows from across the river, who we would give our right arm to beat!"— he was more at ease in front of the mike now, and he had a word for Mrs. Gehrig and for the immigrant mother and father who had made his education, his career, possible. And he denied again that he had been the victim of a bad break in life. He said, "I've lots to live for, honest."

And thousands cheered.

As sad as Lou Gehrig's farewell was for baseball, it was overshadowed in importance less than two months later. Hitler invaded Poland on September 1 and World War II began. But we were still untouched by the storm in Europe and life went on as always, with no one knowing how long it would stay that way.

The American League beat the National League in the seventh All-Star game, 3–1, at Yankee Stadium, and my brother Joe hit the only home run. His classmate from the rookie class of '36, Bob Feller, entered the game in the sixth inning with one out and the bases loaded and forced Arky Vaughan to hit into a double play.

Then Bob pitched three more innings, causing the National Leaguers to complain that Joe McCarthy had violated the unwritten rule of limiting pitchers to three innings. Bob was twenty years old. The American League was dominating the All-Star games. It was its fifth victory in the seven games since the event was started in 1933.

In the World Series, the Yankees blew away the Cincinnati Reds in four games, and Joe helped win the third game with a two-run homer and was one of the leading hitters in the Series with a .313 average.

Two of the greatest movies ever filmed, *The Wizard of Oz* and *Gone With the Wind,* came out in 1939, and baseball players were always grateful for good movies. On road trips they were one of our primary sources of entertainment. Not only that, the theaters were becoming air conditioned, "Air Cooled" as the signs outside said.

Not everything that year was of momentous importance. The words to one of the biggest song hits of the year were:

> Three little fiddies in the itty bitty poo,
> Three little fiddies and the mama fishie too.
> "Fwim," said the mama fish,
> "Fwim if you can."
> And they fwam and they fwam right over the dam.

Presidents are in the news every day, but President Roosevelt was in the news for a different reason in 1939. People were saying he might run for a third term. No American president had ever done that before, and a lot of Americans didn't like the idea. Some of them used the American love of baseball to support their cause, wearing campaign buttons that said:

OUT! STEALING THIRD!

and:

FORCE FRANKLIN OUT AT THIRD!

Even with the Nazi storm troopers spreading death and destruction across Europe, baseball players weren't preoccupied with the international news of the day. That was at least partly due to the fact that in the United States public outcry against the war was slow in building. One of the most vocal isolationists, Senator William E. Borah, called the new world war "that phony little war."

27

Most Americans might not have considered it phony, but a poll by Elmo Roper in December 1939, three months after Hitler started World War II, showed that sixty-seven percent of Americans were opposed to taking sides.

— 3 —

"HELLO, JOE." "HELLO, DOM."

Things didn't get better for the world in 1940, and they didn't start off too well for me, either. After pulling into Sarasota and putting on a Red Sox uniform for the first time, I decided to apply myself gradually to spring training because I was practically in playing condition, and chose to wait until the exhibition games to start before going all-out. But in the first exhibition game, against Cincinnati, I sprained my ankle sliding into home, and my brother Vince was part of the reason.

I was on second base with the bases loaded and our catcher, Johnny Peacock, was on third when Ted got a base hit to the outfield. Peacock hesitated, not sure if it was going to drop in, but I was coming with all the speed I had, never doubting for a minute that it was a hit.

As I rounded third I saw I was catching up with Peacock, and as I started my slide toward the plate, I saw Peacock doing the same thing. I was surprised, because I thought he was going to score standing up. When I saw him going into his slide, I deliberately pointed my right foot away from the plate to avoid stabbing Peacock in the back, but I caught it in the dirt.

Vince in the meantime made an outstanding throw to the

plate, but the Reds' catcher, Bill Baker, dropped the ball. If he had held it, he could have tagged the plate for the force out, but I would have scored. It would have been one of the strangest plays in baseball—a runner scoring from second after a forceout at the plate. The result was a sprained ankle that knocked me out of the lineup for a week or so, but not long enough to keep me from opening the season—in right field.

The Red Sox were loaded with good outfielders in 1940. They had Williams in left and Doc Cramer, who broke into the American League in 1929 and had hit over .300 six times already, in center. Lou Finney was a strong contender for the right field job after hitting .310 the year before. And there was Joe Vosmik, a ten-year man in the American League. The Red Sox must have liked my chances from the start, because in February they sold Vosmik to the Brooklyn Dodgers for $25,000.

I was able to beat out Finney for the job, and when the 1940 American League season opened, there I was playing right field for the Boston Red Sox against the Washington Senators in Griffith Stadium.

My brothers and I were getting an unusual amount of publicity because of the novelty of having three brothers playing in the major leagues at the same time. One magazine ran an article called "The Amazing DiMaggios." My old doubting Thomas from San Francisco, Tom Laird, even got caught up in the enthusiasm. He wrote a feature story in *Collier's* magazine boldly calling me "the greatest twenty-two-year-old player in the game today."

The comment that was the most flattering, however, came from no less an authority than Ty Cobb, who told a writer: "Dom's a throwback to the kind of ball players we used to have."

All of this was pretty heady stuff, especially considering I hadn't played my first big league game. For that reason, I wasn't going to let any of the publicity change the size of my hat. And I learned right away to have a good answer for the question the writers always asked me—"How do you compare yourself to Joe?"

I used to tell them, "I can do two things better than he can—play pinochle and speak Italian."

And when they asked me how it felt to be Joe DiMaggio's

brother, I used to tell them how proud I was of Joe, but then I would remind them, "Yes, he's my brother—and I'm *his* brother."

Any Italian kid from the San Francisco Bay Area had reason to feel at home in the major leagues. As the 1930s were ending, the San Francisco Italians in the major leagues included my brothers and me as well as Frankie Crosetti, Tony Lazzeri, Cookie Lavagetto, and Dolf Camilli, plus an umpire, Babe Pinelli.

Even my manager, Joe Cronin, was from San Francisco. He could never have passed for an Italian, though, with the map of Ireland spread across his face as prominently as it was. Still, I was glad to have him as my manager because I knew he was blessed with the "luck of the Irish"—once when he was a kid, his school burned down.

If I needed any extra care as a twenty-three-year-old away from home for the first time, my brother Joe made sure I would get it. He called me "Min" sometimes, for the three middle letters in my first name, and he told one of his friends in Boston, "Take care of Min—he's my pet."

After opening in Washington, the Red Sox came home for a doubleheader against the Philadelphia A's to open our home season. There I was, playing in one of the most legendary ball parks in baseball, Fenway Park—Green Monster and all. I remember looking around at the historic surroundings.

Behind me beyond the right field wall were Ipswich Street and the Fenway Garage Company. The wall was 304 feet from home plate. Over in left, Teddy's territory, it was 315 feet down the line, with the Green Monster, 37 feet of tin-covered wood and concrete, topped by a 23½-foot net looming in front of Lansdowne Street.

Later in the 1940 season I found my permanent home, in center field, where the deepest corner is 420 feet from the plate. If you think that's deep, imagine what it must have looked like from 1931 to 1934—when it was 593 feet, before a fire burned down the center field bleachers.

With all of its glory and tradition, and as much as I came to love the Boston fans who came there, Fenway Park was not the best ball park for an outfielder with my characteristics. My defensive game was based on speed and a strong throwing arm. I could go a long way to catch fly balls that a lot of other outfielders couldn't reach, and throw out runners trying to move up after the catch.

But Fenway's distances and its configuration were not as ideally suited to my speed as the larger parks like Yankee Stadium, Griffith Stadium, or Municipal Stadium in Cleveland. I loved playing in those big outfields where I could really let it out. Instead of watching fly balls sail into the Fenway seats or up into the left field screen, I could go get them and even turn some of the catches into double plays.

I might have achieved more success as a hitter on a larger field. I was a right-handed hitter, but not a big home run threat, even though I did hit 87 of them in my major league career. That cozy fence in left never helped me that much. I was better in a park where I could move the ball around, be a "spray hitter." I hit over .300 four times in ten full seasons with the Red Sox, made the All-Star team seven times—missing it only because of injury in 1940 and 1947, and finished with a lifetime batting average of .298, the same as Mickey Mantle. I don't feel that I have to apologize to anyone for a career like that. Still, on a bigger playing field . . .

A Boston writer named Joe Cashman agreed with me when he predicted in 1940 that Fenway would limit my skills as an outfielder. He wrote that my defensive ability ". . . will never be fully appreciated in Boston. . . . It's simply because of the way Fenway Park is constructed."

There is another fixture at Fenway besides the "Green Monster." She's a special someone who was there every day in the 1940s and '50s when I was playing and is still there today. She is Elizabeth Dooley, now eighty-six years old, a season ticket holder since the 1930s. She sits in her box seats in the first row of Section 36 right in front of the Red Sox on-deck circle and she never misses a game.

She's so close to the action that she's been hit by foul balls from time to time, including a game when a line drive broke the fingers on one hand. By the time an usher helped her to the first aid room, she fainted from the pain—but she didn't miss the next game. She likes it there. "I'm there to see the game," she explains simply.

She's "Lib" to the players from my era, and if we run into her today around Boston or at Fenway, it's hugs and kisses all around —whether it's Ted Williams, Johnny Pesky, Bobby Doerr, Birdie Tebbetts, me, or someone else. Anyone whose sister makes sandwiches at home so they won't have to leave their seats for even one pitch—which Lib's sister did when we played in the 1946 World Series—is our kind of people.

We had a second loyal lady, Lolly Hopkins, who sat near the on-deck circle on the first base side. She was such a Rabid Red Sox Rooter that she used to bring a megaphone with her so everyone in Fenway Park could hear her words of encouragement. But Lib Dooley is our enduring Number One fan.

Lib was a teacher of physical education and health education for "thirty-nine years and five months" who made baseball her life's interest, and she did it to an extent that any other baseball fan would envy. In addition to our home games, she has been to spring training and used to fly to our road games in other cities. When we were an eight-team league, she made every city except St. Louis— and not just once but several times. She seldom missed our games in New York, Philadelphia, or Washington. She once had a streak where she saw every one of our games in New York for eleven years.

In order to do this she had special arrangements in school: "My students knew that if they misbehaved they wouldn't be kept after school on a Friday if the Red Sox were playing in New York, but they knew they would have to report at eight A.M. on Monday. They knew the same thing applied to afternoon games at Fenway. Nobody was kept after school when the Sox were playing at home, but they knew they'd have to be in Dooley's classroom at eight the next morning."

She had another rule for her students where baseball was concerned: "If you see me in the ball park, pretend you don't. I am not there to talk to you. I'm there to see what's going on between the white lines, and that's all."

The Red Sox selected Lib to throw out the first ball to open the 1985 season. Lib was so closely identified with the Red Sox in the years I was playing that when Jean Yawkey decided to present us with World Series rings in 1986 on the fortieth anniversary of that Series—because the losing team didn't get rings when we played—she chose Lib as the person to make the presentations. "I remembered every one of them, except the relief pitchers," she said recently. I hadn't been to Fenway Park for years, and when I came through the line she said, "Welcome home, Dom." Then she burst into tears.

Ted was behind me, and when it was his turn he looked at her in mock disgust and said, "What the hell are you crying for?"

"None of your business," Lib told him flatly.

In remembering the 1941 season, Lib says: "The games were more fun to go to back then because the people came out expecting to have fun. The fans felt closer to the players. They were easier to identify with instead of the ones today, who are making millions of dollars. Back then we were looking at our heroes."

Elizabeth Dooley wasn't the only famous woman fan in major league ball parks in those years. There was one in Brooklyn too—Hilda Chester. She was a diehard Dodger fan who used to sit in the center field bleachers at Ebbets Field, a lady blessed with the loudest voice anyone ever heard.

The leather-lunged Brooklyn bleacherite was a study in contrast to the refined schoolteacher in Boston. Hilda used to sit and announce, "Hilda's here!" and everybody in the ball park could hear her. Her voice was a legend throughout Brooklyn and the whole National League. The National League players—on all the teams—used to tell us about her, so her fame spread to the American League too.

Hilda came to the games as a peanut vendor at one point in the 1930s but took up her position in the bleachers by the end of the decade. She would scream encouragement to her heroes on the field and was ready to go to war with anybody in the bleachers who dared to criticize any Dodger. That took a unique kind of loyalty, because the Dodgers didn't have a winning season from 1932 until Leo Durocher's first year as their manager in 1939.

34

She suffered a heart attack in the 1930s, and maybe the Dodgers were a contributing factor. The story is that her doctors told her to stop yelling so much at the Dodger games, so she began bringing skillets, pots, pans, and a large kitchen spoon to the games and make her noise that way. Eventually she upgraded her equipment and began using a cowbell.

Mickey Owen, the Dodger catcher in 1941, remembers that Hilda also upgraded her position, moving from the bleachers to the grandstand on the first base side. There she was not only near the players, but she was also close to the Dodgers' "Sym-phony," the ragtag band of five men who played Dixieland music and oompah-oompahed their way through "Take Me Out to the Ball Game" and other ball park traditionals including, of course, "Three Blind Mice" when the three umpires in those days came onto the field before the game.

Hilda never did really stop her hollering, even after a second heart attack in 1941. You could still hear her bellow out for the world to know, "Hilda's here!" Then she'd clang that cowbell, and the whole borough of Brooklyn knew that everything was okay at Ebbets Field—Hilda was there.

The papers made a big deal out of the first game in 1940 between the Red Sox and the Yankees after I won the center field job. It was Dom versus Joe in Fenway Park. It was a long series—five games—and I came out on top that time with eleven hits. Joe had nine. Twenty hits for the family in one series.

The papers also made a story out of our first meeting on the field and what we said to each other. As I trotted in from center field at the end of the Yankee half of the first inning of the first game, Joe was trotting out to the position.

Back then you always made sure to dodge the gloves on the ground. The fielders, all the infielders and the outfielders, used to leave their gloves on the outfield grass just beyond the infield when they came in to bat. They don't allow it anymore, but until the 1950s, everyone did it.

If you were an outfielder, you dropped it in mid-stride as you ran toward the dugout. If you were an infielder, you turned, took your glove by the thumb, and whirled it toward the outfield grass like a Frisbee. If you were superstitious and your glove landed palm up, you'd dash out to where it landed if you still had time and turned it over so it was palm down. Palm up was bad luck.

Shirley Povich remembers that Joe even did that more gracefully than anyone else. We would spin our gloves to the chosen spot in the shallow part of the outfield, like kids skipping flat rocks along a creek, and Povich was right. Joe did it best.

In short center, as I was flipping my glove and Joe was picking his up, we came within hollering distance. I called over to him, "Hello, Joe."

And he answered, "Hello, Dom."

That was it. The writers thought it was a case of two brothers being so reserved, so shy, that they hardly said anything to each other, but it wasn't that at all. We had a game to play, an important game. We couldn't very well stand out there and exchange news from home.

A week later the two teams met again, this time in Yankee Stadium. It was the first time I had seen the stadium. The evening after the first game of the series, I was having dinner with Joe at his apartment. At one point he noted I had played a shallow center field that afternoon, and said, "You're playing too close. That's a big field, and the ball carries well in that part of the ball park."

The next afternoon I played about ten steps deeper than I had the day before. Joe came up and hit one 460 feet. I was able to catch up with it and haul it in, because my brother was generous enough to give me the benefit of having played 77 games a year in Yankee Stadium for four seasons.

When he got back to the dugout, Joe told the other Yankees about the tip he'd given me the night before. Then he added, "I should never have mentioned it to him."

It was the biggest thrill of my rookie year, and I was sure Mom would approve of the way I was listening to my big brother.

One of the papers reminded the fans that our situation could have been reversed, that Joe could have been playing for the Red Sox and I might have been with the Yankees. Boston, like some of the other big league clubs, hadn't wanted to take a chance on Joe's knee, and the Yankees didn't like the fact that I wore glasses.

That used to be one of the stereotypes. Dorothy Parker had written a few years earlier: "Men seldom make passes at girls who wear glasses," and the same attitude prevailed in baseball. If you wore glasses, that meant you wouldn't be able to see well enough to hit, and you couldn't play in the infield because you might get hurt.

It even prompted the nickname that stuck with me—the "Little Professor." After somebody tried to call me "Bunky" in the Pacific Coast League and it didn't stick, somebody else tried to name me "Little Perfection" because they said I did so many things well on the field. But that didn't stick either.

Then someone, probably a writer, started calling me the "Little Professor" because they said I wore a serious expression that, combined with the glasses, made me look like a college professor. Presumably there are many people who have serious expressions and wear glasses but are not college professors, but the name stuck. I've never complained about it. Instead, I appreciated the affection and respect that it implied.

Something else happened in that series with the Yankees. Jimmie Foxx became a catcher again. He was in the final years of his Hall of Fame career, and with all the hitting we had in the outfield, Cronin wanted to find a spot for his heavy bat, so he put him behind the plate, where "Double X" had played a few games earlier in his career.

He caught in 42 games for the Red Sox that year and played another 95 at first base and one at third. With Foxx's versatility, Cronin was able to keep his bat in the lineup enough for Jimmie to hit 36 home runs and drive in 119 in the days before the American League's "designated hitter" rule.

But I remember Jimmie Foxx from the 1940 season for more than that. We shared an apartment in Boston that year, and no future Hall of Famer was ever nicer to a rookie than Jimmie was to me. We ate together, went to the movies together, and when Jimmie wanted to make the night a little longer, which was his tendency, we'd say good night and he'd go on his way.

I wasn't the only one that Double X was nice to—he was nice

to everyone. In fact, he was generous, almost to a fault. I was with him many times at dinner when fans would interrupt our meal and ask for his autograph or start talking baseball while Jimmie's meal got cold. Any other celebrity might have shooed the folks away, but not Jimmie. He'd sit there while his prime ribs cooled off and talk as long as the fans liked. When the fans would finally go back to their table, Jimmie would call their waiter over and pick up their check. He always told me he did it because they had been nice to him.

It's a good thing he was like that. With his brute strength, he could have done some real damage if he'd gone through life with a temper or a chip on his shoulder. I once saw him spin himself around and knock himself right off his feet in the batter's box while trying to check his swing—that's how strong he was.

The distance of his home runs once stopped me in my tracks in sheer awe. We were playing an exhibition game in Cincinnati and I had reached second base on a double, when Jimmie hit one out of the park and over a laundry sign across the street from Crosley Field. I was astounded at the distance of the home run and at the sound of approaching footsteps, woke up to find myself standing transfixed between second and third, admiring the flight of the ball.

Johnny Pesky has a more personal memory of the strength of Double X. As a rookie on one of our train trips, he was trying to do what all rookies had to do—climb into the upper berth—when nice guy Jimmie happened to come down the aisle.

"Hey, kid," he said, "are you trying to get into that berth?"

When Johnny told him yes, Foxx put one hand on Pesky's rear end and hoisted him into the air and then into the bunk all in one motion.

Events of significance were taking place outside the world of baseball as the 1940 season ended with the Reds returning to the World Series and defeating the Detroit Tigers in seven games. The national population reached 131 million, and our life expectancy improved to sixty-three years. We had several good new movies to see during our road trips, including *The Grapes of Wrath* with Henry Fonda and *For Whom the Bell Tolls,* starring Gary Cooper.

Two other movies that year gave us comic relief. One was *My Little Chickadee,* the only movie that W. C. Fields and Mae West ever made together. And the first "Road" picture in the series of seven starring Bing Crosby, Bob Hope, and Dorothy Lamour arrived. It was *The Road to Singapore.*

We were singing and whistling "Oh, Johnny! Oh!" after it became such a big hit for Wee Bonnie Baker, and we were dancing the night away to the music of the Big Band Era—Glenn Miller, Jimmy and Tommy Dorsey, Benny Goodman, and all the others. Those big names weren't the only bands we were dancing to, either. *Downbeat* magazine in 1940 said there were eight hundred dance bands playing every night in America's hotels and ballrooms. If we weren't in a ballroom, we could get the same good music on the jukebox down at one of America's corner drugstores for a nickel a tune.

You didn't even have to leave home to have fun. At home or in a hotel room, radio was our entertainment, especially on a Sunday night. That's when we heard Jack Benny and his carryings-on with Rochester, Phil Harris, and Dennis Day. We heard *Fibber McGee and Molly* and the loud disaster every time McGee forgot and opened his closet door. We heard Fred Allen ridicule the NBC vice presidents, and W. C. Fields feuding with Charlie McCarthy on the *Chase and Sanborn Hour* with Edgar Bergen. We heard *Amos 'n' Andy* and the Kingfish in their Fresh Air Taxi Company and Bob Hope, brought to you by Pepsodent.

On other nights we enjoyed "big band" music by Fred Waring and his Pennsylvanians, Glenn Miller and the Modernaires, Kay Kyser and his College of Musical Knowledge, Horace Heidt and His Musical Knights with their blind whistler, Fred Lowry, or Phil Spitalny and His All-Girl Orchestra.

For drama and thrills we tuned in to *Inner Sanctum, I Love a Mystery, The Shadow, Dr. I. Q., The Green Hornet, The Thin Man, Little Orphan Annie,* or *Mr. Keen, Tracer of Lost Persons.* If all those mysteries and chillers were too heavy, there was always *Grand Ol' Opry, The National Barn Dance,* the *Lucky Strike Hit*

39

Parade and *Major Bowes and His Original Amateur Hour,* where
Ted Mack later got his start, saying " 'Round and 'round she goes,
and where she stops, nobody knows."

Even the advertising on the radio was becoming fun because
things called "singing commercials" were introduced. We heard
quartets and duets singing, instead of just an announcer talking.

> If you want a treat instead of a treatment,
> Smoke Old Gold.

> Pepsi-Cola hits the spot.
> Twelve full ounces, that's a lot.
> Twice as much for a nickel, too.
> Pepsi-Cola is the drink for you.

> I feed my doggie Thrivo,
> He's very much alive-o,
> Full of pep and vim.
> If you want a lively pup,
> Then you'd better hurry up.
> Buy Thrivo for him.

During the day we could listen to the early radio soap operas
—if we wanted to—like *Ma Perkins, Stella Dallas, One Man's Family, Portia Faces Life,* or *Just Plain Bill.*

The listening was getting better every year, and so was the
radio itself. You didn't even have to turn a knob and move the
yellow celluloid dial anymore. The yellow celluloid was gone. Instead, we had something new called "push-button radios."

Things had gotten so much better as we continued to make
our way out of the Depression that now two out of every five
families in the United States owned a radio. Some even had two.

The most important event of 1940 for most of us major league
players didn't even occur during the baseball season. It happened
after the season, on October 29, when the Secretary of War, Henry
Stimson, stood blindfolded in Washington next to President Roose-

velt and a large jar filled with capsules and pulled out the number of the first man to be drafted into the United States Army under the new Selective Service Act.

Tin Pan Alley came up with a new song hit—"Goodbye, Dear, I'll Be Back in a Year." Those poor guys whose numbers were chosen would have to serve in the Army for a year, or so they thought.

— 4 —

THAT WONDERFUL SAMENESS

Drama critics tell us that the baseball movies that have been such smash hits in recent years, especially *The Natural* and *Field of Dreams,* are popular because they are fantasies. But are they?

Maybe we couldn't knock out the lights with a dramatic home run to win the pennant for our team the way Roy Hobbs did in *The Natural,* and maybe "Shoeless Joe" Jackson couldn't really rise out of a cornfield in Iowa still wearing his White Sox uniform from seventy years before. But one reason for the popularity of those movies is that they are *not* fantasies in at least one important sense —their portrayal of the magical hold baseball had on us in 1941 and still does today as we approach the next century.

Even during the Depression, Americans always found a way to come up with the price of admission for a baseball game. To this day baseball ticket prices remain the lowest in professional sports. Even when the Chicago "Black Sox" scandal broke in 1920 with the charges that Joe Jackson and seven teammates threw the 1919 World Series, the fans didn't stay away long, if at all. They found a new hero—Babe Ruth started hitting home runs.

In the years between world wars, men in white shirts and straw hats and women in white blouses and full skirts came to watch and cheer big league games. At bat and in the field players sometimes had trouble following the ball because it was coming out of a solid sea of white formed by the fans in the center field stands and behind home plate. Today many teams don't allow seating in center field for that reason, unless the game is a sellout.

One day a week, often Thursday, was Ladies Day, when women were admitted for half price. On Sunday there was almost always a doubleheader, two games for the price of one. And if a fan couldn't afford the dollar admission for a grandstand seat, there was always the bleachers for fifty cents.

No holiday was complete without a doubleheader—Memorial Day, July Fourth, and Labor Day. This was true especially on the Fourth of July. It was hard finding enough time to do everything you wanted to on that holiday. Picnics—they weren't called "cook-outs" then—the parade, and the evening fireworks were always part of the festivities, but you didn't want to miss the doubleheader either. If you couldn't go, you might be lucky enough to find somebody at the picnic with one of those new battery-powered portable radios you could take wherever you went.

There weren't as many ball park promotions as today. No Bat Day or Seat Cushion Day or—and this really happened—Panty Hose Day. The appeal of the game was enough to make the fans want to come out—by car, bus, or trolley. Some even walked to the games, which wasn't unusual because a lot of the players did too.

There was a strong community identification with the city's baseball team. By the 1941 baseball season, no team had ever left a city in almost forty years, since just after the two-league major league system was established in 1901, and in fact no other team would until the Braves left Boston for Milwaukee in 1953.

Every fan knew the Yankees, Giants, and Dodgers would always be in New York. The Giants and Dodgers move out of New York? You had to be crazy to think a thing like that. And all the way to California? You had to be even crazier.

The Red Sox and the Braves would always be in Boston, the Cardinals and Browns in St. Louis, the Cubs and White Sox in Chicago, and the A's and Phillies in Philadelphia. The Senators would always be in Washington, and the President would always throw out the first ball there on opening day. The Reds, baseball's first professional team in 1869, would never leave Cincinnati, and the Tigers would always play in Detroit, the Indians in Cleveland, and the Pirates in Pittsburgh.

School kids grew up learning their geography by knowing the ten cities and sixteen teams in the American and National leagues. It was that wonderful sameness, year in and year out. We could always count on baseball to be the same warm and sunny game, on the same fields, in the same cities. We loved baseball not only for itself but for the secure feeling of continuity it gave you. We felt a loyalty to baseball, because it was loyal to us.

If you were a kid, you saved the family's empty soft drink bottles and turned the empties into the grocery store for two cents each. If you drank plenty of colas and root beer, and searched for dirty empties that had been tossed into the woods and along the side of the road, you could collect enough pennies in refunds to see a real major league baseball game.

Man or boy, woman or girl, baseball was a special part of our daily lives and our roots, and those of us who remember that the *Saturday Evening Post* never went very long without a Norman Rockwell painting on the cover showing something about baseball have retained that love of baseball and passed it on to those who have followed us.

It's a hold on the American people that began in the 1920s and continues to this day, unlike any other sport. It's still a special part of our life as Americans, just as it was then, when Eddie Joost, Joe Orengo, and I headed for spring training in 1941 at speeds up to forty-five and fifty miles an hour.

Bob Feller was the talk of the baseball world as we prepared for the '41 season. The *Sporting News,* "baseball's Bible," selected him as its player of the year for leading the major leagues in wins in 1940 with 27. Feller had led the American League the year before with 24, and he had led both leagues in strikeouts for three straight seasons. When he struck out 261 men in 1940, it was almost double the amount that Kirby Higbe of the Phillies had to lead the National League—137.

Charlie Keller, the great Yankee slugger who played left field next to my brother Joe, was one of the most feared hitters in baseball in 1941, but even Keller remembers how dazzling Bob Feller was. All of us who used to have to hit against Feller will agree with what Charlie Keller says today about the player known as "Rapid Robert."

"Feller was the toughest," Charlie remembers. "You didn't sleep too well the night before you faced him. His fast ball didn't bother me. It was that curve ball of his—it was better than his fast ball."

Looking back on it today, we can laugh about Feller and his greatness in the years just before and after World War II. Feller laughs himself when he recalls those times. "I remember what Charlie said about my curve ball," Bob says today. "He used to tell people it behaved like an epileptic snake."

While Feller was standing all of us on our heads with a fast ball clocked at more than 100 miles an hour and a curve ball just as good, we wondered just how great this kid would be in the years ahead. There seemed to be no limit to his potential for greatness. His first years with a baseball were a real-life version of the hit movie, *Field of Dreams.* Just as in the movie, his father converted a part of their farm in Iowa to a baseball field, complete with bleachers, so he could form a team of the local boys and schedule games with the bigger teams from Des Moines. In that way, his boy Bob could have a chance to develop into a good baseball player because of the strong competition.

After five years with the Cleveland Indians, he had as many wins as Walter Johnson—82—and a better won-lost percentage than Johnson or Christy Mathewson, with more strikeouts than either one while pitching in fewer innings.

The worst news of all for those of us who had to hit against him was that when our 1941 season started, Feller was still only twenty-two years old.

Buddy Myer, the Senators' second baseman, had the best philosophy about hitting against Feller. Myer was an excellent hitter, the American League batting champion in 1935 and a .300 hitter nine times in 17 seasons in the big leagues. One thing Myer almost never did was strike out.

The 1941 season was Buddy's last, and by then he'd been trying to catch up with Feller's fast ball for six seasons. Feller got him on strikes one afternoon, and Myer came back to the Washington dugout and told his teammates, "Boys, hit what you see, and if you don't see it, come on back."

Despite the way Feller's performances dominated both leagues, another young pitcher from that season, Walt Masterson of the Senators, thought he noticed something different. Walt became my teammate on the Red Sox after the war, but in 1941 he was in his third year in the American League, still just a kid from Philadelphia who was only twenty years old when the season started.

He was talking recently about what he considers the added significance of the 1941 season. "As far as I was concerned," he said, "the 1941 season marked the advent of defensive baseball, especially in the American League. Until 'forty-one it was nothing but sheer strength, with the pitchers throwing their hardest and the hitters ready to challenge the best fast ball the pitcher had to offer."

But Walt remembers that something seemed to happen, and it involved Al Smith, the left-hander with the Cleveland Indians who later in '41 helped to stop my brother Joe's 56-game hitting streak. "The National League was a low breaking ball league," Walt recalls, "and the American League was always a high fast ball league —but then here comes this left-hander with a so-so record in the National League who's traded to our league and he's getting guys out with curves and change-ups. Until Smith came along, the only real curve ball pitchers in our league were Tommy Bridges and Johnny Murphy. Nobody else was throwing curves or changing speeds."

Masterson remembers that Pete Appleton was trying to adopt the same philosophy of pitching by working on a slider, but not everybody was thrilled about it, including his manager when he pitched for the Senators, Bucky Harris.

Appleton gave up a home run with his new pitch, and Harris

told him, "Well, Pete—it slid, all right—all the way out of the ball park."

The New York baseball writers were thinking about more than Bob Feller. At their annual winter dinner at the Commodore Hotel before the 1941 season, they paid tribute to, of all things, the hot dog. They honored the Stevens Brothers concessions firm for promoting the hot dog as the staple food at America's baseball parks, and Tom Meany of New York's *PM* newspaper was even moved to write a tribute called, you guessed it, "Man Bites Dog."

Meany, another winner of the Spink Award for excellence in baseball writing, maintained his journalistic objectivity. He told the crowd, "Historians say the hot dog is fifty years old tonight. I must have had the original at last year's World Series."

The *Sporting News* published an editorial praising the American League for scheduling more doubleheaders for the '41 season. The weekly paper saw the subject as one of the issues of the day, linking doubleheaders to a shorter work week for the players and comparing that to the forty-hour week just won by America's automobile workers in Detroit.

Sporting News also pointed out that doubleheaders on Sundays would give the players a day off during the week. "The sport," the paper said, "must adapt itself to changing times . . . unquestionably the trend is to a shorter week in everything."

We were talking about other things, too, as spring training began. All of us were amused at the "feud" between the front offices of the Indians and the Detroit Tigers. The Indians announced they would be paying Feller $30,000 for the 1941 season, the most money paid to a pitcher since Lefty Grove won 31 games with the Philadelphia A's in 1931.

But the Tigers took great offense to that, saying they paid Buck Newsom $30,000 the year before when he helped to pitch them to the 1940 American League pennant. It was an exercise in oneupmanship, with both teams breaking the unwritten law of professional teams against disclosing a player's salary.

There was a more serious topic of conversation in the Red Sox camp at Sarasota—Bobby Doerr. Bobby was born in Los Angeles, but he moved to a ranch in Oregon after he started playing second base for the Red Sox in 1937. To say that the ranch was in a remote spot is an understatement. It was near the upper reaches of the Umpqua River in the southwest corner of the state. There was no road to his ranch. The only connection with the outside world was a boat that stopped once a day.

Bobby had appendicitis symptoms in 1940, but things calmed down, as they often do with those symptoms, and Bobby was thinking maybe he had gotten lucky. But the appendix flared up again during the off season while Bobby was at his ranch.

He made a snap decision not to take any chances, especially knowing that what happened the year before might have been a warning. Somehow he got himself to that once-a-day boat and a Good Samaritan drove him the last eighty miles to the nearest hospital in Eugene. The doctors didn't fool around. They removed his appendix immediately. If Bobby had missed the boat that day, another twenty-four hours could have meant the Red Sox would be looking for a new second baseman.

But the overriding topic of conversation now was "the international situation." Men were being drafted into the army, and as we limbered up in Florida we realized that before we knew it we could be holding a rifle in our hands instead of a bat.

The conventional things Americans had always done took on an additional dimension in those times, even something as traditional as the New Year's Eve celebration at Times Square. The *New York Times* said on the morning of January 1 that a million people had packed the square the night before, and the headline said they were "Trying to Forget Blackouts Abroad."

The story said: "Everywhere—even in the most hectic whirlpools of the downtown throng—there hovered the realization that London, Rome, Berlin were blacked out; that smoke still rose from the ruins of British buildings; that there were more dark days ahead for countless human beings in other countries, even if this one was fortunate enough to continue at peace. . . .

"Soldiers and sailors dotted the mob; young men who may be soldiers or sailors before next year shouldered along with them."

49

On that same front page there was an article reporting that the navy fleet was being held in Hawaiian waters "until the existing international situation is definitely improved." Another story carried the headline:

HITLER SEES VICTORY IN 1941,
DISAVOWS WORLD CONQUEST;
2 ITALIAN TRANSPORTS SUNK

On page six of the same day's paper, there was an equally ominous story quoting the Japanese foreign minister, Yosuke Matsuoka: "As a New Year greeting it may sound unlucky, but in my innermost heart I fear the coming year will prove a most tragic and unfortunate one for all mankind."

President Roosevelt went on the radio with another of his "fireside chats" in January and told the people: "Never before has our American civilization been in such danger as now."

The outlook was changing in baseball too. We had to keep our minds on our work, but we knew that all around us, "the international situation" was starting to have an effect.

Hugh Mulcahy of the Phillies became the first Major Leaguer to be drafted. He was inducted into the Army on March 8, just as we were beginning spring training, as a member of the 101st Artillery at Camp Edwards on Cape Cod. He was twenty-seven years old, the prime age for a major league baseball player. He had won 13 games the year before for a bad Philadelphia team that won only 50 games.

Hugh didn't let things get him down. People now say that World War II was America's last popular war, and the attitudes and comments of all of us during those years seem to prove that point. What Mulcahy told reporters was an excellent example. Instead of moaning about the interruption to his career, which would have been understandable, he said, "It might be a little tougher and might take a little longer for me to get into shape when I report for spring training next season, but I don't think this year of Army life will hamper my pitching any. Personally I think this conscription bill is a great thing for the young men of today."

For the record, Hugh came back late in 1945 and was able to pitch in only 23 more games before retiring two seasons later.

Before the 1941 season started, the *Sporting News* stepped in with its own contribution. In a special box in its March 6 issue, it announced that the publisher was making the weekly paper available to the players and fans in military camps at the "lowest possible subscription rates permitted by postal regulations," so they "may keep up with baseball."

The paper would be available for half-price, $2.50 per year, "during the period of emergency."

The major league teams weren't the only ones whose operations were being complicated by the draft. The minor league teams were being hurt too. Maybe the worst case happened in Williamsport, Pennsylvania, in the Eastern League in the first months of the draft. The team bought a second baseman, Lou Bush, from Memphis of the Southern Association to strengthen its infield.

But Bush was drafted into the Army. So they got themselves another second baseman, Jerry Lynn. Then he got drafted too.

Even the baseball itself was having problems. The manufacturers got the horsehide to cover baseballs from the Balkans because of the superior quality of the horsehide that came from that region, but with the Nazis controlling central and southern Europe the Balkans were suddenly one of the hot spots of the war. Baseball manufacturers canceled their orders and began looking for sources of horsehide in the United States and South America.

There were other problems in trying to make baseball equipment. The cork for the center of the ball was grown on trees in Spain. Tape for the bat handles was made of rubber from East India and was coated with asphalt from Trinidad. The kangaroo leather from Australia for our shoes was still available, but no one knew for how long.

On the eve of the 1941 major league season, Tom McMahon, a sports announcer for radio station WAGE in Syracuse, sent a letter to the "Voice of the Fan" column in the *Sporting News*. Its sentiments typified the words being spoken and written by Americans everywhere:

Right now Uncle Sam is in a mighty big pennant race. And all America wants to know how to help the United States win that pennant. It is only fitting that America should find the perfect answer to that problem in America's national pastime. For there, across the pages of baseball history, that all America in 1941 may see, is indelibly inscribed the irrefutable premise—If you want that pennant, Play Ball!

Despite it all, President Roosevelt, who five months earlier became the only president elected to three terms, went out to Griffith Stadium in Washington to see the Senators take on the Yankees and threw out the first ball as baseball opened the 1941 season, one of eight times FDR performed the honors. FDR was one of the most enthusiastic baseball fans to occupy the White House, so people weren't surprised when he stayed for the whole game. In Brooklyn, where the Dodgers opened their season, the fans at Ebbets Field recited the Pledge of Allegiance before the start of the game.

While history was being made all around the world in that explosive year, baseball was about to make some history of its own. Not even a war would stop it. After all, the baseball season *always* opens in April.

— 5 —

AN EYEWITNESS TO
BASEBALL HISTORY

The major league season opened as scheduled on April 14, and no one had reason to suspect that we were headed for what has endured as the most historic baseball season of them all. I may have been the luckiest player in either league that year. I was an eyewitness to baseball history from three different vantage points that no one else had for four of the big stories of 1941.

I was Ted Williams's friend and teammate and played right next to him in the outfield during his memorable .406 season. The star who held the whole nation's attention for two months with a 56-game hitting streak was my brother Joe. When Teddy hit the most dramatic home run in the history of the All-Star game, with Joe on first base, I was in the on-deck circle as the next hitter. And when the great Lefty Grove achieved his three-hundredth victory, I caught the last out.

But the anticipation of the exciting achievements that lay ahead and the feeling of optimism that always accompanies the start of the baseball season were tempered by the uncertainty caused by the gathering storm of international events. Buddy Lewis, an outstanding hitter and outfielder with the Washington Senators who already had three seasons with batting averages over

.300 in his first five full years in the big leagues, was a case in point. He asked his draft board for a four-month deferment so he could play the '41 season.

His worried manager, Bucky Harris, asked Lewis what the response was. Buddy told him, "They just smiled."

Benny McCoy, the starting second baseman for the Philadelphia A's in 1940 and again in '41, was feeling the pressure from his draft board, too, in Grandville, Michigan. He was single and caring for his mother and father and supporting them on his salary, but the newspapers said the bonus he got from Connie Mack for signing, plus his annual salary of almost $10,000 a year, "are said to be influencing the board to place him in Class A-1."

The paper meant 1-A, but the draft board meant business. The 1-A classification meant you were fit for military duty and as good as gone. In this day and age, to consider changing a man's military draft classification because he's making an above-average salary is unthinkable and grounds for a lawsuit claiming discrimination on the basis of your income. But not in 1941.

Benny, in fact, did go into the service. He entered the Navy after the '41 season and served in the Pacific all through the war. I know. I served with him. We shared the same tent, just the two of us. He never played in the major leagues again.

We didn't know whether we were going to be wearing our baseball "monkey suits" or an olive-drab uniform, and we found a sympathetic friend in Dan Daniel, the columnist for the *New York World-Telegram*. With all the back and forth involving the draft, who was going, who wasn't, what was grounds for a deferment and what wasn't, Daniel wrote:

> With one draft board insisting that ball players must go and another adopting the policy that since the players must get their entire incomes for the year in five months they should not be inducted until October, with Washington taking the stand that the major leagues furnish national morale-building factors and some fans shouting that the players must go, is it any wonder that the poor guys in the monkey suits are going daffy about the whole thing?

Just before the season started there was an ad in the *Sporting News* from Charleston, West Virginia, for players interested in the minor leagues. The ad sought "experienced ball players for Class C clubs. Give age, experiences, and lowest salary."

Up in the big leagues things were definitely better for at least two of my teammates, both of them pitchers—Mike Ryba and Lefty Grove.

Ryba was a great story for the reporters, and they couldn't resist writing about him. He was a right-handed relief pitcher from DeLancey, Pennsylvania, who was going to be thirty-eight years old in June. The reporters were calling him a "rookie" because he had been out of the big leagues for two years after breaking in with the Cardinals in 1935 and pitching for them for four seasons.

Mike played every position on his way up through the minors and led the International League with 24 wins in 1940 while pitching for Rochester. He even managed briefly in the minors and achieved the distinction of winning the Most Valuable Player award four times in different leagues. He was so versatile—and durable—that in the minors he once pitched the first game of a doubleheader and then caught the second game. He could hit too. He had a lifetime batting average of .235, high for a pitcher, and once hit .380 in the minors.

For all of that, he didn't even get to keep his real name. "Mike" was another Dominic. One of his first managers, Bill McKechnie, kept hollering one day in spring training: "Mike! Hey, Mike!" After a while McKechnie was getting steamed at his player for his refusal to answer him, so he finally walked over and confronted him. "Dammit, Mike," he said. "Why won't you answer me?"

Ryba said, "My name is Dominic. It's not Mike."

McKechnie, using his authority as manager, said, "Well, it is now!"

For the rest of his career, Dominic Ryba was Mike Ryba.

"Mike" was so happy at getting a second chance in the bigs as a thirty-seven-year-old "rookie" that he was able to win 7 games for us in 1941 while saving 6 more and losing only 3. He was also

55

able to stick it out for six more seasons including our 1946 World Series team and ended with a major league career of ten years and 52 victories.

Lefty Grove never had any problem sticking in the major leagues. His case was just the opposite. He was one of the greatest pitchers in the history of our sport, and in 1941 he reached that milestone of pitching excellence—300 wins—and I was proud to play a small part in that.

Therein lies a story. Lefty, whose formal name was Robert Moses Grove, was a quiet, almost moody, six-foot three-inch left-handed pitcher from the coal-mining country of western Maryland. He was a 20-game winner eight times, seven of them with Connie Mack and the Philadelphia A's. He led the American League in wins four times, including 31 in 1931, led the league in strikeouts his first seven years, and led in complete games three times and in earned run average nine times.

Those are Hall of Fame numbers, so it didn't surprise anybody when he was elected to Cooperstown in 1947.

But in 1941 he wanted that three-hundredth win in the worst way, needing seven wins to make it and fully aware that only a dozen or so other pitchers in the whole history of baseball had reached that level. He was beginning to show some signs of aging, slipping from 15 wins and only 4 defeats in 1939 to a 7–6 record in 1940, his lowest number of wins in his 16 seasons to that point. But he was hanging on to get that number 300.

That was when I met him, during my rookie season in spring training at the Red Sox camp in Sarasota. To be more accurate, I didn't meet him—not for a long time. When I reported to camp, Jimmie Foxx and the other veterans all came over to me and introduced themselves, told me they were glad to have me and wished me the best of luck.

All except Lefty Grove.

I knew Grove's reputation as a quiet guy who liked to be left alone. Besides, I was just a rookie, and in those years many veterans took a hard line toward rookies. Their understandable reasoning was that the rookies were trying to take away their jobs, so they extended no courtesies, and something like today's practice of giving hitting or fielding tips to a rookie was frowned on by many of the older players.

Grove was from that school. I accepted that. Some of the others asked me after a couple of weeks why I wasn't speaking to Lefty. After all, he was a star.

I told them that was exactly why I wasn't going to go over to him, intrude on his privacy, and sound like a pushy kid. I thought it was Lefty's privilege to decide for himself when he wanted to talk to the rookie from San Francisco, or whether to talk to me at all. I had no problem with whatever this great pitcher's preference might be, and I was determined to keep my place and not force myself on Grove. Maybe that was wrong, but that was the way I sized it up as the twenty-three-year-old trying to make the team with Lefty, who turned forty during the first week of our 1940 camp.

After a couple of weeks of this, which seemed to be bothering others a lot more than it was bothering me, I was on my way back to our headquarters, the Sarasota Hotel, after visiting a friend in the hospital with another friend of mine in the Sarasota area, Wes Palmer.

As we drew closer to the hotel, Wes asked me, "Why don't you forget your reasoning and just say hello to Lefty?"

I told him, "I don't think I can do that."

Just a few minutes later we were walking across the front porch of this stately old southern hotel, with black wrought-iron chairs, where the guests could relax in the warm Florida breeze and watch the world go by.

As fate would have it, that's exactly what Lefty Grove was doing. He was sitting on the porch with the Red Sox clubhouse manager, Johnny Orlando, and Lefty was right next to the front door. I couldn't avoid him and he couldn't avoid me.

As I came close to his chair, I put out my hand and said, "Hello, Lefty."

With that, this great player bolted to his feet, thrust out his right hand, and said with enthusiasm, "Hello, Dom!"

Then he turned toward Orlando, grabbed him with both

hands and lifted him bodily out of his chair, saying to Johnny, "Get the hell out of that chair! Here, Dom, have a seat."

After that we became friends and admirers of each other. Once in 1940 Lefty lost a 1–0 game in 13 innings to the Senators in Washington, and as we sat on our chairs next to each other in front of the old metal lockers in the clubhouse at Griffith Stadium, Grove maintained a stony silence. The whole baseball world knew of his temper and his complete intolerance for defeat. At one point shortly after the game was over he stood up in silent rage and took his shirt off—without unbuttoning it. He simply ripped the shirt off, with buttons flying in every direction. Then he went back into his solitude.

I didn't dare break the silence. I wasn't too thrilled about the loss either, but after what seemed like forever I thought I'd better say something or we might be in that locker room until dawn, so I got up and turned to him and said, "Lefty, you pitched one hell of a ball game."

He nodded around in the direction of our teammates and said, "If the rest of these guys had played as well as you did, we'd have won in nine."

In 1941 Lefty was determined to win his three-hundredth game, and he finally reached that golden peak on July 25 with a win over the Cleveland Indians in Boston. The final score was 10–6 in what people consider a typical Fenway Park game. Jim Tabor, our third baseman, and Jimmie Foxx helped Lefty. Tabor hit two home runs and Double X had a two-run triple.

I was proud to catch the last out, a fly ball hit by Lou Boudreau. I trotted into the Red Sox dugout on the first base side of Fenway and handed the historic baseball to Lefty myself. It was one of the big baseball stories of 1941. Grove became only the twelfth pitcher in history to win 300 games and only the second left-hander.

Sporting News speculated that Grove might be the last ever to do it, that only Bob Feller of the current pitchers had any chance, and he faced the prospect of induction into the military service. That's exactly what happened. Feller enlisted in the Navy two days after Pearl Harbor and missed almost four full seasons. He won

266 games. A computer expert in Seattle named Ralph Winnie fed data into his computer based on Feller's last three seasons before the war and his first three after and found that Bob might have won 373 games.

Sporting News, however, was allowing only for those pitching stars on the scene in 1941 and not for those who would come later. Although the war cheated Feller out of a chance to reach 300 wins, others later reached that level of pitching immortality—Warren Spahn, Early Wynn, Gaylord Perry, and Steve Carlton.

As for Lefty, he barely made it into that charmed 300 circle. He never won another game.

Mike and Lefty were typical of the major league players from the class of '41 in at least two respects—their love of baseball and their determination to play it every day, regardless of how they felt.

Johnny Mize, the Hall of Fame slugger with the Cardinals, Giants, and Yankees, talked about this at a reception in Washington before the annual golf tournament sponsored by the Major League Baseball Players Alumni Association. "I never heard of a hamstring or a rotator cuff until a few years ago," he said. "If a guy got a sore arm, he sat on the end of the bench, the doctor treated him, and in a week or so he was back in there. Teams carried eight pitchers, and if one got hurt, you went with seven."

My teammate and friend, Johnny Pesky, agrees with Mize, and he has a story to prove his point. We were having lunch at Anthony's Pier 4 restaurant in Boston recently, and Johnny told the story about the time when we were playing under Joe McCarthy, who managed the Yankees in '41 and came to Boston after the war.

"I remember one day when Allie Reynolds hit me with a fast ball right in the upper arm. The pain was killing me, but I wasn't going to give Reynolds the satisfaction of seeing me rub it, even if the damn thing dropped off. So I trotted down to first base and stayed in the game. After it was over, though, I put an ice pack on the arm. I'm sitting there holding the ice on the arm when McCarthy comes by. He was pleased with the defiance I had shown toward Reynolds. He smiled and said, 'I saw what you did out there today, kid—I saw Crosetti do the same thing a thousand times.'

"I almost passed out. He was telling me I had to do it another 999 times to keep impressing him."

Pesky said that day, "We cared about each other. I remember when you hurt your shoulder. I held wet towels against it every day until you were able to play again, and you would have done the same for me. I wanted you back in that lineup. We worried about each other."

Outfielder Taft Wright of the White Sox was playing at Sportsman's Park in St. Louis once even though he was sick from the summer heat. His willingness to play while sick made him the victim of a freak accident. He was chasing a fly ball on that beastly hot afternoon when he missed the catch and ran smack into the wall, face first. His glasses were embedded in his forehead. He had passed out from heat exhaustion even though he was still running for the ball. The only thing that stopped him in his semiconscious state was the wall. But he stayed in the game.

Pesky is right about the way we felt about one another. We felt the same way about the game itself. We loved the game, even doubleheaders—especially doubleheaders. Oh, how I loved them! They gave us the chance to play two games instead of only one. If they had wanted us to play three, we would have been happy to.

With us, the game and the desire to play it were the number one priority. We took a tremendous pride in what we did and in how the public viewed us. The money was well down on the list, maybe the third or fourth or fifth reason we were major league baseball players in 1941.

Walt Masterson remembers the seniority system applied by the veteran players toward rookies: "When I was a rookie, I wasn't allowed to do anything with the other pitchers. I was told to handle the throws back to whoever was hitting fungoes to the outfield. I wasn't allowed to run with the other pitchers in the outfield. They wouldn't let me take batting practice—in fact, they wouldn't even let me have a bat."

Al Simmons, the great Hall of Famer who may have been the

greatest right-handed hitter ever, sent him a message too. In those days the young pitchers were expected to put the ball exactly where the veteran hitters wanted it in batting practice. If they didn't, the veteran would send a hot ground ball back through the middle against the kid pitcher, making him skip rope, or tattoo him with a line drive.

"Simmons hit me seven times in my first week," Masterson says. Then a veteran pitcher, Jimmie DeShong, came to Masterson's rescue, hollering into Simmons in the batting cage: "You SOB! You hit that kid one more time and I'm going to take that bat and hit you over the head with it!"

Masterson remembers the pressure on the young players. "You had to earn your way," he says today. "You had pressure on you every day to compete successfully against so many good players. All the major league teams had a tremendous number of good players not only on their rosters but on their minor league teams.

"I used to run out of gas every September and I never could understand it. I was young and healthy and in good playing condition. Then it dawned on me—it was mental fatigue, the pressure on me as a young player trying to make it. Day in and day out, you were in that caldron."

The Red Sox made the only real challenge to the Yankees in '41 in the race for the American League pennant. We led the league in runs scored, hits, doubles, team batting average, and slugging average, but we were able to challenge the Yankees only briefly. The 1940 champions, the Detroit Tigers, and the team that almost beat them that year, the Cleveland Indians, both finished behind us— and we finished 17 games behind the Yankees.

The real race was in the National League, where the Cardinals and the Dodgers went at each other all season long. Lon Warneke, the "Arkansas Humming Bird," gave the Cards a big lift when he pitched a no-hitter to defeat the Reds, 2–0, in Cincinnati on August 30. It was the kind of game that can start a team on a drive to the pennant as it turns the corner into September, but the Dodgers were able to win the championship over the Cardinals by two and a half games.

61

Maybe the wonder is that the Cards, or anybody else, came even that close to the Dodgers. Brooklyn led the National League in every offensive department in '41—hits, runs, doubles, triples, home runs, team batting average, and slugging average—and the Dodger pitchers topped the league in saves and had the best earned run average.

Brooklyn also had the National League's most-talked-about individual star of the year, Pete Reiser also known as "Pistol Pete." He was a pistol all right, the National League batting champion that year and the daredevil center fielder who was willing to take on any outfield wall in the league, and did.

In those years before warning tracks and padded fences, Reiser banged his body full-tilt into anything that got in his way of a fly ball, suffering various and repeated injuries to his head and body. Eventually that pounding sharply reduced his performance and shortened his career, but in 1941 the baseball world thrilled to his exploits and to his defiant guts.

Reiser was in only his second year of major league baseball that season. He broke in with a .293 average in 1940, playing third base and shortstop as well as the outfield. Then came his career year.

In '41, as the Dodgers' starting center fielder, he hit .343 and led the National League in slugging average as well as batting average. He also topped the league in doubles, triples, and runs scored. The National League players were telling us American Leaguers that the man was destined for the Hall of Fame if anybody ever was. That's how outstanding he was. They were reserving a spot for his plaque on the wall at Cooperstown already, even though he was only twenty-two years old.

In 1942, as he kept terrorizing opposing pitchers with his bat and his own team with his outfield disasters, he hit over .300 again—.310—and led the league in stolen bases. He lost the next three seasons because of military service during the war and never again equaled his stardom of '41. He had only one good season after the war, hitting .309 in 110 games with the Dodgers in 1947.

The Dodgers traded him to the Boston Braves in 1949, and he

ended up playing with three teams in his last four seasons, retiring after hitting .136 with the Cleveland Indians in 1952.

The Dodger fans seemed to have everything going for them in 1941. Their beloved "bums" were a success on the field, and they had Red Barber to tell them about it over the radio. Red, with a soft accent from his Alabama birth and Florida boyhood and a command of the English language as well as the national pastime, had his own way of telling the "Flatbush faithful" what their heroes were doing. If they were staging a rally, they were "tearin' up the pea patch." If they were enjoying a big lead, they were "sittin' in the catbird seat." And if disaster befell them? Then it was, "Ohhhhh, Doctor!"

In New York Mel Allen was telling the fans that the home runs flying off the bats of my brother Joe and Charlie Keller, Tommy Henrich and Joe Gordon, were "going—going—gone!" They had different styles, but today they have one thing in common—they're winners of the Ford Frick Award for excellence in baseball broadcasting.

In Washington, Arch McDonald didn't have a team with that kind of power and excellence to excite his listeners with, so he invented a "Mrs. Murphy," who shared his excitement over the air. He also played a song, "They Cut Down the Old Pine Tree," before each broadcast, although nobody ever really knew what that pine tree had to do with baseball:

> Oh, they cut down the old pine tree.
> And they hauled it away to the mill.
> To make a cabin of pine
> For that sweetheart of mine.
> Oh, they cut down the old pine tree.

Some of the writers covering us in 1941 were as legendary as some of the players they were writing about. That could be both a blessing and a curse in Boston, and it was one of the main reasons for the troubles Ted Williams had with the press there.

A big part of the problem in Boston was simply that we had so many newspapers. We had the *Record,* the *Post,* the *Herald,* the

Globe, the *American,* the *Traveler,* the *Christian Science Monitor*—which had two reporters who were members of the Baseball Writers' Association of America—the *Advertiser* and the *Transcript,* plus an Italian daily, *La Notizia.* It added up to ten newspapers with forty members of the Baseball Writers' Association, and that doesn't even count the radio broadcasters. We had reporters falling all over themselves, and the competition among them for stories often led to the kinds of problems that Ted and others encountered.

Dave Egan of the *Boston Record,* who became Ted's sworn enemy, was one of our most prominent baseball writers in 1941, and so were men like Hy Hurwitz of the *Globe* and Harold Kaese of the *Transcript.* And if you run down a list of the writers' names, it isn't hard to figure out why Joe Cronin was so popular in Boston. There was Egan and Finnegan, Gillooly and Keany, Malaney, Coyne, Cunningham, Fenton, O'Leary, Conway, Drohan, McNamee, another O'Leary, and Noonan.

The list of baseball writers sounded more like the membership roster for the Friendly Sons of St. Patrick.

Even that long ago New York seemed to have the most of everything, and that included baseball writers too. They had more papers than Boston—eleven—plus the wire services, news syndicates, and special publications. Their membership in the Baseball Writers' Association totaled 110.

There was more than sheer volume in their numbers. There was greatness, too, in the persons of writers who became giants as sportswriters or in other fields of American literature, men like Red Smith, who made a significant contribution to baseball as well as to literature when he wrote, "Baseball is a dull game only to those with dull minds." There was also Sid Mercer, Bill Corum, Arthur Daley, Bob Considine, Stanley Woodward, Paul Gallico, Frank Graham, Tom Meany, Quentin Reynolds, Grantland Rice, and Damon Runyon.

There were characters, too, and two of the biggest were John Drebinger of the *New York Times* and Dan Daniel of the *World-Telegram.*

Drebinger was born into cultured surroundings, the son of the first violinist of the Metropolitan Opera orchestra when Caruso sang there. The son became the classical pianist of the Yankee Stadium press box, with an ego as big as some of the athletes he wrote about. So confident was he about his knowledge of any subject that he once got into an argument at the Variety Club about a brass instrument which he insisted was a trumpet.

When the man at the bar disagreed, Drebinger asked in his usual high tone, "What do you know about horns?"

The man he was insulting was Ziggy Elman, Tommy Dorsey's popular trumpet player.

Bill Slocum described Drebinger's attitude best: "Nobody ever won an argument with John."

He wrote the same way. He once told his readers about a routine catch by Babe Herman, the Dodgers' colorful outfielder known for his adventures with the glove, by writing: "Terry flied out to Herman, unassisted."

He was a chess player, an authority on tropical fish, and someone who delighted in imitating celebrities, especially Calvin Coolidge and Theodore Roosevelt.

Dan Daniel was blessed with the same supreme confidence that Drebinger had. Dan was a big, heavy man, slightly round-shouldered, and with a gravel voice and a perpetual scowl. The other writers considered him a warm and generous man with a deadpan wit.

Daniel had a colorful writing style. He wouldn't write that someone "said" something. He used verbs like "declared" and "remonstrated." And he wasn't above inventing a few of his own, either, like "exuberated" and "vehemed."

He felt no reluctance to hand out advice to the experts from his typewriter. In 1946, after we embarrassed the National League in the All-Star game, 12–0, in Boston, with Ted hitting two home runs, Daniel wrote in his column: "The events that transpired yesterday in Fenway Park make it clear that the National League is in imminent danger of becoming a minor league unless certain steps are taken. . . ."

Barely three months later, after the Cardinals beat us in the World Series when Enos Slaughter made his famous dash to the plate to win the seventh game, Daniel wrote: "The autumn classic demonstrated once again that the National League has a distinct margin of superiority over the junior circuit. It is imperative that the teams in Will Harridge's organization look to their farms for new and exciting talent. . . ."

When a friend pointed out that he was contradicting what he had written about the two leagues after the All-Star game, Daniel said simply, "I've warned them both. Now they're on their own."

Pee Wee Reese, the Dodgers' shortstop in '41, still remembers the New York writers with affection and respect. "I got along great with the writers," Pee Wee said recently from his home in Louisville. "If we were someplace having a drink and some of the writers would come by, a lot of the guys would run like a thief. But I used to say, 'These guys aren't going to bite you. Just treat them the way they'd like to be treated. They have a job to do.' I got along very well with them."

Pee Wee says, "I used to go out with them occasionally. I enjoyed being with Dick Young and Al Lang and Roscoe McGowan. Those guys were just terrific people. We had some great writers."

The *Washington Post*'s Shirley Povich, the man who wrote the moving description of Lou Gehrig Day at Yankee Stadium two years earlier, was one of the most respected of the baseball writers in 1941. A modest man who could outwrite and outreport most of his colleagues, he achieved celebrity status in later years not only for his skills but for his name as well.

He could claim one distinction that none of his baseball-writing colleagues could ever accomplish: He became the only man ever listed in *Who's Who of American Women,* along with Elizabeth Taylor, Mamie Eisenhower, and all the other famous ladies of the day. There he was, right smack between Elizabeth Pound and Hortense Powdermaker.

Shirley used to receive questionnaires from the Marquis Publishing Company in Chicago, who published the *Who's Who* books, requesting information for their women's directory. This was even though their own biographical information on Shirley which they sent him for his confirmation showed him to be happily married to a wife named Ethyl and the father of three children named David, Maury, and Lynn.

Sure enough, a few years later he showed up in that *Who's Who* and overnight became one of the most famous "women" in America. He was the guest star on some of the big radio and television shows including Garry Moore's *I've Got a Secret,* where he stumped the panel. He received a telegram from Red Patterson, the vice president of the Dodgers, saying, "My dear Shirley—And to think we roomed together in Miami!" There were other wires, including one from Walter Cronkite: "Miss Povich, will you marry me?"

Povich was used to this sort of thing and was unflappable about all of it. He used to get questionnaires from women's groups requesting certain pertinent information like the one from the League of American Pen Women that asked, "How do you get along with the men in your office?"

Povich filled in his answer: "Fine. I just try to be one of the boys."

Another question asked "Miss Povich" if "her" sex was a handicap in "her" work and he responded, "I can honestly say none whatsoever."

The Revlon Company once went beyond just asking for information. The marketing people wanted a reaction to a new product so they sent him a sample with a letter suggesting that Shirley might want to try it for his menstrual pains.

Povich experienced every kind of situation as a baseball writer, ranging from saving a manager's job to ducking a punch from an angry first baseman.

The manager was Bucky Harris of the Senators. He was about to be fired by his owner, Clark Griffith, and his prospects didn't get any brighter while the Senators were losing a game to the Indians in Cleveland. This was in the days when a team's radio announcers didn't travel with the club, so Arch McDonald was back in Washington getting his information from the Western Union telegrapher who sat next to him in the studios of Station WJSV in the Earle Building in downtown Washington.

At the start of the ninth inning, the Senators were losing by a run. The first two Senators got base hits. Then Cecil Travis, one of the best hitters in baseball, swung at the first pitch and missed. The Western Union operator sitting next to Povich in the press box at Municipal Stadium started to flash the information to McDonald in Washington—but Povich grabbed his hand and said, "Hold it. Tell him 'Travis fouls off the first pitch attempting to bunt.'"

Shirley knew that Griffith would be listening to the radio in Washington and would fire Harris for sure if he knew Bucky wasn't telling Travis to bunt for a sacrifice in that situation. Povich figured it was strike one anyhow, so what difference did it make? As Shirley says, "I'm keeping Bucky off the hook. I'm lying, but nobody's getting hurt."

On the second pitch Travis swung and missed again. The Western Union operator, on more instructions from Povich, flashed the same word to McDonald on the other end: "Travis fouls off the second pitch attempting to bunt."

Then, with two strikes, the hitter is on his own anyhow, and he'll almost always swing away instead of taking the chance of laying down a bunt and having it roll foul for a strikeout. Travis swung at the third pitch, hit a triple, and the Senators won the game.

Bucky Harris got to keep his job not only through the night but through several more seasons, thanks to Povich's journalistic intervention. Today Shirley's colleagues in Washington might call it managing the news, but he sees it as "just helping a pal to keep his job."

The angry first baseman was Joe Kuhel, one of the best and most graceful players at his position in the 1930s while playing for the Senators and the White Sox. But he missed a ground ball one afternoon at Griffith Stadium and the official scorer charged him with an error.

When Povich entered the Senators' dressing room after the game, Kuhel took a swing at him. The scorer was always one of the writers, but Shirley wasn't the scorer that day. That didn't make any difference to Kuhel. In his temper he let fly with a roundhouse swing. Fortunately for both of them, he missed.

Clark Griffith fined Kuhel a hundred dollars when he heard about the incident. He said, "I won't have my players acting like this toward the writers."

Three days later Kuhel received a letter from a fan saying:

Dear Joe—
Here's fifty bucks to pay half of your fine for swinging at Povich. I'd send you the other half if you hadn't missed.

— 6 —

TRAINS—A CERTAIN
SOMETHING

Road trips were much different in 1941 from what they are now.
Jet airliners were something for the future. We traveled by train,
and we'd be gone ten days or two weeks at a time on trips as far
west as St. Louis, north to Boston, and south to Washington. Those
were the geographical limits of major league baseball in '41, and for
another seventeen years until the Dodgers and Giants moved to
California for the 1958 season. In 1941 we went no farther west
than the banks of the Mississippi and no farther south than just
below the Mason-Dixon Line.

    The teams stayed at the finest hotels—the Copley Plaza, Tou-
raine, and Kenmore in Boston; the Belmont, Drake, Del Prado,
Edgewater Beach, and Knickerbocker in Chicago; the Netherland
Plaza in Cincinnati; the Cleveland and Hollenden in Cleveland; the
Commodore, New Yorker, Roosevelt, Governor Clinton, and Bel-
mont Plaza in New York; the Benjamin Franklin, Drake, Warwick,
and Bellevue Stratford in Philadelphia; the Chase, Kingsway, and
Coronado in St. Louis; the Schenley and William Penn in Pitts-
burgh; the Book-Cadillac and Fort Shelby in Detroit; and the
Shoreham and Wardman Park in Washington.

    There was one big drawback to the hotels compared to those

of today: Most of them weren't air conditioned. Johnny Mize, the star first baseman of the St. Louis Cardinals from 1936 until he was traded to the New York Giants before the 1942 season, remembers those conditions. He was talking about them recently in Washington.

"My first year in St. Louis," Mize remembered, "there were ten straight days when the temperature never dropped below a hundred—day or night." Unfortunately St. Louis wasn't the only city in the big leagues where it was hot and sticky. New York could be just as bad, and so could Philadelphia, Washington, and Cincinnati. Even Boston could be miserable at times. Coping with summertime heat was a major project.

"You'd just go into your hotel room, take your clothes off, sit down on the sheet—and jump straight up in the air," Mize said. "You couldn't sit on the sheet—it was too hot. All you could do was go into the shower and turn on the cold water and just stand under it."

When he felt completely cooled down, Mize would walk out of the shower and go to bed without drying off.

Mize's roommate, Lynn King, an outfielder, used a different approach. "He'd take a pitcher of water and pour it over the bed. Oh, it could get hot all right. They used to tell us that the women would put their nightgowns in the refrigerator before putting them on."

Two other roommates on the Cardinals, Enos Slaughter and Terry Moore, found Cincinnati just as close to the boiling point as Mize did. Slaughter says, "I would order up buckets of ice and put them in the bathtub and take our bedsheets off and put them in that ice water and then put them back on the bed. You had the little old circle fan on a table, and that's all you had in the hotel. It was our own version of air-conditioning."

In Cincinnati the players felt the heat for an additional reason. Mize and Slaughter both still talk about the restriction against cabs at Crosley Field. "Cab drivers weren't allowed to pick up the ball players at the ball park," Slaughter says. "We'd play a doubleheader in all that heat and humidity and then have to walk a mile or more to the railroad station."

72

Slaughter's memory agrees with Mize's on the subject of the temperatures while playing at Sportsman's Park in St. Louis. "It was nothing to play a doubleheader in St. Louis when the temperature was 104 or 105 degrees, even at night. In the afternoon it could be 115. I've lost as much as eighteen pounds playing in a doubleheader in St. Louis."

Slaughter was blessed, though. "It never did bother me too much wearing those wool flannels," he says. "I didn't notice the heat then. Maybe it's because we didn't have air-conditioning. That's one of the problems for the players today. They sit around in that air-conditioning and then go out into the heat and it seems hotter."

Walt Masterson of the Senators, who was used to summer weather from his boyhood in Philadelphia and pitching in Washington, had still another way of coping with the stifling heat and humidity in those hotels. "I'd just take a pillow off the bed and sleep on the floor. It was always the coolest spot in the room."

One of the most enjoyable parts about life in those hotels was how we got there—on a train.

Of all the romantic and nostalgic tales about the glory days of traveling by train, the best experts on the subject are the major league baseball players from that era. Maybe the train took much longer than today's jet airliners, and maybe they weren't always air conditioned and the soot from the engine's black smoke came through the open windows and covered everything in gray and made you choke, and maybe the clickety-clack of the wheels speeding along the tracks kept some of us awake at night, but if we couldn't always enjoy the conditions, we could always enjoy one another.

And if we had trouble sleeping at night, there was a suggested remedy that included the name of one of the American League's great hitters from the 1920s and '30s, Heinie Manush. The cure was to listen to the clickety-clack and imagine that the noise was saying to you in a mesmerizing rhythm: "Heinie Manush—Heinie Manush—Heinie Manush."

Air-conditioning was just being introduced in train travel, so

73

we were stuck many times with cars that didn't have it yet. The railroad people kept us cool the old-fashioned way—a large cake of ice at one end of the car, with a fan behind it blowing cool air in our general direction.

There was a hierarchy on baseball teams, and it was evident on the trains. Teams took up three of the cars on a train. The rookies traveled in the third car, the last one—the one that whipped from side to side every time the train went around a bend. If you were assigned an upper berth in the third car, you knew you had a long way to go before you acquired any seniority on that ball club. Your goal was to progress to the point where you would be assigned to Lower 7, Car A. Car A was the front car, the one that remained the steadiest of the three, a lower berth was always preferable to an upper, and the seventh Pullman berth was in the middle of the car, the smoothest riding part of the car because it wasn't over the wheels. When you were assigned Lower 7, Car A, you knew you had established yourself as an important member of the team.

Ball players from the 1940s will tell you to a man that when baseball teams started flying, a certain bonding that held teams together went out of major league baseball. We got to know each other as only you can when you're on a train together for twenty-four hours, or thirty-six or more. You came together as a group, and when you went out onto that field, you came together as a team.

Traveling by plane simply doesn't allow that to happen. Maybe today's teams are close in some cases, and maybe some of them speak in clichés about being "family," but we never used that word when I was in the big leagues. We didn't have to. We were a family and everybody knew it—the writers, the broadcasters, and our fans. And the hours and days we spent together on trains were one of the ties that bound us together. Those trains brought us to our destination, and they also brought us closer to one another.

It was a delightful and at times even a luxurious way to travel. The teams went first class with Pullman cars so we didn't have to sit up in a coach all night, although there was some serious sitting-up done in the club car. Enos Slaughter remembers that the luxuries sometimes didn't start until you actually got on the train. "You had to pay your own way to the ball park and back," he says. "You had to carry your own luggage and see to it that it got on the train and off, and to the hotel. Today all of those things are done for you."

We were heroes on those trains. We'd roll into a station and look out the window and see kids yelling up to us and pointing out to their buddies, "There's Williams!" "I see DiMaggio!" "Look! Isn't that Joe Cronin?" Who wouldn't be happy to sign autographs in that kind of enthusiasm?

Jackie Jensen said once, "I'll never forget those platforms—all those people gathered there just to get a glimpse of us. Train travel meant a lot to baseball and to many of the players."

The National Leaguers used to talk about the effect of train travel on Pepper Martin. Pepper was with the Cardinals during their heyday in the '30s and '40s. In those years we used to carry three-suiter suitcases and wardrobe trunks instead of today's "carry-on luggage" because we'd be gone for up to three weeks. We had to lug that heavy stuff all over the country—but not Martin. His teammates used to say that Pepper took only one white suit and one black shirt. They said by the time the Cards got back to St. Louis, the smoke and soot coming through the train's window had changed the suit into the same color as the shirt.

There was always a card game: poker, gin rummy, hearts—or bridge for the ones with culture. Johnny Mize remembers that Frankie Frisch, the manager, wouldn't let rookies play cards with the veterans, men like Leo Durocher, Dizzy Dean, and Lon Warneke.

"Save your money" was Frisch's simple warning to the first-year men. "Don't let them take it away from you." But Mize remembered something else.

Frisch's advice was unnecessary, he said, because it didn't matter. "You weren't making anything anyway—in the big leagues a rookie was making about five hundred dollars a month."

We read the papers of the city we just left—the front page to see what Hitler was up to, the sports pages to keep up with the other teams, and the comics—"Little Orphan Annie," "Joe

75

Palooka," "Terry and the Pirates," "Smilin' Jack," "Dixie Dugan" and "Tillie the Toiler."

There were some eating and drinking marathons and some escapades that followed. Lefty Gomez of the Yankees was always happy to tell the story of the time Babe Ruth became angry with his manager, Miller Huggins, and held him out over the rear platform, dangling him by his ankles just long enough to scare the daylights out of him as the train streaked up the East Coast from spring training at eighty miles an hour.

Bob Feller remembers the time Rollie Hemsley partook of the spirits beyond his capacity and accidentally set a railroad car on fire on the Indians' train to Richmond, Virginia, for an exhibition game on the way north from Florida.

Every pitcher remembers when he was a rookie and his "helpful" teammates would tell him that the hammock next to his bed was to rest his arm in rather than for storing clothes overnight.

And every raw rookie was vulnerable to the old setup in which a veteran tells him that some thief on the train has been stealing the players' shoes and it was his turn to stand guard. The poor rookie was unaware that if you put your shoes on the floor inside the curtain of your Pullman, the porter would collect them, shine them and return them before morning.

While the unsophisticated rookie was standing guard, the porter would come through and start to take the shoes from each Pullman. The poor, inexperienced rookie would grab the shocked porter and start yelling to his sleeping teammates through their drawn curtains, "I got him! I got him!" It really happened, and more than once.

Bob Lemon remembers the train ride back to Cleveland after the Cleveland Indians defeated us for the pennant in 1948 in the first playoff game in the history of the American League: "What a trip! We had our wives with us and two dining cars. Bill Veeck kept bottles of bourbon and Scotch on each table, and when one was gone he had it replaced. We had forty-five cases of champagne aboard. By the time the train pulled into Cleveland the next morning, we looked like a bunch of bums. Our shirts were filthy and

76

sopping wet, but we were scheduled to ride through the city in a victory parade that started right from the station. Fortunately, it was a cold morning, so most of us took off our shirts and wore our overcoats buttoned to our necks."

Lemon's third baseman on that team, Ken Keltner, says train travel helped the Indians win that pennant and the World Series. "We were more closely knit than teams are now," he says. "On some clubs you don't even know the names of the players. We made our trips on trains and had togetherness. There wasn't much money but we had a lot of fun."

Ken is right on the mark. Those who played when we did will all tell you that it would have been nice to make the megabucks that today's players make, with the minimum salary of $100,000 instead of the $5,000 we were playing for and the average salary in 1990 of almost $600,000 a year, even for good-field, no-hit infielders riding the bench. More than a dozen players are making three million dollars a year. In our day, the whole team of twenty-five players combined might make one-tenth of that.

But all of us will tell you that we enjoyed our work more than today's players seem to. We didn't even consider it work. More money would have been welcome, and there were many times when we would "hold out" for more and refuse to report to spring training until we got what we thought we were worth. But those were either cases of economic necessity or just plain trying to get a fair shake for ourselves.

It wasn't just being able to hold a job and earn a salary that prompted us to choose baseball as our profession. It was the tremendous enthusiasm, even the love, that all of us felt for the sport. We would have played for nothing if we didn't have to eat or have families to support. We loved what we were doing because we loved the game of baseball—and we still do.

With all the times we had, good and bad, and the conditions ranging from luxurious to irritating, traveling by train gave us that special something to enjoy and that strong bond that played such a key role in making us a team. All of us who played in those years have done our share of flying—sometimes first class—but you can be sure that not one of us would take flying over the train if we were still playing.

Two pitchers from the 1940s, Tom Ferrick, who was with the Philadelphia A's in 1941, and Eddie Lopat, who came to the big leagues in 1944, remember another plus for train travel: You became closer to the writers too. They were talking about it between games of a Cardinals-Phillies doubleheader at Veterans Stadium in Philadelphia recently as they snacked on hot dogs and Cokes. Mickey Vernon, the Philadelphia product who won the American League batting championship twice, was there too.

Lopat had to wait a little longer than the rest of us to experience the pleasures and advantages of travel by train. The man who came to be called "Steady Eddie" as a star pitcher first with the White Sox and then with the Yankees started life as a first baseman and struggled for seven years in the minors before making it to the big leagues in 1944.

In 1941, while the rest of us were enjoying life in the major leagues, Eddie was enduring it in Salina, Kansas. Instead of traveling by train, in the minors you traveled by bus, and even that was above Eddie's poverty line. In Salina you didn't get a regular bus— you rode on a school bus.

At the Phillies' doubleheader, Eddie was telling the group: "It was 450 miles from Salina to Fort Smith, Arkansas. And if you were late, you had to sit on the equipment bag in the aisle. It was single-lane roads too. And if it rained, the bus had to go 100 miles out of the way because the roads on our regular route would be washed out."

But when he began the big league life and was able to ride on a train instead of a school bus, Eddie discovered an advantage in addition to the improved creature comforts. "The writers traveled with you," Lopat remembered. "They got a lot of stories by being on the train all day long with the players. We always had our own club car, and we could sit there and talk baseball and give the writer whatever he wanted."

One of the sensitive problem areas of today didn't exist back then—jealousy and discontent among teammates over salaries. Today everybody knows what everybody else is making. Bad feelings result and hurt the ball club, but not in those days.

"There was an unwritten code not to talk or write about salaries, and the writers honored that code," Eddie remembered. Ferrick verified Lopat's memory. "They wouldn't betray your confidence." Tom recalled that the players were grateful to the writers' integrity, and for good reason. "We didn't want anybody to know how little we were making."

Mickey Vernon, sitting between Ferrick and Lopat in the Phillies hospitality room at the top of the stadium, laughed and agreed: "We were too embarrassed."

The writers, however, were the only half of the news media who got to enjoy the pleasures of traveling with the ball club. The radio announcers had to stay home.

Red Barber remembers that none of the broadcasters traveled. "All road games were broadcast by Western Union re-creation. The first all-live games were in 1946, when MacPhail put Mel Allen on the road for the Yankees. Brooklyn announcers started traveling in mid-1948. That's when the Brooklyn games went all live."

Tommy Henrich, "Old Reliable" and the third man in the Yankees outfield in '41 with Joe and Charlie Keller, used to form a comedy team with Joe Gordon during their train rides. Gordon was their All-Star second baseman and the hitting star of the World Series that year. Joe managed to come up with a copy of *Joe Miller's Joke Book,* the old source of material for comedians everywhere. Together Joe and Tommy performed vaudeville comedy routines right out of Miller's book.

As the Yankees headed to the next city, the team of Gordon & Henrich would take to the aisle and go into their routine. They had one advantage that professional comedians don't—a captive audience. Their teammates couldn't get up and leave, so they had to suffer through such shtick as—

GORDON: What time is it, Tommy?
HENRICH: I don't know. I left my watch upstairs.
GORDON: Aren't you afraid it will run down?
HENRICH: No—we have a winding staircase.

79

At which point the comedy team would have to duck the flying Pullman pillows fired at them by the rest of the Yankees.

Johnny Vander Meer, the only man to pitch back-to-back no-hitters, is another player from our era who has nothing but fond memories about traveling by train.

"A big advantage of air travel was that we got a lot more rest," he said. "Ninety percent of the trains pulled out around eleven o'clock or midnight. If we got into our next city at 6:30 or so the next morning, they'd sidetrack us and let us sleep until about eight. We'd get a full night's sleep, once you learned to sleep on those things.

"Today a ball game is over at eleven, the players get to the airport by midnight, they take off at one, fly to the next city by two or three in the morning, sometimes later, and get to their hotels or homes by four or five A.M. They don't get any rest."

Vander Meer never had any trouble sleeping on trains. The Reds had a team physician, a Dr. Rhode, who traveled with the club. "I'd just go to Doc's bag and get two aspirin tablets and go to bed," Johnny remembers. "By the time the road trip was over, Doc's bag would be empty."

All of us remember the togetherness and what ball players called the "camaraderie" created by the train travel and the closeness that went with it. It carried over to our lives together away from the trains too.

Vandie remembers: "I roomed with Frank McCormick, and we always knew where each other was. There was a lot of togetherness, a lot of lobby sitting. We talked about only three things— baseball, hunting, and fishing. Today the players talk about only two things—a little baseball, not much, and the *Wall Street Journal.*"

All of us remember another advantage of train travel over air —the food. In our atmosphere of a real dining room with tables for four covered with a white tablecloths, vases of fresh flowers in the middle, and real silverware, not a plastic fork in sight, we also had waiters in white jackets who met our every need. And the meals sure beat anything on an airplane—ham, chops, casseroles, and in portions you'll never find on an airliner. It was plush living compared to being stuck in an airline seat today, first class or no first class.

The waiters got help from some of the players. Walker Cooper of the Cardinals was one who would borrow a jacket from a waiter and get some laughs waiting on tables for the entire trip.

The record for the longest train may have been set by the 1957 Yankees. Enos Slaughter was on that team, two years from the end of his nineteen-year Hall of Fame career. The Yankees continued to ride the trains right up to Slaughter's retirement after the '59 season.

For their '57 World Series matchup against the Milwaukee Braves, the Yankees chartered a train for the trip to Milwaukee and back. The Braves upset the Yankees with Lew Burdette winning three complete games, but Slaughter remembers that the trip back to New York helped to soothe the Yankees' wounds. Their train was sixteen cars long.

All of us have priceless memories of the pleasantries of all those train trips—to play 77 games a year in seven other cities. Vander Meer and Henrich may have said it better than the rest of us when they expressed their feelings on the subject.

Vandie said, "If I had to play all over again, I'd take the train. There isn't any question about it."

Tommy said simply, "It was a joy."

— 7 —

ALL THIS AND NIGHT
BASEBALL TOO

The 1941 season got off to a happy start, war or no war. Teddy, fresh from a .344 season after hitting .327 in his rookie year in '39, got hot early and stayed that way. My brother Joe was hitting well, and I wasn't doing too badly either after being fitted for special glasses by Dr. Harold Jacobson. He found I had "myopic astigmatism with exophoria," which is a long way of saying I was nearsighted. He said my vision was well below the rating required by the Army, but with glasses my eyes were better than average.

My only problem at the start of the season didn't have anything to do with my eyes. It was my hands. They became tender during the off-season because I spent the winter playing cards in Joe's new restaurant in San Francisco, Joe DiMaggio's Grotto, instead of deep-sea fishing with my father and my other brothers. It got worse hitting against Buck Newsom in Detroit on a cold day. He jammed me twice so I hit two pitches on the handle and my right thumb swelled to twice its normal size. But I got three hits that day with the thumb heavily taped, and four the next day, so I wasn't going to waste my time worrying about it.

My fast start included a good series in Washington. The Red Sox felt confident enough about my potential to trade Doc Cramer to the Senators during the winter and give me the starting job in center field. When we went to Washington, I wanted to show the Senators that the Sox knew what they were doing when they decided to keep me over Cramer. I got four hits in five trips to the plate against the Senators, stole two bases and scored four runs. The *Boston Daily Globe* ran a cartoon showing me hitting .382 and Joe .315, with the fans trying to remember Joe's name.

Our brother Vince was doing well in Pittsburgh after being traded to the Pirates during the 1940 season for Johnny Rizzo, another outfielder. The three DiMaggios were attracting plenty of attention. We weren't the only brothers playing major league baseball at that time, and we weren't even the first. The Cooper brothers—pitcher Mort and catcher Walker—were "the brother battery" for the St. Louis Cardinals in '41 and the Waners, Paul and Lloyd — "Big Poison" and "Little Poison"—were still playing.

There had also been the Cooneys, Johnny and Jimmy, whose father also played in the big leagues, and another brother battery, the Ferrells—Wes and Rick, plus Harry and Dixie Walker. But because there were *three* of us, all playing the same position and all of us doing well, the attention came in different ways. There were articles in newspapers and magazines. There were interviews on the radio. Louella Parsons wrote in her column, "Gossip from Hollywood," that some producer was going to make a movie about our family called *The Great DiMaggio*. It was to be a story about my father and it would feature Joe, Vince, and me. The only trouble with this "scoop" was that the movie never happened.

Grantland Rice, then the most famous sportswriter in America, got so caught up with the fuss that he wrote a poem in his column that went:

> Out the olive trail they go—
> Vincent, Dominic, and Joe,
> Lashing, flashing, steaming hot
> In the fabled land of swat.
> Where the big ash sings its song
> For the glory of the throng,

Or the big mace through the fray
Sends the apple on its way—

Watch them as they whirl, careen,
Over the fields of verdant green.
Rulers of the batting eye,
Where their gaudy triples fly,
In the sunset's shining glow
Who is it that steals the show?
Vincent, Dominic, and Joe.

Even the Red Sox manager joined in. Joe Cronin told Curley Grieve of the *San Francisco Examiner,* "In any all-star outfield you could name today, you would have to select Joe and Dom DiMaggio. They would be one and two on the list. . . ."

I was swinging a 34-ounce bat, heavier than Ted's because he put so much emphasis on bat speed and used one that weighed only 32 ounces—it may not seem like much, but those two ounces can make a lot of difference. Williams started hitting early in the season and simply never quit. He didn't seem obsessed with hitting .400, even though he was around and above that figure all year long. If Ted was obsessed with anything, it was just plain hitting, regardless of what his average happened to be at the moment.

Others had flirted with a .400 season, Bill Terry had done it last in 1930, so the attention early in the season wasn't focused on the possibility that Ted might hit .400. Instead, all the attention was directed at my brother Joe.

Joe started his 56-game hitting streak on May 15, after going 0 for 3 the day before against Mel Harder of the Indians in Yankee Stadium. On the fifteenth, Joe singled in the first inning off Ed Smith, driving in Phil Rizzuto, who had led off the inning with a double.

The only thing notable about Joe's hit at the time was that it drove in the only New York run. The Yanks lost to the Chicago White Sox, and they lost big, 13–1. Ernie "Tiny" Bonham was their starter and loser. It also happened to be Jimmy Dykes Day at the Stadium, honoring the veteran Chicago infielder on the last day

85

of his playing career after twenty-two years. Dan Daniel presented him with a scroll from the New York sportswriters.

The most significant thing about the game as far as the Yankees were concerned was that it continued their slump. It was their tenth loss in fourteen games, their fourth in the last five, and it dropped them below .500 to 14–15. The Indians were in first place with 21 wins and 9 losses.

On the same day, we were having troubles of our own. We were losing to the Indians, 6–4, in Fenway Park, when their manager, Roger Peckinpaugh, pulling out all the stops, brought in their ace starting pitcher, Bob Feller, in relief. That's a rare move, but the Indians wanted to protect their first-place standing, and Peckinpaugh knew what he was doing. We had two on and none out in the bottom of the ninth. Finney had singled to right to lead off the inning as a pinch hitter for Ryba, and I'd walked. That's when Feller came in. He got Stan Spence on a pop-up, one of two things a pitcher hopes for in that situation, a strikeout being the other. With either one, the runners don't advance and you're set up for a double play to end the inning, or, in this case, the game. That's precisely what happened. Hal Trosky, Cleveland's first baseman, leaped into the air and caught a line drive by Ted and then whipped the ball to Boudreau at second to double up Finney and end the game.

The question of the day was whether Cleveland would manage to keep its slender hold on first place after losing the pennant by only one game to Detroit the year before. There was no reason to talk about what anybody on the Yankees did that day.

Ten days later, without knowing it, Lefty Grove became a part of the two most famous batting feats in baseball history to that time. On May 25, he gave up a single to Joe, his only hit in four trips to the plate but the eleventh straight game in which he hit safely. Fourteen years before, on September 27, 1927, Lefty had given up a home run to Babe Ruth, and there's the connection.

Joe went on to extend his streak of hitting in 56 straight games, and Ruth in '27 went on to hit 60 home runs, the most homers in any season and a record that lasted for thirty-four years.

86

When he gave up that hit to Joe, Lefty became the only pitcher to have the distinction of being a part of both achievements. Later in Joe's streak, Ted Lyons of the White Sox joined Lefty in one of pitching's most exclusive clubs, one with only two members.

Five days after Lefty pitched himself into that unique niche in baseball lore, the major league teams showed they were drawing big crowds. Nearly a quarter of a million fans—229,830—attended the eight games played on Memorial Day. The Yankees played us in a doubleheader that day in Fenway Park, and we packed the place with 34,500 fans.

Joe and I had five hits that day, two singles and a double by me and a single and a double by Joe as we split the two games. The Yankees won the first game, 4–3, but we came back to beat the daylights out of them in the second, 13–0, on 16 hits. Nobody was making a fuss about Joe's streak yet, including the New York writers. Sixteen straight games is a nice hot spell, one that can do wonders for a batting average and your team's won-lost record, but at 16 games you're a long way from making history. After all, the major league record was 44 games by Wee Willie Keeler of the Baltimore Orioles when they were in the old National League. How hard would it be to break that record in 1941? Well, Keeler had done it way back in 1897.

In those beginning days of Joe's streak in late May, the news from overseas was growing worse. The Luftwaffe, Hitler's air force, was pounding London every night in its "blitz" that lasted from September the year before until June. Germany invaded Yugoslavia and Greece and prepared to march on the Soviet Union. And relations between the United States and Japan, tense already, were worsening. In the face of this increased international tension, President Roosevelt declared a state of "unlimited national emergency."

As Joe extended his streak into June, he was setting out on his road to history while contending with something Keeler didn't have to worry about—night baseball. Half the big league teams had lights now, and the argument was being heard that night baseball would cause batting averages to drop because it would be harder to see the ball. Maybe that was true and maybe it wasn't, but it's ironic that the two most enduring hitting achievements of our lifetime—Joe's streak and Ted's .406 season—were accomplished at a time when we were beginning to play more of our games at night.

Night baseball became a reality at the major league level in 1935 and reached a new peak of popularity during World War II, when war workers laboring in offices and "war plants," America's factories, during the day were able to see a game at night. It was considered an excellent "morale booster" and thus a great help to "the war effort."

By 1941 the minor leagues had been playing night games for ten years. The spectacle of games "under the lights," as the writers used to say, was introduced into the major leagues by Larry Mac-Phail. MacPhail was the general manager of the Cincinnati Reds, a bombastic kind of a guy, never afraid to take on the whole world if he thought he was right—and he always did—and never reluctant to ram through something new.

That's what he did in the case of night baseball. He won permission from his fellow owners in the National League to play seven night games in 1935, one against each team, beginning on the evening of May 24 against the Philadelphia Phillies. In addition to having the guts of a combat hero, MacPhail had the promotional genius of a circus owner. He got President Roosevelt to agree to push a button from the White House that "magically" turned on 616 lights at Crosley Field, to the delight of 20,422 fans. Ford Frick, a former New York sportswriter who had become president of the National League, threw out the first ball.

Clark Griffith, the owner of the Senators and one of the pioneers of the American League, was not convinced about this new phenomenon until the war came along and he realized that all those government workers in Washington would be happy to turn out at night to root for his Senators. But until the war, Griffith remained a staunch opponent of night games. He even predicted its eventual failure. "There is no chance of night baseball ever becoming popular in the bigger cities," he announced, "because high-class baseball cannot be played under artificial lights."

On May 28, 1941, he swallowed his words and the lights came on at Griffith Stadium. MacPhail moved to the top job with the Brooklyn Dodgers in 1938, and immediately outdid his success of three years before in Cincinnati. Even with three major league teams in New York, no team was playing night games there. Mac-Phail put an end to the dark ages on June 15, when night baseball held its New York premier at Ebbets Field. Once again he didn't overlook a thing.

He recruited Jesse Owens, America's hero of the 1936 Olympics in Berlin, to put on a series of sprinting and broad-jumping exhibitions before the game. He trotted out his new coach, Babe Ruth, for an enthusiastic greeting. Then, somehow or other, he got Johnny Vander Meer to pitch his second straight no-hit game.

With all the pregame hoopla and the problem of jamming the overflow crowd into the ball park, the game didn't start until 9:45. The attendance totaled 38,748, the largest crowd in Ebbets Field history. Included were several hundred fans from Vander Meer's hometown of Midland Park, New Jersey, who came to Brooklyn by bus to watch their hero. When the hometown folks turn out, it doesn't always make for a great game by the player concerned. As Johnny says, "Usually that gets you into the clubhouse by the third inning."

The good folks of Midland Park and the rest of the crowd had no particular reason to suspect something even more special than the first night game in the history of New York was in the air. Neither did Vandie. He'd pitched a no-hit game four days earlier against the Boston Braves. It's safe to say not one person in Ebbets Field that night, including Vander Meer, thought for one second about the possibility of a second consecutive no-hitter. There was good reason not to give it a second thought: no pitcher in major league history had pitched two no-hitters in a row—and it hasn't happened since either.

But it happened that night, and thousands of people who lived in Brooklyn in 1938 are still telling their friends and grandchildren that they saw the first night game in New York City's history and Johnny Vander Meer's second straight no-hitter—on the same night.

Vander Meer threw enough pitches for two games that night, one on the field and one in the bullpen. He kept warming up, then sitting down because of delays in getting the game started. "Mac-Phail kept selling tickets," Vandie says. "The ball park was over-crowded. They were sitting in the aisles and everywhere. The fire marshal wouldn't let the game start because of the crowded condi-tions. I don't know how many pitches I threw by the time the game started, but when I got up to get ready for the first inning, it was the fourth time that I was up and throwing."

Johnny began setting the Dodgers down without trouble ex-cept for an occasional walk. Only one batted ball from the Brook-lyn hitters was a tough chance, and Johnny took care of that one himself. It was a sharp ground ball back through the pitcher's box by Buddy Hassett in the middle of the game. Vandie knocked it down and threw him out.

"I was real quick in the second game," Vander Meer said recently. "I threw a couple of curve balls in the second, third, and fourth innings, but they hung a little bit. You don't usually have the great curve ball and the great fast ball on the same night, so I threw about ninety percent fast balls. Then in the eighth and ninth I went back to the curve when everybody was looking for the fast ball."

Did he know he had another no-hitter going later in the game? "In Brooklyn, they let you know in the first inning."

He got early help from his teammates. The Reds scored four runs in the third inning and went on to a 6–0 win. Vander Meer was struggling with his control throughout the game—he walked eight batters—but in the ninth inning, with the drama almost un-bearable, Johnny's historic performance was almost undone by Leo Durocher, Brooklyn's brassy shortstop.

"I didn't go for the no-hitter until the ninth inning in either game," Johnny says. "I had seen too many games broken up in the sixth or seventh. But by the ninth inning in the Brooklyn game, I decided to go for it. I figured I had twenty-one good pumps left. And they were going to have to hit something good. They weren't going to hit any let-up curve balls, or change-ups or nickel pitches. I had to go with my best."

Vander Meer's best was plenty good. He led the National League in strikeouts three years in a row—1941, '42 and '43—with a fast ball that commanded respect from every hitter in the league.

He came close to using up his allotment of "twenty-one good pumps" in a hurry—by walking the bases loaded with one out. Then something happened that Vander Meer says was the best play of the game—"not a great play but a smart play."

Ernie Koy, Brooklyn's rookie center fielder, a .299 hitter that year and one of the fastest Dodgers, hit a ground ball to Lew Riggs at third base. Riggs in an instant made the decision not to risk trying for an "around-the-horn" double play from third to second to first. Instead, he went to the plate with his throw and got the force out.

Then, in the same moment, another smart decision was made —by Ernie Lombardi, Cincinnati's catcher. Lombardi was ready to try for the double play at first, but he saw that Koy was running inside the base line, in the way of the throw Lombardi would make, so he held the ball rather than take a chance of making a wild throw into right field.

That brought up Durocher with two outs, the bases loaded, and Vandie's no-hit, no-run game still intact. "Leo the Lip," who hit a total of 24 home runs in seventeen years as a big leaguer, was in his first year as the Dodgers' shortstop after ten years with the Yankees, Reds, and Cardinals. He lined Vandie's first pitch down the right field line. A .247 lifetime hitter was about to ruin a once-in-history pitching performance. But fate stepped in, and the ball curved foul.

Durocher then made the final out of the amazing feat by sending a routine fly ball to Harry Craft in center field, and Vandie got a new name. Since that night fifty years ago, he has been known as Johnny "Double No-Hit" Vander Meer.

Johnny was saying last year that as a kid growing up in New Jersey during the Depression, he saved his nickels so he could go to see the Giants at the Polo Grounds once a year. "I used to watch Carl Hubbell," he said. "I watched the way he laid his glove down and the way he wouldn't step on the base line when he crossed it, and I mimicked him.

"When we came into New York early in my career, I made my second or third start of the season and it was against Hubbell. He was on a long winning streak. The game went into the ninth inning

91

with the score 1–1. Both of us were taken out for pinch hitters and the game went into extra innings. But it was a big confidence boost for me. It made me believe in myself. I had stayed with Hubbell, my idol. When I walked downtown that night, I was floating on air."

On the night of his second consecutive no-hitter, he floated on the New York air again.

Following MacPhail's lead in Cincinnati and Brooklyn, the Washington Senators installed lights at Griffith Stadium in 1941 after Griffith's change of heart. He approved the installation of an "eight-tower floodlighting system" in Washington. Westinghouse took out newspaper ads telling readers that Griffith Stadium was the sixth big league ball park to be "sportslighted" by Westinghouse. The ads also said the Senators could expect an increase of 250,000 in their attendance, which may have had something to do with Mr. Griffith's change of heart.

Night baseball was an immediate hit. More people were able to go to the games at night and still work during the day, at a time when days off were not nearly as easy to get as today, especially with America preparing for the growing possibility of another world war.

Most of us were able to make the adjustment to night baseball. We learned to see the ball as well as in day games, and some even thought night games gave them an edge. Enos Slaughter was one. "I enjoyed night baseball," he says. "I could follow the ball a lot better at night than during the day."

Bobby Doerr also thought there was a distinct advantage of night ball over day games. "You didn't have to contend with the sun on those white shirts in the center field bleachers," Bobby says. "That's always a potential problem for hitters in afternoon games, because when the pitcher delivers his pitch, that white baseball can get lost in that background of white shirts and the hitter has trouble seeing it. The sun hits those white shirts and magnifies the brightness.

"The place I appreciated night baseball most of all was in Yankee Stadium, because I didn't have to contend with the shadows that always showed up in the middle part of the day games there, plus those white shirts in center field."

In Bobby's opinion, the worst ball park for problems with the sun and the shirts was Wrigley Field in Chicago. "I played there in the 1947 All-Star game," he says. "Johnny Sain was pitching, and he threw me two curve balls and I don't think I saw them, because of those shirts. Then he threw me a fast ball up around the eyes, and I wasn't going to let that get by. I got a base hit off that one."

Slaughter agrees with Doerr on the subject of the white shirts in the center field bleachers during day games, especially at Sportsman's Park in St. Louis, where the Cardinals and the Browns played their home games. "It was awful," Enos says. "A ball in the lights was nothing like that sunshine out there."

Slaughter even got to participate in an experiment that baseball people still talk about from time to time. He played a game with a yellow baseball in a night game at Brooklyn in 1938, an innovation that a few people—including Chuck Finley, the former owner of the Oakland A's—have advocated on the theory that it was easier to see an orange ball at night.

Slaughter's first-hand conclusion: "I didn't see any difference."

In the minor leagues the trend was just the opposite—away from night games—but for a related reason, particularly in the South. A prolonged drought was reducing the amount of electricity available from the dams of the Tennessee Valley Authority. Teams in the Southern Association, the South Atlantic League, the Appalachian, and the Georgia-Florida Leagues were switching their night games to afternoons to save the electricity so it would be available for the country's defense buildup.

Even when minor league teams were playing at night, things didn't always go as planned. The lights were often dim and created a shadowy effect on the field, a far cry from the superior systems being installed in the major leagues. Tommy Henrich is blunt and to the point on the subject of lights in minor league parks: "They were the lousiest lights you ever saw."

There were other light-related problems too. In the Georgia-Florida League in 1941, Tex Willoughby came to bat for the Waycross Bears. He hit a high fly ball to right field, and just as it was coming down, the lights went out. The ball dropped into the out-field without being caught.

The umpires held a conference and ruled that Willoughby would have to bat again. That was fine with him. He would have been out anyway if the lights hadn't gone out. So he stepped back into the batter's box and got himself a triple.

On June 2 Joe hit in his nineteenth straight game with a single and a double against Bob Feller in Cleveland as the Indians defeated the Yankees, 7–5. New York might have lost the game, but the Yankees succeeded in breaking a different streak, one by Feller. Bob had pitched 3 straight shutouts and had a scoreless string of 31 innings until the Yanks finally got to him.

Something else happened in that game. Ken Keltner hit a long shot to center field and Joe was able to make an outstanding catch, robbing Kenny of an extra base hit. Keltner would get his revenge a month and a half later.

The last sentence of the article in the *New York Times* on the game said: "DiMaggio, incidentally, has hit safely in nineteen straight games." But Joe wouldn't have been the biggest story in the baseball world no matter what he did. That was the day Lou Gehrig died.

The headline said:

GEHRIG, IRON MAN OF BASEBALL, DIES AT THE AGE OF 37

The end came at Lou's home, 5204 Delafield Avenue in the Fieldstone section of the Bronx, seventeen days before his thirty-eighth birthday. Newspaper stories reported he was twenty-five pounds underweight. The outpouring of sentiment for Gehrig and sympathy for his family was immediate.

All of us knew Lou's health was failing, but we didn't know much about amyotrophic lateral sclerosis in those days. In fact, public ignorance of ALS and its characteristics was so common that the year before one New York paper reported that the collapse of the Yankees in mid-August, after winning the pennant in '39, was due to the fact that several Yankee players had been infected by Gehrig. That the Yankees got hot and drove from fifth place in the American League standings into the thick of the race in September didn't satisfy Lou. As mild-mannered as he was, he was so furious about the story he sued the newspaper for a million dollars for libel. The paper withdrew the story, printed an apology to Gehrig, and told its readers that the disease is not communicable. Only then did Lou withdraw his lawsuit.

We heard early in the 1941 season that Lou was only a shadow of what he was in 1939 when he stood in front of those 61,808 teary-eyed fans in Yankee Stadium on July fourth and haltingly said what has endured to this day as an immortal farewell: "Today . . . I consider myself . . . the luckiest man . . . on the face of the earth."

The day before Lou entered the Mayo Clinic following his farewell to baseball, the Hall of Fame at Cooperstown was dedicated as part of baseball's centennial year. The Baseball Writers' Association of America, which makes the selections, voted Lou into Cooperstown immediately. Only one other player, Roberto Clemente, who was killed on a mercy mission to aid victims of a hurricane in Puerto Rico on New Year's Eve in 1972, has been so honored.

Following Lou's death, the Gehrig story was all over the papers, with features about his career, his life, and his family. The *New York Times* reported that the top salary for one of the greatest sluggers in the history of baseball was the $39,000 he earned in 1938. The *Times* said that after his rookie salary of $3,750, Gehrig "moved into the big money class. He never dropped out of five figures for the rest of his career."

Shirley Povich wrote that Gehrig never got the top billing he deserved, even at the time of his death. Shirley recalled that on the day Lou hit four home runs in one game, John McGraw was the big story of the day because he announced his retirement. Throughout his career, Gehrig played in the shadow of Babe Ruth. Finally, when he died, he would have center stage for himself. But it didn't happen. Kaiser Wilhelm died the same week, prompting Povich to write, "Even in death, Lou could never get top billing."

Babe Dahlgren succeeded Lou when he took himself out of the lineup in '39, and Dahlgren was luckier than the other first basemen in the Yankee organization over the years of Lou's streak of 1,230 consecutive games dating back to 1925. Two outstanding prospects, George McQuinn and Buddy Hassett, were traded out of the New York farm system at their own request because Lou was always such an established figure at first base. McQuinn became a star with the St. Louis Browns and Hassett had a successful career with the Braves and Dodgers. They knew nobody was ever going to take Lou Gehrig's job away from him.

The fans stood in line—5,000 of them—to see Lou as he lay in state the night before his funeral. It rained the next day, but the Christ Protestant Episcopal Church in the Bronx was full for his funeral, and five hundred more fans stood outside under umbrellas. Inside, baseball's biggest celebrities paid their respects—Commissioner Landis, presidents Will Harridge of the American League and Ford Frick of the National League, Ruth, Bill Dickey, Lou's last manager, Joe McCarthy, Yankee players, and even the Yankee batboy, Timmy Sullivan.

The Reverend Gerald Barry told the congregation there would be no eulogy. He said: "We need none because you all knew him." No one could argue with the Reverend Barry's reasoning. Lou Gehrig delivered his own eulogy by the life he led.

On the same day that the headlines reported Lou's death, another headline said:

HITLER AND MUSSOLINI CHART WAR MOVES IN 5-HOUR TALK

While Joe continued his hitting streak deep into June, other players, including me, faced challenges of our own. The Senators' Walt Masterson was notified by his draft board that he might be called for his physical soon. His teammate, Cecil Travis, who had a higher batting average than Joe for the month of June, got better news from his draft board. The folks in Fayette, Georgia, granted his request for a sixty-day deferment so he could complete the 1941 baseball season.

The Selective Service announced that the limit of drafting 900,000 men would be lifted. And those one-year hitches were going to be eighteen months now or longer. So much for that hit song about being back in a year. The guys were going to be in for "the duration and six"—the national emergency and six months more.

Every ball player was concerned. Bob Feller remembers: "Most of us were making our minds up during the season what we wanted to do. If you weren't, you had to be living in a cave somewhere."

One of our pitchers in 1941, Charlie Wagner, remembers the feeling vividly even today. "The war threat concerned us deeply," he says. "It was always on your mind. You talked about it all the time. On the train or in the hotel lobby we'd ask each other, 'What are they doing overseas now?' You knew it was coming."

Moe Berg was a catcher with the Red Sox in 1939, the year the war started with Germany's invasion of Poland. Berg was one of the most sophisticated men this country has produced in any field. A graduate of Princeton, he was fluent in at least six languages and read French and Italian, studied for two years at the Sorbonne in Paris, and held a Ph.D. His thesis on the Sanskrit language of the Middle East is on file in the Library of Congress. And he was a U. S. spy during the war. When the war ended, Moe didn't have any visible means of support, so my guess is that he continued to work for the government as a CIA agent.

Charlie Wagner remembers that Berg used to keep us up-to-date on developments in Europe and explain their significance. When Hitler invaded Poland, Moe told the Red Sox players, "It's bad. It's very bad."

As Charlie says today, "The discussions about war were always there because the subject was always in the back of your mind. In 1942 it became even worse. When the day's game was over, the war was always talked about, not baseball."

To find out more about my own situation, I paid an unpublicized visit to the Federal Building in downtown Boston early in the season to see if I could enlist in the Navy either after the season or right then and there if necessary. They checked my eyes and said my vision wasn't good enough, and that I had only a fifty–fifty chance at best of being accepted by the Army. In other words, I didn't have to worry about getting drafted because I'd probably flunk the physical and be declared 4-F, physically unfit for military service.

That wasn't good enough for America's young men in those days, so I pressed the doctor in charge. I asked about the possibility of a letter to the examining physician recommending that an exception be made in my case because I was a professional athlete in tiptop physical condition. I was told yes, there were cases where the ruling doctor might consider other factors, especially in the case of a professional athlete, and decide that the pluses out-weighed the minuses. They offered to provide me with a letter recommending that extra consideration be given to my overall athlete's condition as something that would offset the simple fact that I wore glasses. They asked if I would like such a letter for use when my number came up. I told them, "By all means."

My timing couldn't have been better. Shortly after my visit to the Federal Building, while we were in St. Louis for a series with the Browns, my draft board in San Francisco ordered me to report to Board 18 in Boston for a physical examination. The 1941 major league season was one-fourth over and I was hitting .342. A notice from your draft board is not the kind of thing you want to have on your mind, especially when you're hitting that well and trying to keep it up. But in 1941 the draft was a fact of life.

The doctors in the Federal Building had been right. I flunked the exam because of poor eyesight. But that wasn't an acceptable answer to a young man in 1941. There was no rejoicing if you were declared 4-F. Every man in his twenties or thirties wanted to do his part in helping America prepare for whatever dangers we would face as a nation in the near future. And society was beginning to attach an unspoken stigma to those in the 4-F category. Before long, and especially after Pearl Harbor, 4-Fs were viewed with suspicion, and there were often behind-the-back whispers.

American baseball players weren't the only ones facing an

uncertain future. Even the Cuban and Venezuelan players were vulnerable, like Roberto Ortiz and Alex Carrasquel of the Washington Senators and Bobby Estalella of the St. Louis Browns, who was traded to Washington in September. The Justice Department issued a ruling requiring the Senators' owner, Clark Griffith, to post a bond as a guarantee that the Cuban and Venezuelan players "will not become public charges." The government didn't want those players drawing welfare checks in the U.S. if they didn't stay on their teams.

Even with the uncertainty facing most of us, ball players were still a lot better off than some other men our age. Lives were being lost on the other side of the Atlantic. Hitler's prize warship, the *Bismarck,* his biggest and most destructive fighting vessel, sank the British dreadnought *Hood* off the coast of Iceland, and the British Royal Air Force and navy got their revenge by chasing the *Bismarck* all over the Atlantic and eventually bombarding her to the bottom of the ocean in a rain of death and destruction that were page one headlines all over the world.

As the next step in the escalation of the war, the German navy formed its submarines into "wolf packs" to attack ships in the Atlantic—American ships as well as others—and our Navy had to begin protecting our own interests and people on the high seas.

Back home we could try to take our minds off the war by whistling Duke Ellington's new song hit, "Take the 'A' Train," or seeing Orson Welles's new movie, *Citizen Kane.* When we went to the movies, Fox Movietone News, narrated by Lowell Thomas, and the Universal newsreels with Graham McNamee as the narrator, showed us the new monument carved out of stone on Mount Rushmore in South Dakota with its sixty-foot-high faces of Washington, Jefferson, Lincoln, and Theodore Roosevelt.

Trips to the movies didn't really take our minds off the war, though. On the contrary, the newsreels showed us scenes from the war in Europe.

As June progressed, Joe kept right on hitting, and by now people were paying attention. Not just baseball fans but the whole country. It was in every paper and on every radio newscast. The people at Hillerich & Bradsby Company in Louisville, the makers of the Louisville Slugger bats, had to be loving it. They ran an ad that said:

A pitched ball travels 100 miles an hour. A batter's swing travels 200 miles an hour. That is the best reason we know for SHORTER LENGTH BATS that have a FASTER SWING SPEED!

And right there in the ad, in the middle of Joe's streak, was the hottest hitter in baseball at various stages of his batting stroke.

Then, in the midst of all the attention, it looked as if the streak might end after 37 games. The Yankees were playing the St. Louis Browns in Yankee Stadium on June 26, and the Brownies were stopping Joe cold behind Eldon Auker, a six-foot-two right-hander who won 16 games for them the year before. The Browns were never much of a team at the time, but on that day they were sharing the baseball spotlight with Joe. The Browns were losing the game, but in the only real story in that game, they were winning.

Joe flied out to left in his first time up. On his second trip he hit a ground ball to the St. Louis shortstop, John Berardino, who today is Dr. Steve Hardy on the television soap opera, *General Hospital.* Johnny was a good shortstop, usually able to handle what anybody hit to him, but he had trouble with this one and bobbled it.

Dan Daniel of the *New York World-Telegram* was the official scorer, and he charged Berardino with an error, a gutsy call with the Yankee players looking up to the press box from the dugout and the 8,692 fans vocally disagreeing with the decision. Joe grounded out in the sixth inning and faced the possibility that he might not get another chance to bat. But Tommy Henrich, "Old Reliable," showed just how reliable he could be and got another chance for Joe.

It happened in the eighth inning. Johnny Sturm, the Yankees' rookie first baseman, led off the inning by popping up. Then Red Rolfe, their third baseman, walked. Now Henrich was the hitter.

As Joe moved toward the on-deck circle, Tommy went back to the dugout to confer with his manager, Joe McCarthy. He was afraid he might hit into a double play and deprive Joe of another chance. How about a bunt?

The Yanks were already winning, 3–1. You don't bunt with a 2-run lead in the eighth inning. But then, when do you ever have a teammate trying to make baseball history who is hitting right behind you in the batting order? McCarthy gave Henrich his okay to lay it down. He did, and then Joe hit Auker's first pitch for a double—a line drive past Harlond Clift at third base. Marius Russo, a left-hander born in Brooklyn, had a no-hitter going for the Yankees into the seventh inning and ended with a one-hitter, a home run by George McQuinn, but the drama over Joe's streak had the United States of America so preoccupied by now that nobody paid any attention to Russo's bid for a no-hitter.

Henrich had a unique reason to want to bunt. "I could hit Eldon Auker," he said in Arizona recently. "I was afraid I might hit a line drive right to an infielder. I also knew Auker. He was a class guy. He wasn't going to take the easy way out and walk Joe."

Joe had long since broken the Yankees' team record for hitting safely in consecutive games. That was 29, held by Roger Peckinpaugh and Earle Combs. He'd passed Rogers Hornsby, holder of the post-1900 National League record with 33 straight games. Now the really big targets were in sight—George Sisler's "modern" record for the twentieth century of 41 straight games, and the all-time mark of 44 by Wee Willie Keeler, the man who explained his batting success with the simple strategy, "I hit 'em where they ain't."

Joe was handling all the attention from the press and fans well. That 61-game streak with the Seals might have been good preparation for what he was going through. He was the only thing people in baseball were talking about at that point in the 1941 season, even though Ted Williams was crushing the ball just as consistently and was flirting with the rarefied atmosphere known only to the .400 hitter. But it was only June and too early to be getting hopes up that someone might hit .400 again. What my brother Joe was doing was happening right now, and the tension was here and now. Ted's would come in September.

I didn't notice any change in Joe during the streak. We had

dinner a couple of times when the Yankees and Red Sox played each other, and we visited on the field. I was glad to see him holding up so well. It's asking a lot of an athlete to maintain his stability and disposition—and keep on excelling—while the world is placing a heady additional burden on him. Roger Maris found that out in 1961 and had some problems with it, and understandably so, but Joe was hanging right in there. I was proud of what he was doing on the field and how well he was performing off the field. He was a credit to baseball and to us DiMaggios.

I was able to keep up-to-the-minute on Joe's streak when we were playing at home. Ted was friendly with the man who operated the scoreboard in left field at Fenway Park, Bill Daley. Each time my brother would get a hit, Daley would holler out to Ted in left field through an opening in the score board, and then Ted would yell over to me, "Hey, Dom! Joe just got a double!"

Joe and his streak held such a magical grip on the nation's attention, and was such a welcome relief from the war news overseas, he became the subject of a hit song recorded by Les Brown and His Band of Renown:

> Who started baseball's famous streak
> That got us all aglow?
> He's just a man and not a freak,
> Joltin' Joe DiMaggio.
> Joe . . . Joe . . . DiMaggio . . . we want you on our side.
>
> From coast to coast, that's all you hear
> Of Joe the one-man show.
> He's glorified the horsehide sphere,
> Joltin' Joe DiMaggio.
> Joe . . . Joe . . . DiMaggio . . . we want you on our side.
>
> He'll live in baseball's Hall of Fame,
> He'll get there blow by blow.
> Our kids will tell their kids his name,
> Joltin' Joe DiMaggio.
> Joe . . . Joe . . . DiMaggio . . . *we want you on our side!*

— 8 —

THE STREAK AND
THE STOLEN BAT

With the approach of Fourth of July, the wave of patriotism stemming from the threat of war grew stronger. Eleanor Roosevelt urged the women of America to knit items for soldiers and sailors. Her husband urged Congress to enact daylight savings time so the country could save 736 million kilowatt hours of electricity a year.

While Americans continued to prepare for war, we also continued to make advancements in our way of life. Trans-World Airlines announced that flights from New York to Chicago on its new Stratoliners would take only four hours and ten minutes. In New York, advertisements in newspapers proclaimed the benefits of the new Emerson AC/DC radios "with easy-carry handle" for $12.95. Better than that, you could "charge it, no money down, no interest charge," if you agreed to pay off that $12.95 under a ninety-day installment plan at Davega City Radio.

Not all of us had our minds on the preparations for war. Mickey Rooney became engaged to Ava Gardner, and a man named Tommy Manville, who was the heir to the Johns-Manville insulation fortune, made the news by getting married the fifth time. It seemed that every time things threatened to get dull, Tommy Manville took another bride. This time he married one Bonita

Francine Edwards, a showgirl. It may be just as well that we didn't stage any national celebration for the Manvilles. The marriage lasted seventeen days.

Maybe we weren't as rich as Manville, but at least we were getting paid. That was a distinct improvement over the Depression of only a few years before, and when you think back, you remember how much lower the prices were.

Baseball players could buy a pair of Riddell baseball shoes for $4.50. On a trip to New York, Red Sox wives could buy a pair of shoes at Saks Fifth Avenue for $5.85 and a "luxurious imported French suede" handbag for $2.98 at Arnold Constable, with a dollar off "for lucky early birds"! Satin gowns were on sale at Stern's for $1.69.

Men's suits were $31.50 at B. Altman & Co. Shops for Men (regularly $35.00), and a white broadcloth shirt to wear with it was $1.39.

As the spring days of June turned into the summer dog days of July and August, we could go to those air conditioned movie houses and see the latest productions from Hollywood like *A Yank in the RAF* starring Tyrone Power and Betty Grable, *Buck Privates* with that popular new comedy team of Bud Abbott and Lou Costello. Carmen Miranda was wearing a pile of fruit on her head in *That Night in Rio,* and George Sanders and Walter Pidgeon were starring in a new thriller, *Man Hunt.* But no movie in America was attracting the attention that Joe was.

The Hollywood writers turning out scripts for all those movies couldn't have written anything as dramatic as the story of Joe's streak. He went after George Sisler's 41-game modern record in Washington during a doubleheader that was played in hundred-degree heat. In the first game he tied the record with a double off Dutch Leonard, one of the best knuckleball pitchers of his day, in the sixth inning. Shirley Povich remembers that the pitch was low and away, but Joe managed to pull it to left anyhow. Then a crazy thing happened.

Between games a fan ran into the Yankee dugout and stole Joe's bat. Joe had to borrow Tommy Henrich's bat for the second game. I don't know if I have ever heard of that happening, and even if it has, it's a million-to-one shot. But not only did it happen to Joe, it happened just as he was waiting for the second game and his chance to break the modern record.

Borrowing a teammate's bat is fine, but it's never really the same as your own. A ball player has his own kind of bat—length, weight, and model—because that's the kind he likes. Some players sand the handle, and Joe was one of those who did that. Every bat doesn't feel the same to every player any more than tennis racquets or golf clubs.

Even so, something like the different feel of Henrich's bat became a trifling matter to someone as invincible as Joe was during his streak. In the second game he was batting against the Senators' six-foot four-inch second-year right-hander, Sid Hudson. Sid had caught everyone's attention the year before as a rookie by winning 17 games, the most in his career, for a seventh place team that finished 26 games below .500. He was on his way to winning 13 games in '41 for a team that was destined to finish seventh again, both times ahead of Connie Mack's Philadelphia A's.

Joe flied out to Buddy Lewis in right in the first inning, and then hit a line drive to Cecil Travis at short in the third. In the fifth he flied out to Doc Cramer in center.

In the seventh he was facing Red Anderson, the Senators' six-foot three-inch right-handed pitcher who was in his third attempt to make the big leagues. He broke in with Washington in 1937 "for a cup of coffee," as baseball players say, just long enough to appear in two games. He was farmed out in 1938 and '39 and came back for two games in 1940. In '41 he appeared in 32 games, won 4 and lost 6, but never played in the major leagues again.

Anderson had relieved Hudson, and on his second pitch, a fast ball, Joe sent a line drive single to left field and broke the modern major league record by hitting in his forty-second consecutive game. Then, as the gods continued to smile on Joe, some loyal friends traced the trail of his pilfered bat to a kid in Newark, New Jersey. Joe got it back just in time for another doubleheader two days later in New York—against us.

New York was always one of the major league's hottest, sticki-

105

est cities in those years, with all its skyscrapers, miles and miles of concrete, and heavy traffic. St. Louis, Philadelphia, and Washington weren't much better, if at all, but New York in July was what the people there used to call "broot-*uhl.*"

The temperature was in the mid-90s that afternoon, July 1, but 52,832 fans showed up for one reason—to get a firsthand answer to the question people all over the country asked every day, "What did DiMaggio do today?" Whenever I heard that question I was tempted to answer, "Oh, I got two for four, and thanks for asking."

Joe and I were talking on the field before the start of the first game, and I told him it seemed he couldn't do enough. He had broken the consecutive game hitting streaks for both leagues—now he had to try and break a record set in the last century. It seemed irrelevant to me. Everybody knew about Wee Willie Keeler, but who ever heard of his 44-game hitting streak? Besides, Keeler did it under different rules, including not getting charged with a strike for hitting a foul ball.

As far as I was concerned, Joe had the major league baseball record. I wondered if the writers, and maybe the Yankees' front office, dug up Keeler's record because they knew they had a good thing going.

In the first game Joe popped out foul to Lou Finney at first base and then grounded out to Jim Tabor at third. In the fifth inning, against our ancient "rookie," Mike Ryba, Joe hit another ground ball to Tabor, who was playing Joe deep, like some of the other third basemen in the league at that time, including Cleveland's Ken Keltner. Tabor had trouble making the pickup and then made a bad throw to first allowing Joe to continue on to second base.

In the press box Dan Daniel was the official scorer again. He signified "hit."

There might have been some raised eyebrows around Yankee Stadium at that point, just as there were in Joe's thirty-seventh game when Daniel ruled that Joe's grounder to Johnny Berardino was an error. But it didn't make any difference. On his last trip up, facing Ryba again, Joe hit a line drive to left field for a solid base hit, and there wasn't a thing that Ted Williams or I could do about it. And Joe took Daniel off the hook. The noise was ear-splitting as the 52,000 fans in the 95-degree heat made themselves even hotter with a standing ovation that lasted several long minutes. Joe's streak was now at 43 games, only one shy of Keeler's nineteenth-century achievement.

Joe may have outhit me in that game, but I beat him on distance. I hit a home run, but it didn't help. We lost to the Yankees, 7–2.

In the second game Joe didn't fool around. In the first inning against Jack Wilson he lined a single over Joe Cronin's head at short. The crowd went crazy again. Now Joe had tied Keeler.

As things turned out, it was a good thing that Joe got that hit when he did. The second game lasted only five innings, called on account of darkness. He was able to get three trips to the plate because the Yankees got ten hits and beat us, 9–2, but the umpires—Joe Rue, Ed Rommel, Bill Stewart, and Bill Summers—called the game after five innings. Time of game: One hour and five minutes.

The next day, July 2, was just as hot, so bad that Lefty Grove asked Cronin to start someone younger in his place. The assignment fell to Dick Newsome, a rookie right-hander. Even though he was a first-year man, Newsome was on his way to winning 19 games. He slipped badly the next two seasons, winning only 8 each year, and 1943 was his last year in the major leagues.

In '41, though, Newsome was tough, and if Joe was going to break Keeler's record, he was going to have to do it against a good pitcher. Joe was hitless in his first two at bats, but on his third trip to the plate, Newsome got behind Joe, two balls and no strikes. No pitcher wants to get behind 2–0 or 3–1 to a good hitter, because then he has to come in with a strike to avoid either walking him or being only one pitch away from it. The hitter knows this as well as the pitcher. Good hitters' eyes light up when the count is 2–0 or 3–1.

On the next pitch Joe hit a home run over the left field wall. It was his only hit of the game.

After the game, Lefty Gomez, the colorful Yankee pitcher who was Joe's friend and roommate, told the people in the clubhouse that Joe broke Keeler's record by following Keeler's advice. "He hit it where they ain't," Lefty said.

Bobby Doerr still speaks in awe about Joe and his streak. "You had to admire him," Bobby was saying in talking about 1941. "I thought Yankee Stadium was the hardest ball park to hit in for a right-handed hitter in all of baseball. You had shadows beginning in about the fourth or fifth inning and, boy, it was tough to see. Most of the time, you'd have a white background from the white shirts of the fans sitting in the center field stands. I remember thinking, 'How does anybody ever hit here?' I have to say that if Joe had played in any other ball park, his stats would have been even greater."

The crowd was small, only 8,682 fans, but they seemed to make as much noise as the 52,000 the day before. I was surprised that there weren't more people in the ball park, but it was a Wednesday afternoon, the middle of the week, and many fans had probably decided to spend their money on the doubleheader the day before or on the doubleheader coming up on July Fourth, two days later.

Something else worth remembering happened in New York that week, something with enormous long-range meaning for every sport. The Federal Communications Commission authorized the start of commercial television broadcasting in the spring of 1941. The first commercial broadcast took place on the new TV station, WNBT, on July 1. Antennas on the top of the Empire State Building sent signals to 4,000 "receivers" within a radius of fifty miles that could receive the "telecasts."

The first WNBT commercial program gave the time, temperature and weather, followed by three 15-minute programs—the news with Lowell Thomas, *Truth or Consequences* and *Uncle Jim's Question Bee*. The first sponsors were Bulova Watch, Lever Brothers, Procter & Gamble and Sun Oil.

Larry MacPhail was ahead of everybody else on that subject too. The same man who pioneered night games in the major leagues in 1935 produced the first televised big league game in 1939. MacPhail did even more than that. He also broke New York City's "radio ban."

The Yankees, Giants, and Dodgers had an agreement among themselves that had lasted for five years—no radio broadcasts of home games. Their fear echoed what we would hear when television became popular: Don't broadcast your home games because, if you do, the fans will stop coming to the ballpark. MacPhail put an end to that in 1939 simply by breaking the radio ban and hiring Red Barber as his play-by-play announcer. A little later Barber found out from a friend of his at NBC, Alfred "Doc" Morton, that the network had televised a college baseball game between Princeton and Columbia on May 17, at Columbia's Bakersfield, with Bill Stern broadcasting the play-by-play.

Morton asked Barber to see if MacPhail would agree to allow a Dodgers game to be televised. A new idea always appealed to MacPhail. In addition to night baseball, he is credited with introducing season tickets and air travel for his teams. He said yes to this one too, with one condition: NBC would have to put a TV set in the press box so the Dodger officials and the writers could watch. The viewing audience itself wouldn't be much bigger than that. There were only a few hundred television sets in the whole New York area at the time.

On August 26, 1939, the first major league game ever televised began when Red Barber leaned toward the mike at Ebbets Field at the start of the first game of a doubleheader between the Dodgers and the Cincinnati Reds, and said: "This is Red Barber speaking. Let me say hello to you all."

There were two television cameras, both situated on the third base side of the field. One was at ground level near home plate, and the other was in the second deck, right in among the fans. That's where Red had to sit. He didn't have a monitor, so he couldn't tell what the viewers were seeing on their sets. He didn't have a script for the commercials so he ad-libbed his between-inning plugs for Mobil Motor Oil, Ivory Soap, and Wheaties.

He dutifully told his viewers about the quality of the motor oil, that Ivory Soap was "99 and 44/100ths percent pure" and about Wheaties, "the breakfast of champions." Afterward he conducted television's first postgame interview, talking to the two managers, Leo Durocher and Bill McKechnie, and several of their players.

It was a primitive effort, and Harold Parrott's review in the *Sporting News* said as much: "The players were clearly distinguishable, but it was not possible to pick out the ball."

A half century later in his autobiography, Red remembered that those associated with the pioneer telecast sensed they were a part of something special. "Everybody knew it was the beginning of something big," he said. "We just didn't really know what."

A million TV sets were sold in the United States in 1941 after the FCC authorized commercial television, but its development was halted by the war until, in the words of one of the song hits of the day, "the lights go on again all over the world."

When they did, television exploded into our lives, and into baseball.

Red recently verified that because of what his 1939 telecast might lead to, he asked NBC for a souvenir of the event. The network gave him an engraved silver cigarette box, a prestige gift in those days. NBC made sure to engrave a properly historic message on it:

To
Red Barber
Pioneer Television Sports Announcer
In Grateful Appreciation
National Broadcasting Company
August 26, 1939

Inside was a bill for thirty-five dollars.

— 9 —

"THE MOST THUNDEROUS CLIMAX IN HISTORY"

After becoming the first man in major league history to hit safely in 45 straight games—in any century—Joe got a rest. Heavy rain forced the Yankee front office to postpone the July Fourth doubleheader with the Philadelphia A's. July third was an open date, so Joe had a rare treat for any major league player—two days off in a row.

The Yankees had reason to be elated about what Joe was doing for them. He was not only attracting huge crowds to all of their games, including the ones on the road, but he was bringing them to the top of the American League standings. From their .500 record when he started his streak, they were now in first place, leading the Indians by two and a half games. In the National League, the Dodgers were a game ahead of the Cardinals. The baseball tradition in those years that the teams leading the two leagues on July Fourth would be in the World Series was going to hold true again.

The rain in the East didn't dampen the patriotic fervor that was growing throughout the country. This July Fourth had a national theme—"A Birthday Present for the United States." Americans were showing their red, white, and blue with patriotic observances to a degree not seen since the days of "the great war." To add to it, a story of heroism against the odds that came out of that war, *Sergeant York,* starring Gary Cooper, opened in movie theaters around the country that week and the next.

Baseball fans were doing their part even when attending the traditional doubleheaders. In Los Angeles, where fans could only see major league players during their October barnstorming tours, those attending the Los Angeles-Oakland doubleheader in the Pacific Coast League filled two dump trucks with aluminum for "the national defense program."

It was only the latest example of how baseball fans were showing their patriotism in 1941. On May 27 President Roosevelt had delivered a radio address to the nation on national defense. His speech was broadcast over the public address system to the crowd at the Polo Grounds who were watching the Giants play the Boston Braves. It was a close game, with Jim Tobin pitching for the Braves and Hal Schumacher for the Giants. The score was 1–1 after seven innings, and then time was called so everyone could listen to the President.

FDR's speech lasted forty-five minutes, and when play was resumed, both managers lifted their starting pitchers. Casey Stengel, the Braves' manager, removed Tobin and brought in Manny Salvo, followed by Dick Errickson. The Giants, under Bill Terry, brought in their Hall of Fame star, Carl Hubbell. The Giants won, 2–1, on a single by Hubbell.

After the Fourth of July celebrations across the country, baseball again made history, with the most dramatic All-Star finish the game had ever seen. Only one man could have knocked my brother Joe out of the headlines by then—Ted Williams—and, oh, did he ever. But it happened in a way that required help from all three of us—Joe, Ted, and myself.

It was an All-Star game with a cast to match. In the American League we were proud of our record of having defeated the National League in five of the first eight All-Star games, dating back to the start of the event in 1933 in Chicago. But the National League fielded a formidable lineup in '41—Johnny Mize, Stan

Hack, Terry Moore, Billy Herman, Arky Vaughan, Pete Reiser, Bob Elliott, Eddie Miller, Enos Slaughter, Mickey Owen, Al Lopez, Mel Ott, Paul Derringer, Bucky Walters, Joe Medwick, Claude Passeau, Bill Nicholson, Frank McCormick, Whit Wyatt, and Terry Moore.

We had a lineup on our side that would knock your eyes out, too, stars like my teammates—Ted, Joe Cronin, Bobby Doerr, Jimmie Foxx—plus Bob Feller, Red Ruffing, Joe Gordon, Cecil Travis, my brother Joe, Rudy York, Bill Dickey, Charlie Keller, Luke Appling, Ken Keltner, Lou Boudreau, and Frankie Hayes.

Ted Williams, the hero of that game, became one of the greatest hitters in the history of baseball for two reasons:

1. He had more talent
than the rest of us.
2. He worked harder.

Ted was the toughest taskmaster I ever knew, harder on himself than he was on anyone else, but plenty hard on us, too, especially if you were the leadoff hitter, which I was. If I led off the game by making an out, I would be headed past Ted on my way back to the dugout while he was on his way to the on-deck circle. As Johnny Pesky stepped into the batter's box, Teddy would be giving me the third degree:

"Where was that last pitch, Dommie?"

"What's he throwing?"

"What did you hit?"

His timing was always the worst in that situation. I was fed up with myself and in no mood to talk about it, so I'd tell him in my disgust, "I don't know."

To Williams, ignorance was worse than not getting a hit. "How the hell can you not know?" he'd bark. "What kind of a dummy are you? No wonder you didn't get a hit. Don't be so damned dumb!"

He was always grilling everybody, to learn as much as he could about hitting and about his professional enemies—pitchers.

113

With Ted every trip to the plate was an adventure filled with excitement, a challenge of wits and physical ability to see who would defeat whom. With a Louisville Slugger in his hand, he was a hitter possessed.

They still tell the story about his first day in Sarasota as a rookie, when Bobby Doerr pointed out Jimmie Foxx, one of the most feared sluggers in baseball and said, "Wait till you see Foxx hit."

Ted supposedly said, "Wait till Foxx sees *me* hit."

His sworn purpose in life was to be such a great hitter for so many years that after he retired, people would always point to him and say, "There goes the greatest hitter who ever lived."

Many people have said exactly that after Ted hit a home run in Fenway Park on the last day of the 1960 season in the last time at bat of his career. When people ask me who was the greatest hitter I ever saw, Ted or my brother Joe, I tell them in all honesty that Joe was the greatest right-handed hitter I ever saw, and Ted was the greatest left-handed one.

Teddy's career was brilliant from beginning to end. He played 19 seasons and missed 5 more because of duty as a Marine fighter pilot in World War II and the Korean War. Even with those five years knocked out of his career, he still finished with the tenth most home runs, the tenth most runs batted in, the second most walks, the sixth highest batting average, and the second highest slugging average behind only Babe Ruth.

What he did at the end of his career was just as impressive as what he did in his prime, maybe more. In 1957, at the age of thirty-nine, he led the major leagues in hitting with a .388 average, 37 points higher than Stan Musial's average at the top of the National League. In 1958, when he turned forty in August, he led the American League again with .328, beating out his teammate, Pete Runnels, who was ten years younger.

In Ted's last year he was, as always, a .300-plus hitter. He hit .316 with 29 home runs. He was forty-two years old.

The computer specialist in Seattle, Ralph Winnie, has projected that without losing those five years because of war duty, Ted would have been the all-time leader in runs scored and runs batted

114

in and second only to Hank Aaron in home runs with 743 instead of the actual career total of 521.

Winnie also computed that were it not for the war, Joe would have hit 525 home runs instead of 361 and would have achieved the third highest runs-batted-in total in history, the eighth most runs, and 1,017 more hits, raising his total from 2,214 to 3,231.

Teddy was blessed with exceptional eyesight, but he was also blessed with a determination and self-discipline that put him into a universe above us merely mortal hitters. His powers of concentration exceeded any I've ever seen. Before a game, while the rest of us were socializing on the bench, he sat with his eyes locked on the opposing team's starting pitcher as he warmed up on the sidelines, searching for any little tipoff in his delivery and analyzing what he was throwing.

During the game, when the opposing manager brought in a relief pitcher to face him in the late innings, Ted would slyly inch closer and closer to the plate from outside the batter's box after each warmup pitch, trying to see what the guy had. Eventually the home plate umpire would have to shoo him out of there, reminding him it was against the rules for a hitter to be standing that close to the batter's box during a relief pitcher's warmup pitches.

Ted was an authority on bats as well as on hitting. Bobby Doerr remembers that Ted was not only the first to go to a lighter bat, but the first to order a set of postal scales for the clubhouse so he could weigh each of his bats with precision. As Bobby was saying recently, "We used to think that with a heavier bat you had a better chance of getting a base hit out of it. But Ted's theory was that with a light bat, you had better bat speed and better control."

One spring when we were barnstorming our way north after spring training, Doerr and Williams visited the Hillerich & Bradsby factory in Louisville, where they make the Louisville Slugger bats. They got there a half hour before the plant opened, and Bobby says Ted was jumping out of his skin—"he was just dying to get in there."

During their visit Ted went to the man who operated one of the lathes and said, "Anytime you see any pin knots in the wood, stick those bats in my bag." Bobby remembers Ted's preference for

115

pin knots. "He always thought you'd have a harder spot in the bat any place where you had those little pin knots."

Much to Doerr's surprise, the lathe operator followed through on Ted's request. "By golly," Bobby says, "that guy did it. But the thing about it was that when Ted walked away, he handed the guy a $20 bill. So he got pin knots in his bats."

When we went to Detroit for the All-Star game in 1941, where Ted's hitting skills made All-Star history, he ran into Mr. Hillerich himself in the lobby of the Book-Cadillac Hotel. Doerr remembers the conversation:

WILLIAMS: "Mr. Hillerich, I want to get some thirty-two-ounce bats."

HILLERICH (throwing up his hands): "Ted, you can't get good wood with a bat that light."

WILLIAMS: "What good is the wood if you can't handle it?"

In those days, the rest of us were swinging bats that weighed thirty-four, thirty-five, or thirty-six ounces. But Ted's reasoning was that with a thirty-two-ounce bat, you could be quicker and make better contact.

Ted had a memory like a computer, and still does. Bob Feller struck him out on a slider in Old League Park in Cleveland early in their careers. Feller says, "He missed it by a foot. I got him on a one-two pitch with the bases full. And he still mentions it."

Ted did special exercises in the locker room to strengthen his arms, wrists, hands, and fingers, even after the game when the rest of us were dog tired and ready for something cold to drink and a chance to stretch out and get our second wind. Then, after strengthening even his fingers, he'd recruit one of our pitchers, wait for the crowd to finish filing out of the stadium, and then go back onto the field for another thirty or forty-five minutes of batting practice.

He didn't confine his practice swings to the playing field. "Broadway Charlie" Wagner, one of our pitchers and one of the flashiest dressers in the big leagues, was Ted's roommate from the

After my first season with San Francisco Seals, Vince (on the left) and Joe came back to the Seals for an exhibition game. All of us played our minor league ball for the Seals.

With the Seals, I made the switch from shortstop to center field and learned about hitting from Lefty O'Doul.

My brother Vince as a rookie with the Boston Braves in 1937.

My rookie year with the Boston Red Sox, 1940.

Joe, Ted Williams, and I take time out for the photographers before the Yankees' home opener in 1942.

National Baseball Library, Cooperstown, N.Y.

I didn't always make it with this much to spare, sliding into third base against the St. Louis Browns as a rookie in 1940.

The Yankees' catcher, Bill Dickey, and one of our outfielders, Pete Fox, come to my aid after I was beaned by Charley Stanceu at Yankee Stadium on August 11, 1941. The umpire calling time out is George Pipgras. I was hospitalized overnight for observation and then released.

Babe Ruth gives his long-time teammate, Lou Gehrig, a bear hug at home plate in ceremonies at Yankee Stadium on July 4, 1939, when Gehrig said good-bye to baseball. He died on June 2, 1941.

Part of the crowd of fans who lined up outside the church on a rainy morning for Lou Gehrig's funeral.

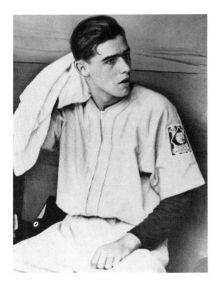

Washington pitcher Walt Masterson says the pressure of competing against so many outstanding players every day always had an exhausting effect by season's end.

Bob Feller of the Cleveland Indians led both leagues in wins and strikeouts in 1941.

"Broadway Charlie" Wagner, who roomed with Ted Williams in 1941, was knocked out of his hotel bed in St. Louis by one of Ted's practice swings.

Johnny "Double No-Hit" Vander Meer remembers the first night games and the long train rides as well as he recalls his back-to-back no-hitters. He was the National League's strikeout king in 1941.

AP/Wide World Photo

Lefty Grove takes his stretch in the top left photo, delivers his pitch at bottom, and follows through while winning his 300th game. It happened on July 25, 1941. I caught the fly ball that sealed Lefty's victory.

Joe McCarthy, manager of the New York Yankees in 1941.

Connie Mack, owner of the Philadelphia Athletics and their manager for 53 years.

Joe Cronin was the Red Sox manager in 1941 when we finished second behind the Yankees. Joe managed the Red Sox and the Washington Senators for 15 seasons, and for 13 of those years he managed the hard way — while also playing shortstop.

President Franklin D. Roosevelt receives his annual season pass to major league games from Clark Griffith, owner of the Washington Senators.

Red Barber (left), the radio voice of the Brooklyn Dodgers in 1941, interviews Bob Quinn of the Red Sox.

Shirley Povich of the *Washington Post,* speaking at the Hall of Fame's induction ceremonies in 1955 as president of the Baseball Writers' Association of America, covered every major event in baseball's historic 1941 season.

Joe and Ted reenact the boyhood game of "choosing up sides" before we played New York in Yankee Stadium on July 1, 1941. Ted was hitting .402, and Joe had just broken the major league consecutive-game hitting streak.

Ted Williams is greeted by Joe and coach Marv Shea, number 30, after his 1941 home run in Detroit with two outs in the bottom of the ninth inning won the All-Star game for the American League. It was my first year as an All-Star, and I had one of the best spots in the house for the most dramatic home run in the event's history. I was the on-deck hitter.

Three men who stopped my brother Joe's hitting streak after 56 straight games were pitchers Jim Bagby (upper left) and Al Smith (above) and third baseman Ken Keltner (left). Ken made two sensational plays on hot smashes that carried him into foul territory behind third before he could straighten up and throw Joe out. It happened in Cleveland on the night of July 17, 1941.

My brother Joe lines a sharp single to the outfield in Cleveland against Joe Krakauskas, the last hit in his unmatched feat of hitting safely in 56 consecutive games. The date was July 16, 1941. The catcher is Rollie Hemsley.

Pete Reiser, one of the stars of 1941. His roommate, Pee Wee Reese, said, "He played hard—damn he played hard." Reiser led the National League that year in hitting, slugging, total bases, triples, and runs scored. Pee Wee Reese (left) played in 84 games as a rookie with the Brooklyn Dodgers in 1940 before being injured, then came back to play in all but two of their 154 games in 1941.

Johnny Mize of the Cardinals was one of baseball's most feared hitters in 1941, leading the National League with 39 doubles and hitting .317, fifth highest in the league.

Enos Slaughter of the St. Louis Cardinals never forgot his manager's words about hustling all the time.

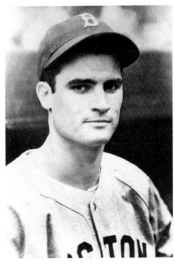

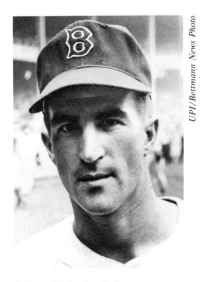

Bobby Doerr, our second baseman, remembers the white spots on the bats used by Ted Williams in 1941, proof of Ted's hitting consistency.

Johnny Pesky broke in as our shortstop in 1942 and received a lesson from Ted on how to hit against one of the Yankees' ace pitchers, Spud Chandler.

Charlie Keller hit 33 home runs for the Yankees in 1941, second in the American League behind only Ted Williams, who hit 37—while also hitting .406. Charlie's double in "the Mickey Owen game" clinched the win for New York.

Mickey Vernon, who later won the American League batting championship twice, came within one point of hitting .300 in his first full season in 1941, but catcher Bill Dickey of the Yankees unknowingly foiled a plan.

(Above) Ted Williams and Joe Cronin at Fenway Park with its fabled "Green Monster" in the background. Going into the last day of the 1941 season, Joe offered to let Ted sit out our doubleheader to insure his .400 batting average. Ted refused—and raised his average six points. (Left) The classic Ted Williams batting form in 1941.

The fans line up outside the Ebbets Field bleachers in Brooklyn for tickets to the third game of the 1941 World Series. Note the price of a ticket.

This is the storybook moment in the 1941 World Series when Brooklyn's Hugh Casey (left) seemed to have defeated the Yankees to tie the Series at two wins each. But his curve ball striking out Tommy Henrich gets away from catcher Mickey Owen. Both Henrich and Owen still have their eyes on the ball as umpire Larry Goetz signals strike three and Henrich alertly breaks for first base. He kept the inning alive by reaching base and the Yankees rallied to win the game and the Series. Dodger fans began their annual chant, "Wait till next year."

rookie left fielder's arrival with the Red Sox in 1939 until Charlie's retirement in 1946.

Broadway remembers that Williams once knocked him out of bed while practicing his swing. It happened at the Chase Hotel in St. Louis in 1941. Ted was swinging a bat in front of a mirror between the twin beds, accidentally hit the bedpost on Charlie's bed, and broke it. Broadway tumbled out onto the floor.

Charlie says Ted's only reaction was to say, "Call down and see if you can get another bed." Wagner says it didn't occur to him to apologize because with Ted the swing was the only thing he was interested in.

Instead, Ted just said, "Man! What power!"

Williams had his own inflexible rules of hitting, and he couldn't understand why the rest of us didn't follow the same code. The truth is we tried, but not everybody can hit like Ted Williams. And even though we couldn't apply his rules as successfully as he could, none of us argued with the wisdom of what he preached:

1. *Wait on the pitch.* That way you will be able to make a better decision on whether to swing at the pitch or take it, because you'll have a longer look at where the pitch is and whether it's something you want to hit or pass up.
2. Once you start your swing, *you have to be quick.* With that unlimited boyish enthusiasm of his and with his voice getting higher as he warmed to his subject, he used to say, "It's wait, wait, wait and then quick, quick, quick!"
3. *Get a good pitch to hit.* If it's a fraction of an inch out of the strike zone, don't swing at it, because once you start doing that, you'll find yourself swinging at pitches that are more and more off the plate. Don't start compromising. "Hit strikes" was the way he put it.

The 1941 All-Star game was my first. I entered the game in the sixth inning, and in the eighth I received one of those once-in-a-lifetime thrills, or once in ten thousand lifetimes. In my first time at bat in an All-Star game, in front of 54,674 fans, I singled—and

117

drove in my brother. It's enough of a thrill to get a hit in your first All-Star at bat, and to drive in a run with it makes it an even bigger thrill. But imagine how it feels when the runner you drive in is your own brother.

Then came the ninth inning.

The game was played in Detroit that year, in what was then called Briggs Stadium and is now known as Tiger Stadium. Regardless of its name, it's always been known as a hitter's ball park, and on that eighth day of July, its reputation was confirmed.

The National League was winning, 5–3. Feller started the game for us and pitched 3 shutout innings. Thornton Lee pitched the middle 3 and gave up only one run, but the National League scored 2 runs in the seventh off Sid Hudson and two more in the eighth against Edgar Smith to get its lead. Going into the ninth inning, the hitting star of the game unquestionably was Arky Vaughan of the National League with 3 hits, including two 2-run homers, the first time any man hit 2 home runs in an All-Star game.

The National Leaguers were in a great position to win their fourth game of the 9 played so far. Whitlow Wyatt, Paul Derringer, and Bucky Walters had limited our team to 3 runs in 8 innings. To protect the lead, they had Claude Passeau on the mound, who won 20 games for the Cubs the year before. With Passeau out there, that 2-run lead looked like money in the bank.

Frankie Hayes, the catcher for the Philadelphia A's, led off the inning and Passeau got him on a pop-up. Ken Keltner, the Indians' third baseman pinch hit for Edgar Smith and singled off the glove of Eddie Miller at short. That brought the potential tying run to the plate in Joe Gordon, the Yankees' second baseman.

Gordon, who was nicknamed "Flash" after the popular comic strip character of the time, singled to right. Now things were beginning to get sticky for the National League. The tieing run was on first and we had three of the greatest hitters in baseball—Cecil Travis, Joe DiMaggio, and Ted Williams—coming up. We found out after the game that another one of the American League's best hitters was an interested spectator, a soldier in the right field stands whose presence was never announced to the crowd. Private Hank

Greenberg was sitting out there, in the same seats where so many of his home runs had landed for the Tigers.

Now Passeau faced Travis, one of the best left-handed hitters in baseball. Even though Travis played for the Washington Senators in the American League, nobody had to tell a National Leaguer like Passeau how good Travis was. Going back to his rookie year in 1933, his only average below .300 was .292. His other years sounded like the time of day between three and four o'clock—.319, .318, .317, .344, .335, and .322. In this season, when Ted hit .406, Cecil Travis was the reason my brother Joe didn't finish second even with a 56-game hitting streak. Joe hit .357, but Travis hit .359.

Maybe Passeau knew too much about Travis. He walked him. Now we had the bases loaded and only one out, with Joe coming up and Ted on deck.

Joe stepped in, having hit in 48 straight regular-season games, the most feared hitter in baseball if Ted wasn't. Joe had doubled in the eighth before I drove him in. This time he hit one of his smoking ground balls—Joe always hit the ball so hard—to Miller at short. Eddie fielded it cleanly and shoveled the ball over to Billy Herman at second to start a double play that would end the game.

But Travis, a good team player as well as an excellent hitter, came in hard at second with a shoulder block that knocked Herman off balance and forced a wide throw to first that pulled Frank McCormick off the bag. Travis was out at second, but Joe was safe at first. People seem to have forgotten how fast Joe was. They never mention it, but he was exceptionally fast. He got down the first base line faster than anyone, but he moved so gracefully you were unaware of his speed.

Bobby Doerr, who was playing in his first All-Star game that year, too, and who shot home movies with Ted's camera before the game—he still has the films—talks about Joe's speed even today. "I remember I had Joe in a rundown once between first and second. I had the ball and he wasn't that far away from me. I made up my mind I was going to run him down rather than jockey around with him. I had a running start, and I just barely tagged him out. It

119

surprised me how fast he could accelerate from a standstill. You really had to hustle to throw him out on a ground ball."

Keltner scored on the forceout at second, and now we're only one run behind with two on and Williams up. And I'm in the on-deck circle as the next hitter if Ted gets on.

Now the wheels started turning in everyone's head. Should the National League manager, Bill McKechnie, take the unusual step of loading the bases by walking Williams intentionally? Ted was hitting .405, and McKechnie could always take his chances by pitching to me instead, even though I was hitting over .300. Ted's run wouldn't mean anything anyhow. Gordon at third was the potential tying run, and Joe at first was the winning one. They were the only ones that counted.

Passeau had struck out Williams in the eighth, and that may have entered McKechnie's thinking, plus a reluctance to move Joe into scoring position. I was hoping for the chance to win the game for the American League in my first All-Star game.

The National League asked for time out to talk about it. Meanwhile, our third base coach, Art Fletcher of the Yankees, was getting irritated with some talk coming from the box seats that Arky Vaughan was the hero of the game. Artie turned to the fans and said, "He ain't no hero yet. This game ain't over."

McKechnie decided to let Passeau pitch to Ted, and he immediately had reason to question the wisdom of his own decision. Ted hit the first pitch over the right field fence—foul. The count went to two balls and one strike, and then the home plate umpire, Lou Jorda of the National League, called for the ball. He inspected it for any scratches or blemishes that could affect its flight, threw it out of the game, and put a new one into the game.

On the next pitch Ted hit his famous home run—all the way to the roof of Briggs Stadium, and a line drive at that. The ball hit the facing of the third deck 90 feet above the 325-foot sign. Gordon and Joe scored ahead of him, and Ted went leaping around the bases with those skinny arms and legs flying all over the place in his jubilation. The fans came streaming out of the stands and on to the field.

I hurried from the on-deck circle over to the plate to join the welcome-home committee as Ted rounded the bases. There was a man there in street clothes too—our starting pitcher Bob Feller. He had showered after his performance and changed into civvies, but had stayed in our dugout for the rest of the game. When Ted hit his homer, Bob was one of the first American Leaguers out there at home plate to help carry him off the field in victory.

When Feller was asked about it recently, he laughed and said, "I wanted to get in on the reflective glory."

It was the first time an All-Star game had been won in the ninth inning. Judson Bailey of the Associated Press wrote that it was "the most thunderous climax in the history of baseball's All-Star spectacle," and it still is.

After the game Ted was beside himself with excitement. He told the reporters: "I just shut my eyes and swung. I had a feeling that if I got up there in the ninth, I'd go for the downs. Boy, I feel great! There's nothing like hitting a home run."

Ted said he hit a waist-high fast ball, and over in the National League dressing room, Passeau said the same thing. One newspaper article the next day said the National Leaguers "were a mad, snarling, and disgusted flock of players as they stormed into their dressing room. They kicked at their trunks, slammed equipment around the room, and began a chorus of cursing in an attempt to explain the defeat."

My All-Star teammates carried Ted off the field. Joe, Feller, and I were among the first to reach him. In our dressing room there was high-decibel bedlam. Del Baker, who managed our team because he won the American League pennant the year before with the Tigers, gave Ted a big kiss on the cheek, but only one kiss made Baker a piker compared to Artie Fletcher's demonstration of affection and worship. Artie must have kissed Williams more that night than all the women in Boston before or since.

The reports the next day said Passeau slumped down into a chair in Briggs Stadium's visitors dressing room and hung his head in silence for a few moments. Then he "rolled his uniform and tossed it into his grip. He rinsed his mouth with a swig of cold beer." Then he told reporters how hard it is "to lose when you had two chances to beat them in the ninth."

That was Enos "Country" Slaughter's first All-Star game. He got a base hit to left center off Sid Hudson his first time up, but he did something else that day. He was playing right field for the National League when Ted's home run hit the facing of the third deck.

"The ball bounced back on to the field," Enos was remembering last summer. "I picked it up and stuck it in my pocket and kept it for forty-four years."

When Slaughter was inducted into the Hall of Fame in 1985, he gave the ball to Ted. Williams had Enos sign it, and today the ball is in Cooperstown right there with Country and Ted.

For the DiMaggio boys, the game was just as sweet as it was for Williams. The next day one of the San Francisco papers said, "From the San Francisco angle, we are unable to judge which was the mightier hit—Ted Williams's home run that won for the American Leaguers yesterday in the ninth inning, or Dominic DiMaggio's single in the eighth, driving in brother Joe."

I thought they had a good point.

— 10 —

OF STREAKS AND BROTHERS

America was building herself up in more ways than just defense. Some new things called vitamins were introduced into our daily lives. We were told they were good for our health, and so were minerals. A national nutrition program was begun, and vitamins and minerals were added to milk, bread, and other everyday foods. The national attention given to what America was eating and drinking was spotlighted by school kids all over the country who wore big blue-and-white buttons that said:

Drink More Milk.

The German "wolf packs" continued to stalk American ships in the Atlantic Ocean, especially tankers. They were sinking so many that the oil and gasoline supply to the East Coast was sharply reduced. Because of that, gas stations in seventeen eastern states were placed under a curfew and ordered to reduce the number of hours they could sell gasoline and oil.

FDR and Winston Churchill met in the North Atlantic in early August, signed the Atlantic Charter, and agreed on long-range objectives toward "the final destruction of the Nazi tyranny." It was America's latest act of cooperation with its British ally. Earlier in the year Roosevelt succeeded in getting Congress to pass his lend-lease program, under which the United States would lend billions of dollars to help England meet the German threat. The bill was symbolically numbered House Resolution 1776.

It was hard for most Americans to doubt the need to help England or to prepare here at home for what most thought was an unavoidable world war. Our awareness was made greater by dramatic radio broadcasts from overseas by the newest name in American journalism, Edward R. Murrow, who stationed himself on rooftops in London and broadcast eyewitness accounts of Hitler's relentless nightly bombing during the London blitz.

This was something new for people everywhere, not just in America. The sounds and voices of war were brought into living rooms every night as listeners huddled around radios, heard the crackling interference, and then Murrow's deep and solemn voice from across the ocean: "This—is London."

Despite these advancements in communications through the magic of radio, public opinion polls showed that one third of all Americans were still opposed to getting involved in the European conflict.

War news and the baseball news generated by Joe's streak continued to dominate the front pages of America's newspapers. On July 15, Roosevelt recommended to Congress that the draft be extended because two-thirds of the draftees in uniform would be discharged over the next few months and "greener recruits" must be drafted to replace them. On the same day, Joe collected a single and a double off Edgar Smith of the White Sox in Chicago to extend his streak to 55 games.

The next day he got three hits against the Indians in Cleveland. His last hit of the day came off Joe Krakauskas. The question was who was going to stop Joe—or whether he was ever going to be stopped. A headline in the *New York Times* said:

CARDS BEAT DODGERS IN NIGHT GAME;
YANKEES ROUT INDIANS
DiMaggio Hits 56th Game in Row
And Yanks Crush Cleveland, 10–3

The next night, Thursday, July 17, some 67,468 fans showed up at Cleveland's Municipal Stadium on the shores of Lake Erie to see if Joe could make it 57 games in a row.

On that night, Hitler's army was bearing down on Moscow with his fanatical idea of trying to capture the Soviet Union. While the Yankees were on the road, Ted Lewis was on the stage at Loew's State Theater on Times Square back in the city that Joe now held in the palm of his hand. Ginger Rogers was starring in *Tom, Dick and Harry* with George Murphy, Alan Marshal, and Burgess Meredith at Radio City Music Hall. And another war comedy, *In the Navy,* with Abbott and Costello, was at the Metropolitan on Fulton Street in Brooklyn.

A new draft call was announced for 750,000 twenty-one-year-olds. The first number was pulled out by Staff Sergeant Robert W. Shackleton, who was stationed at Fort Dix, New Jersey, but was sent to Washington to pull the number blindfolded from a bowl full of capsules. Brigadier General Lewis Hershey, the deputy director of Selective Service, was on hand, too, but they let a sergeant do the job.

Joe's streak was stopped that night on two great plays by Ken Keltner at third base and another by Lou Boudreau at short. The Cleveland pitchers who managed to stop "Unstoppable Joe" with such great help from the left side of their infield were Al Smith and Jim Bagby, Jr. They were well known to baseball fans already, but they became national celebrities that night and the next morning.

Keltner was the one who had the most to do with stopping Joe, and today when people talk about the end of the streak, they say: "That was the game when Ken Keltner made two great plays at third base." Saying they were "great plays" may be an understatement. Joe hit two shots down the line at third, and the players who were there will tell you that Ken backhanded both of them with his own momentum and the force of Joe's shots propelling Keltner into foul territory. When he straightened up to make his throws, he was behind the bag and both of his feet were still in foul territory. Both his throws were strikes to Oscar Grimes at first base.

Early in the '41 season, Keltner began playing Joe closer to

125

the third base line than usual. As the streak wore on, he moved still closer each time the Indians played the Yankees, making it as hard as he could for Joe to hit a double down the left field line on one of his patented hot smashes on the ground.

"And I played him farther back," Ken was saying a few months ago, "because he never bunted. I was playing a deep third and close to the line to keep him from going for two." The presence of Smith and Bagby on the mound gave Keltner even more reason to be ready for some DiMaggio shots.

"Neither one of them was a fireballer," Ken remembers, "so Joe had to be pulling the ball down that line."

Joe's grounders to him that night "were hit like bullets, both of them." Then, with his modesty, Keltner adds: "Let me tell you, they were unconscious plays—but they were in the glove. Then I had to straighten up and throw the ball over to first. I got him each time, just by an eyelash."

Looking back on it now, maybe Ken feels good about that night, but he wasn't thrilled about it at the time. "We lost the ball game," he says. The Indians staged a two-run rally in the bottom of the ninth, but the Yankees held on to win, 4–3. "People kept coming up to me after the game and thanking me for making those stops, and I would say to them, 'What do you mean, thanking me? We lost the ball game, didn't we?' "

Joe was so enormously popular, especially that year, that Ken remembers something else that happened. After the game he met his wife, Evelyn, and as they started to walk together toward the stadium parking lot, they were picked up by a police escort, who saw them to their car.

Ken remembers going to the front office the next day to complain about the police escort and find out just why anybody thought it was necessary.

"What's the big idea of the police escort out to the parking lot?" he demanded.

One of the members of the front office staff said, "Joe has a lot of friends here in Cleveland. We just wanted to make sure you got home safely."

That's how popular Joe was, and not just in Cleveland but everywhere.

Some time later Joe gave Ken an autographed picture of himself. He signed it:

To My Dear Friend—The Culprit.
Joe DiMaggio

Today Ken is a member of that large group of major league players from the 1940s who say, as Ken puts it, "Joe was the greatest player I ever saw. He did it all. Williams was the greatest hitter I ever saw, and Joe was the greatest ball player."

Did Keltner play Williams differently because he was having such a great year in '41 too? "No, because he was left-handed he didn't bother me at all. I was happy I was playing over where I was."

He was even more grateful every time he heard Williams in the on-deck circle rubbing his hands on his bat handle so hard he made it squeak, the habit that bothered Bob Lemon when he turned to pitching several years later. "I used to hear it too," Ken says today. "He'd be over there making that bat screech."

Keltner remembers something else about playing third base for the Indians. He won the job with an outstanding rookie season in 1938. He was a sensational third baseman, and showed he was an excellent hitter, too, with 31 doubles, 26 home runs, and 113 runs batted in as a twenty-two-year-old kid from Milwaukee.

When Lou Boudreau came up to the big club at the end of that season after an all-American collegiate career at the University of Illinois, the best he could do was get into one game as a third baseman. Then the Indians made a shortstop out of him because nobody was going to keep Keltner out of the lineup.

Lemon came along as a third baseman in 1941, and the same thing happened. He got into one game at third, but Keltner was an established star by that time, so the Indians made Lemon a pitcher.

"They both came up as third basemen," Ken points out. "One goes to short, the other goes to pitching, and I'm still playing third base. And now they're both in the Hall of Fame. Figure that one out. They didn't get my job—that's what it will tell you."

In Chicago that night I was having better luck. I hit a triple and a home run against the White Sox and drove in three runs. We were able to beat Chicago, 7–4, and break another streak on that same night—Thornton Lee's 16 straight complete games for the White Sox.

You can appreciate the enormity of Joe's accomplishment even more when you look at the statistics from his streak. In those 56 games he hit .408. He had 91 hits including 35 for extra bases—16 doubles, 4 triples and 15 home runs. He batted in 55 runs and scored 56. In 223 times at bat, he struck out only seven times.

He carried the Yankees to a record of 42 wins and only 13 losses during his streak, with 2 games ending in ties when they were stopped by rain. New York, which was struggling at the .500 level when Joe began his sustained achievement, roared into first place when Joe's streak reached 37 games. The Yankees stayed there the rest of the season. We finished second, 17 games behind.

Charlie Wagner still remembers Joe's consistency that year, not just his streak. Charlie was one of our best pitchers that year, winning 12 games for us. He was in his fourth year with the Red Sox, so he had seen enough of Joe to form some definite impressions of him.

"Joe was so tough in the clutch," Charlie said recently. "He was just a cool guy going on about his business every day. But when he was out of that lineup, the Yankees looked like a whole different ball club. You could see it in their mood. I'd ask Rizzuto, 'Isn't the big guy playing today?' And he'd get a worried look on his face and say, 'No—jeez, I hope he gets back soon.'

"You noticed Joe doing the things the great hitters do. He was a tough out with two strikes, like Ted. He'd almost give you two strikes. But on the third strike, as a pitcher you didn't know where to go with your pitch because he was going to hit almost anything you threw up there. You could feel that pressure when you were pitching, and you had to be aware of it or you'd be backing up third."

Mickey Owen, the Dodger catcher who would become famous himself that year for a different reason, studies baseball statistics every night of his life and compiles charts to illustrate his findings. He rates Joe as "the most consistent player in the history of baseball." Then he explains why:

"Joe is the winningest player who ever put on a major league uniform. Anyplace he went, you win. He played for thirteen years, and ten of his teams won pennants. His team never finished worse than third. He played in ten World Series, and the Yankees won nine of them. Nobody comes close to that."

The emotional letdown after the constant publicity and the pressure of keeping his streak alive would have gotten the better of many other players. What did Joe do? He started another streak, against Bob Feller no less, and hit safely in the next 16 games, 14 of which the Yankees won. Johnny Niggeling, a thirty-eight-year-old right-hander for the St. Louis Browns, stopped him the second time, after Joe hit safely in 72 games out of 73. The season was 154 games long in those years, so Joe came only 4 games short of hitting in every game but one for half of the season.

To put it another way, if Keltner and Boudreau had not come up with three spectacular plays in one game, Joe would have hit in 73 straight games. And no one has even come close to 56.

On the subject of hitting streaks, Joe and I crossed paths again eight years later, when I set the Red Sox record of 34 straight games, which still stands. Vic Raschi of the Yankees stopped me. And who made the catch on my last time up? Joe.

It was a line drive to center field, the hardest ball I hit in the whole game, but it was right at my brother. The next day the Poston papers headlined the story, saying:

JOE DIMAGGIO'S CATCH STOPS BROTHER'S STREAK

Both of us got a kick out of that. Joe laughed and said, "If I had let the ball go through, it would have hit me right between the eyes."

I'm proud that my streak is still the Red Sox record, and proud that the man who made the final catch against me was my brother. Hitting in 34 straight games is a rare achievement—only fourteen players have accomplished it—and I know from my experience how difficult it was to do, so I can appreciate even more than most players just how nearly impossible it is to do what Joe did.

He broke a record that stood for forty-four years against hitters like Cobb and Terry, Sisler, Hornsby, Ruth, and all the rest. And Joe didn't just break it by one game—he broke it by 12, plus his double in the All-Star game that actually gave him a streak of 57 games.

Joe hit his way into a class by himself.

Almost as incredible as Joe's streak was the attitude that the Yankees' management showed when it came time to talk about his contract for 1942. Ed Barrow, their general manager, wanted Joe to take a cut in pay. He offered my brother a contract calling for five thousand dollars below what he earned in 1941.

Barrow wasn't above reminding Joe that "our boys in uniform" were making twenty-one dollars a month. The owners were perfectly willing to play on your patriotism, but they were never willing to say if they had taken a pay cut themselves.

The sad fact is that many of the baseball owners in those years were something less than model employers. They beat players down for every dollar they could when negotiating contracts for the next season, and they always had you over a barrel because of baseball's notorious "reserve clause" that was in every player's contract until the courts struck it down in the 1970s.

That reserve clause bound you to your team, and if you didn't like what your team was offering in salary, too bad. People in other occupations could work for somebody else if they wanted to, but not baseball players. The reserve clause stated that if you decided not to play for your team, you remained the property of that team anyhow. It's hard to imagine that slavery still existed in America in the twentieth century, and harder yet to imagine it wasn't overthrown until the 1970s.

These restrictions weren't limited to life in the big leagues, either. It was just as bad in the minor leagues. Some big league teams had six hundred or eight hundred players on their minor league rosters, with a team in almost every one of the forty-two minor leagues in the country at that time.

It got so bad in the minors, with big league teams stockpiling players and preventing them from moving up to a higher level from one year to the next—even having college players on minor league teams under assumed names—that Judge Landis, the first commissioner of baseball, released seventy-four minor leaguers from the farm system of the St. Louis Cardinals in 1938 and ninety-one from the Detroit Tigers in 1941. Landis simply declared them free agents and gave them the option to sign with any team they wanted to. That's how Tommy Henrich became a Yankee. In fact, it was his letter to Landis asking for clarification as to his status that prompted Landis to investigate the practice of stockpiling minor leaguers and then take his actions.

Johnny Mize could relate to the attitude the Yankees showed to my brother Joe after his streak. Mize was one of the most feared hitters in baseball, from his rookie year with the Cardinals in 1936 until his retirement from the Yankees after the 1953 season. He's a member of the Hall of Fame now, and no wonder. He was that rare combination of talent—the ability to hit for a high average and the power to hit home runs consistently.

He led the National League in home runs four times and runs batted in three times. He led the league in hitting in 1939 with a .349 average, and had the highest slugging average four years out of five. Some of his hitting accomplishments testify to his greatness —batting averages in his first nine years ranging from .302 to .364, home run totals as high as 40, 43, and 51 and years when he had 125, 137, and 138 runs batted in.

Yet Mize has bitter memories about the way he was treated in those years by the Cardinals' owner, Sam Breadon, and their general manager, Branch Rickey. After winning the National League batting championship, Rickey told Mize before the 1940 season: "You're not hitting enough home runs."

It was a strange statement to make to the man who also led the league in home runs with 28 in '39 and already had 99 homers

131

in his first four seasons in the big leagues. Nonetheless, Mize responded to Rickey's suggestion, hit 15 more home runs in 1940 than in '39, and led the league again, this time with 43, breaking the St. Louis team record. Along the way he managed to drive in another 137 runs, leading the league in that department, too, and giving him 553 RBIs in his first five seasons.

When they sat down to talk about a new contract for '41, Rickey told Mize he should take a pay cut because his batting average was only .314. Mize says today: "So I had to hit better than .349 and hit more home runs than I ever had to get a raise."

Mize remembers that Breadon, as the St. Louis owner, was never willing to give an annual raise of more than five hundred dollars. With Rickey still unwilling to grant Mize a raise after the 1940 season, even though Johnny had delivered on Rickey's request for more home runs, Mize held out and refused to report to spring training.

Eventually he signed a two-year contract, something else that was unheard of in those days, but told the Cardinals he wanted it understood that if he were traded, the contract, giving him the same salary as in '39, would be voided and he would be free to negotiate a fairer salary with a new team. The Cards told him okay.

With that understanding Johnny Mize went out to meet minimum goals for the 1941 season, so he could point to a decent year but still force the Cardinals to trade him. "All I wanted to do in '41," he says today, "was hit .300 and drive in a hundred runs. I just wanted out of St. Louis. I knew I wasn't going to get any more money there."

Johnny hit .317 that year—three points higher than the year before and the fourth highest in the league. He finished third in slugging average behind only Pete Reiser and Dolph Camilli, both of the Dodgers, and drove in exactly 100 runs, third behind Camilli and Babe Young of the Giants. His home run total dropped from 43 of the year before to 16, but he tied Camilli for the league lead in doubles with 39.

The Cardinals went down to the wire with the Dodgers in their battle for the National League pennant, and Johnny Mize was the biggest batting star in their lineup. He led the team in batting

132

average, home runs, and runs batted in. In the field he tied Cincinnati's Frank McCormick for the fewest errors by first basemen with only 8.

With all of that production out of one man in a year when they almost won the pennant, the Cards traded Mize in December to the Giants for three players, Ken O'Dea, Bill Lohrman, and Johnny McCarthy, plus $50,000.

Both sides were elated. The Cardinals wouldn't have to worry anymore about Mize and his requests for a raise in pay for one outstanding season after another. And Mize could go to New York, where he stood a better chance of getting what he had deserved all along.

Enos Slaughter confirms Mize's stories about life in the Cardinals' organization. Enos was born in Roxboro, North Carolina, still lives there, and is still called "Country" by his friends. He knew what it was like to play for starvation wages, whether it was in the country or later in the big city of St. Louis.

His first year in the minor leagues was with Martinsville, Virginia, of the Bi-State League in 1935. His salary was $75 a month. He was promoted to Columbus, Georgia, in the South Atlantic League, Class B ball, a jump of two levels in the minor league system when the starting level for a minor leaguer would be one of the Class D leagues. Then it was Class C, Class B, Class A, Class AA—called "Double A"—and then the highest level in the minors, Class AAA or "Triple A." When Enos made his first big jump in the minors, from D ball to Class B, he was given the princely raise of $25, from $75 a month to $100.

He had another good year and was promoted to the Triple A level—Columbus, Ohio, in the American Association, in 1937 for a monthly salary of $150. Then he found out it wasn't always going to be that easy, and the dollars weren't always going to be that plentiful. This was back when the Cards had so many players stashed away in minor leagues all over the nation that the players used to call their minor league system "the St. Louis Chain Gang."

In Triple A ball, Country hit .382, so he asked Branch Rickey for a bonus.

133

"He jumped down my throat," Slaughter says. "He said the older fellas had been talking to me. I didn't get any bonus."

Country found out that things didn't get any better when you made it to the major leagues, at least not with the Cardinals. His salary as a rookie in 1938 was $400 a month. Enos began to play more after Frankie Frisch was fired in September of Slaughter's rookie year. Ray Blades managed the Cardinals in '39 and '40, and Country headed out on the road to stardom.

He hit .320 as a second-year man and led the National League in doubles with 52. He was also becoming an outstanding outfielder, leading the league in putouts and assists.

For all of this he was paid $700 a month.

Mickey Owen, the Dodgers' catcher in 1941, also testifies to the struggles facing minor league players in those years, especially in the Cardinals' organization. Owen found the shortest route to the big leagues—catcher. Some say it's still true today that not that many kids are willing to catch, so there isn't that much competition at that position.

It was especially true with the Cardinals. "The Cardinals didn't have any catchers—not even in their minor league system," Mickey said. "That's why I got to the big leagues. Rickey would always sell them off. And their scouts weren't signing any. It's hard to find catchers, especially good ones, because good ball players don't catch. They don't have to."

The problem in the St. Louis organization was to get a fair salary, but Mickey remembers that at least he didn't have the problem encountered by those in the Yankees' farm system, where the hard part was getting a chance to advance.

"More good ball players suffered in the Yankees' chain than in the Cardinals' chain. Rickey would sell you. They needed money. And they didn't draw. But the Yankees didn't need the money. They had a rich owner, the old boy who owned that brewery—Ruppert—and they drew over a million people every year, so they had money. You couldn't buy their ball players.

"They'd keep you down there in the minors, and there were lots of young ball players who lost the bloom and never developed as good ball players because they didn't get to play against the good competition quick enough."

Mickey points to a fellow catcher as an example. "Buddy Rosar never got to play. He sat around with the Yankees for four years. You lose a lot when they make you do that. The Yankees had a lot of college players in those days, and they'd say to themselves, 'I have a good education. I'm going home and get a job in the school system or someplace else,' and they'd drop out.

"They lost a lot of young players like that. They almost lost Keller that way, and yet he went on to become one of the most underrated ball players in the history of baseball. He should be in the Hall of Fame. So should their right fielder—Henrich."

Johnny Vander Meer agrees with Owen on the subject of the control exerted by two men over the fate of players and their salaries. They were Branch Rickey, the Cardinals' general manager, and Ed Barrow, the GM for the Yankees. "Two men controlled the pay scales," Vander Meer says—"Rickey in the National League and Barrow in the American. The other owners and general managers reacted to what they were paying. And as players we didn't have any way to go to arbitration in those days."

Eventually we had our fill of that kind of treatment. Shortly after the war Johnny Murphy of the Yankees started rallying the troops and warning the owners that they were forcing us to unite in some fashion. Some of the rest of us joined in—Allie Reynolds, Fred Hutchinson, Bob Feller, Eddie Yost, and myself.

Later we were joined by Robin Roberts, Ted Kluszewski, Sherm Lollar, and others who came up behind us in the late '40s and early '50s. Our work, and the continued attitude of the owners, led to the establishment of what today is the Major League Baseball Players Association—the players' union.

But in 1941 that's the way the owners treated us. Even if a player hit in 56 straight games or led the league in everything you could name, trying to convince management to pay a fair day's wage for a fair day's work never was easy, even though the Bible says that should be the arrangement.

— 11 —

SAVING THE BEST FOR LAST

People remember the .406 season by Ted Williams in 1941, but most of them seem to have forgotten that he suffered two injuries that would have prevented a lesser man from reaching that immortal level.

In spring training Ted chipped a bone in his ankle while sliding into second base. It was a frightening way to start the 1941 season, both for Ted and for the rest of us. He was becoming the brunt of our batting attack. Jimmie Foxx, Bobby Doerr, Joe Cronin, and others were still productive, but it was clear after he played only two seasons that Ted was becoming the most important man in our batting order. When he went down with that injury, we were afraid our season was going down with him.

The Red Sox had finished fourth in 1940, behind the Tigers, Indians, and Yankees, and we thought we could move up in 1941. We were only eight games behind the first-place Tigers. Detroit nosed out Cleveland by one game and the Yankees by two, so with only eight games separating the top four teams—in what we used to call "the first division"—we felt there was no reason why we couldn't climb over the whole pack and win the pennant in '41.

Ted had added 17 points to his rookie average of .327, and any team that has a .344 hitter batting in the third spot in the batting order knows it's going to do all right, and maybe a whole lot better than just all right. Lou Finney hit .320 in 1940, I hit .301 as a rookie, Doc Cramer had a .303 season, and Jimmie Foxx had a .297 average with 36 home runs, the second highest in the American League and only five behind Hank Greenberg.

Doerr, Cronin, and Jim Tabor weren't exactly automatic outs either. Bobby hit .291, and Cronin and Tabor both hit .285. Four of the eight starters in our batting order, excluding the pitcher's position, batted in more than 100 runs—Foxx, Williams, Cronin, and Doerr. If we could get the pitching, we could win it all, because there was no doubt about our ability to score runs.

That's why we kept our fingers crossed when Ted went down with his ankle injury. For the first two weeks of the season he couldn't do much more than pinch-hit while the rest of us kept rooting for his speedy recovery. At the time, we would have settled for a .306 season instead of wishing for something as unthinkable as an average 100 points higher than that.

As it was, sitting out those first few weeks of the season except for limited duty probably didn't hurt either Ted or the team. Those first two weeks can be miserable in Boston, with rain and cold temperatures and sometimes wet snow thrown in for good measure. Ted hated those days, and so did the rest of us.

It was hard to get loose. Besides, even with all the enthusiasm that marks the beginning of the baseball season, who the heck wants to play baseball when it's forty degrees and drizzling? And if you want food for speculation, think about this: although he would have had more hits for the season, Ted could have missed .400 because he might have gotten off to a slow start over the two weeks he missed. Besides, he was using the time to sharpen his skills. We had gotten Joe Dobson the previous December in a six-man trade with Cleveland. The Red Sox sent Gene Desautels, Jim Bagby, and Gee Walker to the Indians in exchange for Dobson, catcher Frankie Pytlak, and infielder Odell Hale.

While he was recuperating from the chipped bone in his ankle, Ted took batting practice every day with Dobson as his pitcher. Dobson had a good curve ball, and Ted wanted the challenge of hitting good pitching. No batting practice fast balls this time. He wanted quality pitching, so that when he came back to full-time duty, he would be ready to take on the American League's pitchers.

When he did come back to play on an everyday basis two weeks later, he was as unstoppable as any hitter I've seen in my life. He was hitting everything they were throwing up there. On June 6 in Chicago, he hit a double and a home run off Johnny Rigney in four trips to the plate and raised his average to .436, an average that is almost impossible for any player to imagine. When he soared to such heights, we began to think that this was going to be an exceptional season for him, even by the high standards he had set in his first two years in the big leagues. And it didn't seem to be just another hot streak. Others have hung around the .400 mark in June and even later than that, but when someone is hitting 36 points over .400 in June, people start talking about it.

Ted, with his ability to rise to the drama of the occasion, had more people than ever talking about him after that home run in the All-Star game. His average was .405. Then another dark cloud appeared on his horizon.

After the All-Star game, Ted went 0 for 4 against the Tigers in Detroit. In the second game of that series, he walked on each of his first three trips to the plate, and then a freak thing happened. The field was wet from a light rain, and as he was trotting down to first base on his last walk, his spikes caught in the soft dirt. The same ankle was injured again. He was hitting .397 when it happened. This time he was out for ten days except for four trips to the plate as a pinch hitter. His average dropped to .393.

Ted wasn't the only one on the Red Sox team with injury problems. I came up with one, too, and it was a beaut. We were beating the Yankees in Yankee Stadium in August—shutting them out—and I was having a field day. I reached base five times, but on two of those times I did it the hard way. I hit a home run and two singles, but I was also hit by a pitch twice.

Marv Breuer hit me in the third inning, but in the ninth Charley Stanceu really zonked me. The ball hit me in the back of the head and knocked me unconscious at home plate. They told me later that Joe came dashing in from deep center field immediately. I got up eventually and made it down to first base, but Stan Spence replaced me in the bottom of the ninth.

Luckily, I wasn't seriously injured. I had plenty of company in getting "beaned" that season. Skeeter Newsome, our substitute shortstop behind Joe Cronin, was hit in the head twice that year, and so were Pete Reiser, Mickey Owen, and Dolph Camilli of the Dodgers, Bill Dickey of the Yankees, Hank Leiber of the Cubs, Roy Weatherly and Jeff Heath of the Indians, and Frank McCormick of the Reds.

Batting helmets were unheard of at the time. But Newsome got smart and started wearing a helmet, twenty-five years before they came into mandatory use in the major leagues. The Dodgers went one better. They developed the "Brooklyn Dodger safety helmet" in the 1930s and ordered it worn by all their players, including those on their farm teams in the minor leagues.

Nevertheless there was still widespread opposition to using batting helmets or warning a pitcher on a close pitch, let alone throwing him out of the game. One newspaper reporter wrote: "It has been suggested that when a hitter is struck, the pitcher be expelled. This would bring on the worst epidemic of hit batsmen in the history of baseball."

As for the talk about batting helmets, which some people were calling "cap plates," Paul Waner, the Hall of Famer with the Pittsburgh Pirates who formed the brother combination of "Big and Little Poison" with his brother Lloyd, said: "When we have to wear helmets, I'll go home."

Three days after Teddy's return to the lineup, he was back up to .400, and he kept on going. He reached .414 twice and stayed above .400 all the way to the last weekend of the season. He even got some help along the way from Harry Heilmann, the last player in the American League to hit .400. He hit .403 for the Tigers in 1923.

Heilmann was a radio broadcaster for the Tigers then, and when we played a series in Detroit in August, Harry told Ted he was rooting for him to break .400. He reminded him not to be tempted by the fences in friendly Briggs Stadium. Ted applied that reminder around the rest of the league's ball parks as well as in Detroit, but he was managing to hit the long ball anyhow. It is another one of the forgotten facts about Ted's .406 season that he also led both leagues in home runs that year with 37.

Something else about Ted was overlooked that year and every year he played—his ability as an outfielder. As the center fielder who played next to him for ten seasons, I can vouch for his talent on defense. He knew as much about the left field wall at Fenway as he did about hitting. He covered a lot of territory, had a strong arm, and always threw to the right base because of his sharp baseball instincts. We never bumped into each other in all our years together because we communicated so well, many times without saying a word. But Ted never got the credit he deserved as an outfielder, because people always focused on his phenomenal performances as a hitter.

By September 10, Ted was hitting .412. He was leading the league all right—by 49 points. Cecil Travis was hitting .363, and my brother Joe was third at .355.

Charlie Wagner remembers his roommate's consistency in 1941. "It wasn't just another day at the ball park for Ted," Charlie says. "You could see him getting one, two, three hits a day, and that's what you have to do if you're going to hit .400. For Ted that year, every day was a day of greatness."

Ted took care of himself too. He and Charlie were a good combination for roomies. Neither of them smoked or drank, and they both made sure they got their rest. They liked to go to the movies together, and Bobby Doerr used to go with them. Williams never agreed with that old fear spread by Rogers Hornsby that movies were bad for your eyes and would interfere with your ability as a hitter. Ted was just the opposite. He went to every movie he could, especially the cowboy ones.

Broadway remembers that Williams would grab the local paper our first day in a new city and flip through the pages until he found the movie section. Then, with that kid's enthusiasm that he still has, he'd say, "Oh boy! Here's a Western!"

Another pitcher, Johnny Vander Meer, didn't wait for Ted's 1941 season to predict greatness for him. He did it the year before.

"We were playing the Red Sox as we barnstormed our way through Alabama and the Carolinas after spring training," Johnny said last summer. "Our two teams did that in a lot of those years. It was a perfect combination. They had the good hitters and we had the good pitchers, so it was beneficial to both ball clubs.

"I faced Ted in the ninth inning of one of our games against the Red Sox in Tampa. I struck him out to end the game. I turned over a fast ball and made it sink. He took it for strike three. It was a good pitch, too close to take with two strikes, but he wouldn't have done anything with it even if he had hit it, because it was sinking.

"As I was walking off the field, Ted caught up with me and asked me, 'Did you turn that ball over?'

"I said, 'Yes, I did.'

"And he said, 'I thought so. I saw those stitches turning the other way.'

"I figured any hitter who watches the ball that close and can tell when the pitcher has reversed the usual method of releasing his fast ball is destined for bigger and better things. So when I got into our clubhouse, I said to Joe Beggs, one of our relief pitchers, 'That guy's liable to become a pretty good hitter.' "

Our hopes at the beginning of the season that the Red Sox might be able to climb over a couple of teams were being fulfilled to a certain degree. We were in second place behind the Yankees—but twenty and a half games behind them! They clinched the American League pennant on September 4, which is still the major league record. We had an expression in those days about a team that was as strong as the Yankees were that year. We used to say, "They'll win the pennant by Labor Day." Well, in 1941 the Yankees almost did. They missed it by three days.

Those who were baseball analysts—and some who were not— were quick to say that my brother Joe was the big reason the Yankees won the pennant. Their feeling was that Joe simply had

142

carried the biggest share of the load for the Yankees in 1941, and they had strong evidence to support their contention.

The team had only two .300 hitters—their rookie shortstop, Phil Rizzuto, hit .307—and they didn't have a single 20-game winner on their pitching staff. Lefty Gomez and Red Ruffing were tops with 15 wins each, and Johnny Murphy had 15 saves, the most in the league.

Murphy said in later years: "DiMaggio won us the pennant that year, no question about it." Murphy pointed out that the Yankees in those years emphasized team unity rather than relying on a one-man team. "But in 1941," he admitted, "it was one of the great individual performances in the history of baseball."

Almost fifty years later, when Paul Molitor of the Milwaukee Brewers made a run at Joe's record, Shirley Povich wrote in the *Washington Post* that he used to feel there were three things in life that would never happen: Man would never walk on the moon, an actor would never get elected president, and nobody would ever break Joe's streak.

Povich may have been wrong about the first two items, but at least he got the most important one right.

While the Yankees were celebrating winning the American League pennant, Ted was continuing his assault on the .400 target. He entered the last day of the season with a batting average of .39955. Rounded off, he was hitting .400 right on the nose.

Tommy Henrich says: "I can't prove it, but I don't remember catching a fly ball off him that season. He was making such great contact. He hit several line drives out my way that sank for base hits, and if the ball didn't sink, it was gone."

Bobby Doerr remembers the same thing. "He must have hit a hundred line drives to right field that year that were sinking liners between the second baseman and the right fielder," Bobby says. "On his bat, there would be a white spot on the fat part, where he was hitting every ball. Not just on one bat, but a lot of bats. That's how sharp he was.

"Ted was the first to use a substance on his hands to get a sticky grip on the bat. It was a combination of olive oil and resin.

143

Later players went to the pine-tar rag. Ted's bats would get so colored up from the olive oil and resin and the dirt from his hands, the white spot on his bats became even more pronounced. It was an amazing thing to see—that little four- or five-inch white spot on the fat part of every bat."

Bobby remembers the story Bob Lemon used to tell about the times he was trying to pitch while Ted was kneeling in the on-deck circle with that olive oil and resin. Ted would actually make the bat screech as he twisted it in his hands. Lemon says: "Here I am out there on the mound concentrating on the hitter knowing that Ted is next, and he's over there making his bat screech."

Henrich remembers the attention Ted was getting from his fellow players around the league. "From his rookie year," Henrich says, "his presence in the batting cage prompted other players who were warming up to stop and watch him hit. That's how great he was."

The last day of the season was unusual for another reason—it was a doubleheader, something rare on the final day. We were in Philadelphia to end the 1941 season with the A's, and our Saturday game was rained out, so we had to play two on Sunday.

Some 10,000 fans turned out, and every one of them must have been there to see if Ted would become the first man to hit .400 since Bill Terry hit .401 for the Giants in 1930 and the first one in the American League since Heilmann's .403 in 1923. The fans could have been disappointed for a reason they might not have anticipated, because if Ted had accepted an offer from Joe Cronin, they wouldn't have seen him at all.

On Saturday night Joe went to Williams and offered to hold him out of both games so he would be assured of the .400 season that had become the biggest baseball story since Joe's streak ended. But Ted wouldn't hear of it. If he was going to hit .400, he was going to do it swinging the bat, not sitting on the bench. Ted pointed out later that Jimmie Foxx lost the American League batting championship to Buddy Myer of the Senators that way in 1935. Double X sat out the last game while Myer got two hits. Myer finished with .349, three points higher than Foxx. Of course, no one was threatening Ted's batting championship. But Ted wasn't going to try to achieve anything by sitting in the dugout.

It was a decision that I've always admired him for, one that all of us were proud of and one which I could relate to in my own way. I had faced the same kind of decision once before, although on a much smaller scale. It happened in my first year with the San Francisco Seals.

I was hitting just under .300 going into the last day of the 1937 season. Any hitter is proud to reach .300 because of the respect which that average carries. I'm proud that I hit .300 four times in my major league career and just missed it two other times.

In 1937 I wanted that .300 average in the worst way as we prepared to play a doubleheader on our last day of the season against the Angels at Wrigley Field in Los Angeles. A .300 batting average would make people notice me and establish me as a legitimate major league prospect. And it would start to make believers of people like Tom Laird, the San Francisco columnist who wrote that the Seals signed me only because I would be a drawing card as Joe DiMaggio's brother. A .300 average in my first year of professional baseball would show the Tom Lairds of the world that *Dominic* DiMaggio could play this game too.

My roommate that year was Larry Woodall, and we were the young and the old. Larry was hitting just under .300 himself, but he was in the final stages of his professional career after spending ten years as a catcher with the Detroit Tigers. He'd left the major leagues in 1929 and was forty-three years old by this time. On the morning of our last day of the season we shook hands, wishing each other good luck in finishing the season with a .300 average.

Then Larry said to me, "Kid, if only one of us gets to do it, I hope it's you. I've had my career, but you're just starting out."

I picked up a couple of hits in the first game of our doubleheader and was hitting a point or two over .300. Just as Joe Cronin did with Ted four years later, Lefty O'Doul came to me between games and asked if I wanted to sit out the last game. He knew how much .300 meant to any kid in his first year in the minors. He also knew that the opposing pitcher, "Jittery Joe" Berry of the Los Angeles Angels, was someone who had given me trouble throughout the year. I hadn't had much success against him, and Lefty knew it.

When he asked me if I wanted to sit out the second game, I gave the same definite, almost defiant, response that Ted did. "Hell, no," I said to O'Doul. "I want to *hit* .300. Besides, I owe this guy."

I appreciated Lefty's thoughtfulness, but no thanks. I was going to play. The story has a happy ending. I was able to get a couple of hits off Jittery Joe, who came up to the big leagues in the 1940s and pitched for the Cubs, A's, and Indians, and I finished with a batting average of .306. That's why I was doubly proud of Ted's determination on that last day in 1941.

Charlie Wagner remembers that on the night before, his roommate seemed to expect to hit .400. "He was very confident," Charlie says today. "It wasn't a nervous confidence. We didn't talk about it because there was no discussion on hitting between us, ever. All Ted wanted to know was who was pitching. In those days teams didn't list the pitchers for the next day because everyone was afraid of the gamblers' influence. It was not unusual for guys to call the managers about the pitching rotation and say they were reporters, but they weren't newspapermen at all. Cronin would always give them some silly name, maybe some guy who'd pitched twenty years ago. So Ted always had to wait until he got to the ball park to see who was pitching.

"That's the only thing he concerned himself with on that last night. Ted never allowed himself to get too high or too low, all through his lifetime. There was nothing special the night before the last day of the '41 season. Ted was an early-to-bed, early-to-rise guy, and I was too.

"At the ball park the next day Cronin asked him again if he wanted to finish the season in the lineup or sit out the doubleheader, and Ted said, 'You're damned right I want to finish.' "

The books of baseball history show that Ted responded the way champions do. It was a cold day, the kind that hitters usually don't like. It's hard to get loose, and the bat stings your hands when you hit the ball. As I watched Williams perform that day, I

146

could tell that the weather wasn't going to bother him at all. I don't think he was even aware of it.

When he came to bat in the first inning, Ted heard from both the umpire and the catcher. Bill McGowan was the home plate umpire, one of the greatest of all time. As Ted stepped in, Mc-Gowan held up his hands to signal time out, then stepped out to the front of the plate. He bent over to dust off the plate, with his rear end facing the pitcher the way umpires are taught to do so the pitcher will be able to see the umpire's "stop sign" and know not to throw a pitch.

As McGowan started to sweep off the plate with his umpire's whisk broom, he said to Ted without looking up: "To hit .400 a batter has got to be loose. He has got to be *loose.*"

It's ironic that to hit a baseball, which Ted himself admits is the hardest thing to do in any sport, you have to have intense concentration—while staying relaxed. If a batter tenses up, his muscles will not be able to respond fast enough to give him the quickness he needs.

But if he relaxes too much, he'll lose the concentration that is also needed to determine what the pitch is, where it's going to be, and what you need to do to hit it. Hitting requires a delicate balance of these skills simply because you're using a round object to hit another round object coming at you at speeds up to 100 miles an hour thrown by a man standing on a hill only 60 feet 6 inches away.

No wonder the man with the highest career batting average in history, Ty Cobb, was able to get a hit only 3.67 times out of every ten times up. Or to put it another way, out of every ten times he went to the plate, Ty Cobb failed almost seven times. And he was the most successful hitter in history. That's how hard it is to hit a baseball well.

It was a class act for Bill McGowan to remind Ted to stay loose. It might have helped Ted a little too. Bobby Doerr and some of the rest of us remember that Ted was plenty pumped up that day. He remembers how keyed up Ted was on the bench during our at-bats. Bobby says: "He was yelling and screaming all day. He was playing on even more adrenaline than usual."

Right after McGowan's reminder, however, the A's catcher, Frankie Hayes, looked up at Ted through his mask and told him about some orders the A's had received just before the game from their owner-manager, Connie Mack. Mr. Mack was the grand old man of baseball in those years, the only man besides Burt Shotton of the Dodgers who was allowed to manage in street clothes. He always presented the same picture—ramrod-straight at six feet one inch, a man who never seemed to gain an ounce over his playing weight of 170 when he was a catcher with Washington, Buffalo, and Pittsburgh in the 1880s and '90s. His real name was Cornelius McGilicuddy. He always sat in a corner of the A's dugout in a business suit, a white shirt, a starched high collar that was a relic from the 1920s, and a necktie, holding the day's score card in one hand, using it to wave his outfielders around and position his infielders.

He was considered the gentleman's gentleman, the very model of dignity and integrity. It was that integrity that prompted him to give his players special orders before that last day of the season and Ted's attack against .400. When Ted stepped into the batter's box in the first inning, Frankie Hayes said, "Mr. Mack told us if we let up on you, he'll run us out of baseball. I wish you all the luck in the world, but we're not giving you a damn thing."

Almost as soon as Ted stepped into the batter's box, we knew McGowan's advice to him about being patient was as unnecessary as it was thoughtful. Ted looked as loose that day as any hitter I ever saw.

In the first inning he lined a single to right against Dick Fowler. The next time up he hit a home run off a new pitcher, a kid named Porter Vaughan, a left-hander who broke in the year before. Third time up, another single. Fourth time up, another hit. After four trips, he's 4 for 4. On his fifth trip to the plate, he reached base on an error.

Between games Ted still could have taken Cronin up on his offer. But his determination remained, just as all of us on the team knew it would. He was hitting a point or two above .400 by now, and Cronin made the same kind of offer he made the night before.

"You can do it one way or the other," he told Ted, and Ted said bluntly, "I'm doing it the other."

I remember he ate a sandwich, but whatever he felt, it wasn't showing. That's just the way Ted was. He never allowed what he was thinking to show.

In the second game, the one the writers called "the nightcap," Ted hit a single and a double in his first two times up. The double broke a loudspeaker above the right field wall. On his third trip to the plate, his eighth time up that afternoon, the A's got him out for the first time. We heard in the spring of '42 that the A's had to replace the speaker over the winter.

Ted was 6 for 8 for the day and .406 for the history books. The clubhouse at Shibe Park seemed only slightly larger than a phone booth that afternoon. You almost had to turn sideways to get past your teammates. Ted didn't bother concealing his emotions after that second game. You could see both the elation and the relief, and he talked about his achievement willingly and enthusiastically. Not only could you see the joy, you could even feel it.

What Ted did that year—and that day—is my definition of greatness. In the half century since, only one man, George Brett, ever made a serious run at that standard of excellence—and he missed by 16 points.

Joe's streak and Ted's .400 season placed pressure on many different people, including their teammates. Tommy Henrich's bunt to make sure Joe got another time at bat in his thirty-eighth game was an example of how his teammates tried to help him keep the streak alive. In Ted's case, the people hitting right behind him—Jimmie Foxx and Bobby Doerr—needed to maintain a high batting average themselves. If they didn't, other teams would be able to pitch around Ted, giving him bad pitches, unafraid of walking him if the hitters behind him weren't hitting well enough to drive him in.

There was pressure on the scorekeepers around the American League, as Dan Daniel found out when he charged Johnny Berardino with that error instead of giving Joe a hit. And there was pressure on the umpires.

We were blessed with good umpires in those years. I'm inclined to think television has not helped the quality of umpiring in the major leagues. There seems to be a tendency for certain umpires to "perform," to slip into the mistaken and always harmful attitude that the fans came out to the park or turned their TV sets on to watch the umpires as well as the players.

The best umpire is the one you don't notice. He makes good calls, is always in position, and keeps the game moving. Because he's doing a good job, the players have no arguments with him. Thus the good umpire goes almost unnoticed.

Even if a disagreement develops, the good umpire maintains his composure and tries not to show up the player, because he doesn't like it if the players try that on him. I think too many of today's umpires in the major leagues have a short fuse, sometimes almost asking the player to knock the chips off their shoulders. Too often today the umpire loses his temper before the player does—while the camera catches his performance.

In 1941 we had better than that. Some of the most legendary names in umpiring history were in the major leagues that year—McGowan, Cal Hubbard, Al Barlick, Beans Reardon, Eddie Rommel, Larry Goetz, and three guys named Bill—Grieve, Stewart, and Summers.

Two of the umpires of 1941 are worth special mention because one of them was finishing a great career, and the other was just beginning. They were Bill Klem and Jocko Conlan.

Klem was called the dean of umpires in 1941. He was known throughout baseball for claiming, "I never called one wrong in my life." By '41 he had been calling them right as a professional umpire for thirty-nine years.

He had a series of classic run-ins with John McGraw, the manager of the Giants. In one of them, McGraw disagreed with Klem so vigorously he yelled, "I'll have your job for this!"

Klem always addressed players, managers, and coaches as mister, so he said to McGraw calmly, "Mr. McGraw, if you can take my job away, I don't want it."

During another Klem-McGraw clash, Klem, who did not have a lot of formal education, was explaining a rule and said, "I learned you that rule last year."

McGraw, who had a college education, said, "And it's about time you learned something about grammar. You can't *learn* anything to anyone. You can *teach* him, but you can't learn him."

Klem had an answer for that too. He said, "Mr. McGraw, it begins to look as though I can neither learn you nor teach you. You're hopeless."

Klem was called the "Old Arbitrator" by many people, including himself, because he made it clear from the start of his career that his word was final. His quick, firm decisions added to his stature. He had a majestic, autocratic manner, but he was said to have done more for umpires than any other man who ever lived.

He began umpiring in the Connecticut League in 1902, a time when umpires put their game clothes on in their hotel rooms and rode streetcars to the ball park. Klem demanded that umpires have dressing rooms of their own—with showers—and other basic necessities equal to what the players had, and he got them.

He also demanded that umpires be treated with respect on the field and not be subjected to the abuse that had characterized their profession. He was so effective in commanding respect himself that his colleagues followed his example, and the umpiring profession was elevated to a new level.

When their careers were over, John McGraw said simply, "If there ever was a good umpire, it was Bill Klem."

When Klem died in 1951, the United Press story called him "baseball's best known and most widely respected umpire." Ford Frick, who covered many of Klem's games as a sportswriter, said flatly, "He was the greatest umpire who ever lived."

Jocko Conlan was a rookie umpire in 1941. One of the reasons he became one of the best umpires of his era was his background. He had been a major league player before becoming an umpire. In fact, he was an umpire *while* he was a player.

Jocko was a reserve outfielder with the Chicago White Sox in 1934 after spending fourteen seasons in the minors. He broke his thumb during some clubhouse clowning with his friend, Ted Lyons, and was on the bench unable to play while his teammates struggled to survive the summer heat in a game against the Browns in St. Louis.

They made it through the game, but one of the umpires didn't. Red Ormsby was the base umpire while Harry Geisel worked behind the plate. Even in the big leagues in those years there were only two umpires, one behind the plate to call balls and strikes and the other to umpire on the bases. Even though Geisel as the home plate umpire had a much hotter job than Ormsby that day, Ormsby was the one who passed out from the heat.

Conlan offered to fill in so the game could be completed, and both managers, Jimmy Dykes of the White Sox and Rogers Hornsby of the Browns, accepted Jocko's offer. Dykes, however, quickly posed a problem for his player-turned-umpire.

Luke Appling, Chicago's star shortstop, slid into third base on a close play, and Conlan called his teammate out. Dykes, who was a colorful character himself and one not reluctant to take on an umpire, came charging out of the White Sox dugout and yelled at his substitute outfielder, "What kind of player are you? Calling one against your own team!"

Jocko had the perfect answer: "I'm an umpire now."

At that point Appling looked up and said to Dykes, "Jocko was right—I was out."

And an umpire was born.

He umpired again the next day as Ormsby rested. The American League paid him fifty dollars. Over the winter he decided to abandon his career as a player and enter the umpiring profession in the New York-Penn League. By 1941 he was breaking into the National League after being rejected by the American League the year before for being too small at five feet seven and a half inches. It was an evaluation I could relate to at five nine and having heard when I was playing for the Seals that I was too small for the major leagues.

In the American League we didn't get to see him every day, but we saw his ability and his control of a game in six All-Star games and six World Series. Jocko himself probably gave the best description of his performance as an umpire. In his autobiography he said, "I was a strong umpire, and I was a good umpire. I always respected the ground a ball player walked on, and I respected the player himself. But, in turn, I demanded respect from each and every player I came across. And I got it."

Jocko wore one thing that no other umpire in either league wore—a polka dot bow tie—and one thing no other umpire in the National League wore—the inflated "balloon" chest protector that was worn on the outside, a standard item in the American League. The National League umpires preferred the inside padded protector.

Conlan was the son of an Irish cop in Chicago who grew up near Comiskey Park, the home of the White Sox, as one of nine children. He was an amateur boxer before becoming a minor league baseball player, and perhaps that's why he never backed away from a tough situation. He had some classic showdowns with Leo Durocher and enjoyed the same kind of relationship with Leo that Bill Klem had with John McGraw. In one of them he came close to using his boxing experience. He was steaming at something Durocher had said, but instead of going after him, Jocko told Durocher, "Take a punch at me."

Leo was surprised. "Why?"

Jocko said, "So I can knock you out. Right here."

He made all his calls with his left hand, even the strikes. When a player started calling him names, he would tell the offending party, "I ain't what you say I am."

Then he would point toward the clubhouse with his left hand and say in his final words of the discussion, "You are outta here."

Tom Ferrick remembers that his manager in 1941, Connie Mack, enjoyed a luxury with umpires that no other manager did. Mack wasn't just the manager of the Philadelphia A's. He was their owner too. And it didn't hurt that he had been one of the founders of the American League, along with Washington's owner, Clark Griffith, forty years before.

He commanded a certain respect that no other manager could. He was "Mr. Mack" to everyone in baseball, a power in the American League until his death in Philadelphia in 1956, not three months after Griffith died.

Ferrick remembers that in 1941, Mr. Mack, who turned seventy-nine that year, was still very much in charge of things. "He made all the changes," Tom says. "He decided on pinch hitters and relief pitchers—he was still sharp."

His stature as one of the league's powers used to show up when he disagreed with an umpire's decision. His son, Earle, worked with him and even played for the A's in 1910, '11 and '14 —a major league career that added up to five games.

Ferrick says that when Mr. Mack would disagree with the umpire's call, he'd turn to Earle in the dugout and say, "Tell so-and-so I want to see him." And Earle would go out onto the field and tell the umpire, "Dad wants to see you."

Would you believe it? The umpire would walk all the way over to the A's dugout and listen to Mr. Mack's argument.

— 12 —

HUGH, MICKEY, AND TOMMY

The Red Sox were not playing that badly, but the Yankees just seemed to be off in another league of their own, head and shoulders above the rest of the teams in our own league, and maybe that much better than anybody the National League had to offer.

Joe wasn't the only DiMaggio who had a good year in 1941. Our brother Vince hit 21 home runs and drove in 100 runs in his first year of playing center field for the Pittsburgh Pirates. I was able to hit .283 in my second season with 165 hits plus 90 walks and finish third in the American League in runs scored, behind Ted and Joe.

If anything, the Yankees won the pennant that year not only on the strength of Joe's bat but also with their defense. Their catcher, Bill Dickey, had the highest fielding average for catchers in the league, and Ruffing led the pitchers in fielding. And their excellent young second base combination—Rizzuto at short and Joe Gordon at second—led their positions in double plays.

On top of that they had one of the most successful managers in baseball history, Joe McCarthy. Jimmy Dykes, the White Sox manager, called him "the push-button manager," claiming that the Yankees had so much talent that all McCarthy had to do was push a button and the right man for the occasion would automatically pop up.

That, of course, isn't as easy as it sounds, even if it were that simple. You still have to know which button to push. McCarthy managed his way into the Hall of Fame with teams that won 2,126 games in 24 seasons. He has the highest won-lost percentage in baseball history. He managed his teams into nine World Series and guided them to the championship in seven of those Series. In World Series competition he also has the highest won-lost percentage.

A manager can't maintain that level of success over twenty-four years by just pushing buttons. One of the reasons for Mc-Carthy's success was his emphasis on teamwork. The Yankees had more than their share of individual stars in '41, but they were even tougher to beat because they played as a team. McCarthy demanded it. After he came up to Boston to be our manager from 1948 until he retired after 94 games of the 1950 season, he was the same way.

Tommy Henrich remembers that Charlie Keller was an example of McCarthy's emphasis on a team attitude. Keller was a straightaway left-handed hitter at the beginning of his career, but Joe could see his power and convinced him to start pulling the ball so he could reach the close seats in Yankee Stadium's famous right field porch.

Keller did what his manager asked and hit more than 30 home runs three times and also drove in more than 100 runs three times. In '41, he hit 33 homers—second only to Ted Williams, drove in 122 runs—third behind my brother Joe and Jeff Heath, and scored 102 runs. He had some high batting averages too—hitting over .300 three times and finishing with a career average of .286 for 13 seasons. Henrich remembers: "Charlie could have had thirty more points on his average, but he had learned to pull the ball at Mc-Carthy's urging."

Tommy also tells a story that illustrates Joe McCarthy's insistence on teamwork. It involved the time that McCarthy was talking to some writers on the field before a game. He said, "I'll show you a team player." Then he called to Joe Gordon to come over to where McCarthy and the writers were standing.

McCarthy asked his All-Star second baseman, "Joe, what's your batting average?"

Joe said, "I don't know."

"What are you fielding?"

"I don't know."

McCarthy turned to the writers and said, "That's what I like. All he does is come to beat you."

McCarthy was also smart enough to warn his players about the dangers of distractions. Henrich remembers that during the 1941 season, while the Yankees were opening up their big lead over us on their way to the pennant, McCarthy told his players, "There are three subjects I don't want to hear discussed on this ball club. One is politics. One is religion. And the other is war."

Meanwhile the Dodgers and the Cards were fighting each other for the National League pennant, a race that wasn't decided until the last week of the season, with the Dodgers finally winning by two and a half games. The Cardinals were alive until they went into Cincinnati needing to take three out of four games from the Reds. But Cincinnati had a starting pitching staff composed of Bucky Walters, Johnny Vander Meer, Paul Derringer, and Lee Grissom. The best the Cards could do was split the series, and the Dodgers were the champions of the National League.

If Johnny Mize of the Cardinals had been a happier player that year, who knows who would have won the pennant? They certainly got help from Enos Slaughter, who hustled his way into the Hall of Fame in a nineteen-year career in which he achieved a lifetime batting average of an even .300. Slaughter hit .311 in 1941 and stayed healthy all the way into August. That was unusual for the Cardinals that year. Country remembers that there were only four games out of the entire 154-game season when the St. Louis starters were in the lineup at the same time.

Slaughter's turn to be struck down by the injury bug came on August 11, when he broke his collarbone in Sportsman's Park trying to catch a fly ball to right center by Stu Martin. Martin was an infielder who played for the Cards from 1936 through 1940 and was then sold to the Pirates. As his fly ball started to drop, Slaughter dashed in and was ready to dive for it. Then he saw Terry Moore, the center fielder, leaving his feet, also trying for a diving catch. Country jumped over Moore—while Moore actually caught the ball between Slaughter's legs.

Enos hit the ground and was out for four weeks with his broken collarbone. The Cardinals called up a kid from the minors to take Slaughter's place—Stan Musial. In the first 12 games of his major league career, Musial came to bat 47 times and hit .426. The next year he hit .315 to help St. Louis win the pennant and drove in the winning run in the Cards' first victory in their World Series upset defeat of the Yankees.

When Musial came up to the Cardinals, it wasn't the first time Slaughter had seen him. Musial began his minor league career fresh from his hometown of Donora, Pennsylvania, as a left-handed pitcher. He injured his arm later and turned to playing the outfield and first base, but in Columbus, Georgia, in 1938, Country singled off Musial in an exhibition game when the Cards were coming north after spring training. Mize and Moore did better than that— they both hit home runs off the future "Stan the Man."

Slaughter returned to the lineup in mid-September in a way that was typical of the Cardinals and of Enos himself. The Cardinal team surgeon, a man famous throughout athletics in those years for his surgical skills, was Dr. Robert Hyland. He pulled the wire out of Slaughter's collarbone in the morning. With blood running down his arm, Country left for the ball park and played that afternoon.

His explanation was simple: "I was trying to win a pennant."

Throughout those years Slaughter was famous for running everywhere, even to first base on a walk, but he wasn't always that way. When he was playing his second year of pro ball five years before, at Columbus, Georgia, he had an experience he never forgot. He hit .325 that year, but he made the mistake of trotting in from right field at the end of an inning and slowing to a walk after reaching the third base line. His manager, Eddie Dyer, met him at the top of the dugout steps.

Dyer told him simply: "If you're tired, kid, I'll get some help for you."

Slaughter said, "I vowed never to walk on a ball field again." The story goes that he got his nickname in a contest at Columbus when one of the writers ran a contest to pick a name for the city's popular rookie. The fans submitted their suggestions, but Slaughter was to be the final judge. According to the story, he picked "Country" for himself.

Eleven years after picking up his new name, Country Slaughter showed in historic terms that he was keeping his promise to himself to hustle all the way on a ball field. He hurried home from first base on a hit by Harry Walker to win the 1946 World Series for the Cardinals. Unfortunately he did it against us Red Sox in his first year back from the war, and mine too.

The Cards' manager that year was the same man who needled him about his pace in Columbus, Eddie Dyer.

With the 1941 Dodgers, Leo Durocher had a winning blend of veterans and kids. Their star was Dolph Camilli, their thirty-four-year-old home-run-hitting first baseman, who led the National League that year with 34 homers and 120 runs batted in. Some called him the "Dodgers' Joe DiMaggio," and, like Joe, he won his league's Most Valuable Player award that season.

On the other end of the age spectrum was their gifted, hell-for-leather twenty-one-year-old center fielder, Pete Reiser, who led the league in hitting with a .343 average. Then there was their ever popular right fielder, Dixie Walker, the "Peepul's Cherce," who hit .311, his best year in the 10 seasons he'd been in the big leagues.

The Dodgers also had a young leader from our Red Sox farm system at shortstop, Pee Wee Reese, who played his first full season that year and led the National League's shortstops with 346 putouts. Their third baseman was another Flatbush favorite, Cookie Lavagetto, whose presence used to inspire the Dodger fans to yell, "Lookie, lookie, lookie! Here comes Cookie!

The Dodgers had Johnny Mize's old teammate from the Cardinals in left field, Joe "Ducky" Medwick, who had a .318 average for the Dodgers that year as one of baseball's best bad-ball hitters. Medwick frequently swung at pitches outside the strike zone but managed to hit well enough to compile a .324 lifetime batting average in 17 seasons. An Italian kid who watched him in St. Louis adopted Medwick's bad-ball hitting habits and slugged his way into the Hall of Fame too—Yogi Berra.

Brooklyn had a talented pitching staff in '41, with two 20-game winners, Whitlow Wyatt and Kirby Higbe, who tied for the most wins in the National League with 22 each, plus "Fat Freddie" Fitzsimmons. Fitzsimmons, who was to play a pivotal role in the World Series, turned forty in July of the 1941 season, but he could still help a team win a pennant. He already was a 200-game winner in a career that began in 1925. For the Dodgers that year he won six games and lost just one and allowed only 2.07 earned runs for every nine innings he pitched. Freddie didn't pitch enough innings to qualify for the ERA championship, but if he had, he would have beaten Elmer Riddle of Cincinnati, who won the title with 2.24.

The Dodgers also had Larry French, Curt Davis, and Hugh Casey for pitchers, and a talented young catcher named Mickey Owen, who had more putouts that year than any other National League catcher. He was considered one of the best, most dependable catchers in the major leagues. He was full of confidence behind the plate and was capable (almost) of catching any pitch that anybody threw.

Owen still remembers the pitchers who threw to him and their characteristics, especially Casey and Higbe. "Hugh Casey," Mickey said last summer, "was the best relief pitcher who ever played baseball, and his record shows it. He's the leading relief pitcher of all time with a .728 winning percentage. No other relief pitcher is even in the .700s. Nobody else could touch him.

"Higbe was a big, strong guy who could throw hard and do a lot of pitching. He was exceptionally good in hot weather. He could be fogging them out there when the other fellas were struggling, because the heat didn't bother him a bit."

Then Mickey mentions another pitching plus for the Dodgers in '41: "Whitlow Wyatt was as good a pitcher as there was in baseball that year."

How Owen came to be on the Dodgers in the first place is a story in itself. He and Durocher were teammates on the 1937 Cardinals,

160

and they liked each other and each other's style of play. Owen says today that Durocher thought Mickey could handle low-ball pitchers like Higbe and Casey and still throw out base runners, so he traded Gus Mancuso to the Cardinals with minor league pitcher John Pintar, and $65,000 for Mickey on December 4, 1940.

But Mickey remembers that there was always another reason behind any trade involving Mancuso. His managers were always afraid he'd take their jobs. Gus played for five teams in 17 seasons and was one of the most capable catchers of his day. But he moved around a lot. He played for the Cardinals twice, the Giants twice, and the Cubs, Dodgers, and Phillies.

Mickey to this day says Mancuso was "as smart a catcher as ever got behind the plate." And he says that being constantly traded was Mancuso's most serious problem, even though five Mancuso teams won the National League pennant.

"Every manager would trade him off in a hurry," Mickey remembers. "He wouldn't stay very long. He wasn't a guy to undercut you, but they were all getting rid of him because they knew if they started off on a losing streak, they were liable to get fired, and Gus would be put in as manager.

"Bill Terry got rid of him from the Giants to the Cubs. Gabby Hartnett had a meeting with his pitchers early in the season and asked them, 'Who would you rather have catching—me or Mancuso?' And they said Mancuso."

So he was traded to Brooklyn, stayed for only one year under Durocher, and was traded to St. Louis for Mickey.

The Cardinals' starting catcher, Walker Cooper, who was only twenty-six years old himself, was injured early in the 1941 season, and Mancuso caught 105 games, catching the veteran Lon Warneke and Mort Cooper—Walker's brother, who was the other half of the famous St. Louis brother battery—and Max Lanier. But where Mancuso really stood out was in his handling of the Cardinals' outstanding young pitchers—Ernie White, Howie Krist, Harry Gumbert, Howie Pollet, and Johnny Beazley.

A fellow catcher like Mickey Owen would remember all those good young arms on one staff. He says, "I always said that if Cooper had gotten hurt earlier, with that experienced old head

Mancuso in there, the Cardinals would have won the pennant in 1941."

The next year, after helping the Cardinals so much in 1941 in his only full season with them, Mancuso was sold to the Giants.

Pee Wee Reese remembers the makeup of the Brooklyn Dodgers in 1941: "Our ball club was a very unusual one—everybody came from some other team. I don't think anybody at all came up through our farm system. When you think about it, Dolph Camilli came from Philadelphia, Billy Herman came from the Cubs, Cookie Lavagetto came from Pittsburgh, and Mickey Owen and Pete Reiser came from the Cardinals."

Reese and Reiser, the two kids on a club of veterans, had their injury problems. Reiser was showing more and more of a fondness for crashing into outfield walls and fences, and Reese was still getting over the effects of two disabling injuries in his rookie season in 1940. He was hit in the head by a pitched ball and was hospitalized for eighteen days shortly after he joined the Dodgers from Louisville, where he had been the star shortstop for two years. Then he broke his ankle after only 84 games and was out for the rest of the 1940 season. In '41 he was still fighting off the lingering effects of those injuries.

The head injury was scary, and Pee Wee says today that the experience bothered him from time to time for the rest of his playing career. It happened in Chicago—and those white shirts in the center field stands at Wrigley Field played a part.

"A kid named Jake Mooty released the ball, and I never saw it. It hit me in the head. I was batting about .280 at the time. When I got back into the lineup, it was at Ebbets Field. In my first game back, Joe Medwick got hit in the head by Bob Bowman of the Cardinals. It scared the hell out of me. Every once in a while after that, the thought of getting beaned used to bother me at the plate."

The circumstances surrounding the Medwick beaning said something about the personality of the Dodger team that year. "Durocher had had some words with Bowman before that," Pee Wee says, "and Medwick and Durocher were great friends. Bowman couldn't hit Durocher, so I guess he decided to hit Medwick.

It looked like he killed him. Even Larry MacPhail ran out of the stands and onto the field. It was a wild scene." Ducky was out of the lineup for four days.

What was it like to be a young player under the explosive Durocher in those years? "Durocher was very tough on young players," Reese says today. "But when I look back on it, the things he got on me about were a big help. It was probably one of the best things that happened to me."

Pee Wee remembers how Durocher used to drive the Dodgers in 1941, motivating them to their success. "He got on the other clubs pretty strongly too." In those cases, Durocher wasn't motivating opposing teams. He was berating them. "We could wake up anybody, even a last-place ball club," Pee Wee says. "They wanted to beat us, because they wanted to beat Durocher."

In '41 Reese opened the season wearing an ankle brace. "It was a long year for me," he says. His batting average dropped from .272 in his rookie year to .229. Durocher, still an active player as well as the Brooklyn manager, filled in for Pee Wee in 12 games at short. "It was a great relief," Pee Wee says, "when the season was over and we had gotten into the World Series."

Like their teams of the postwar years, the Dodgers seemed to top everybody in nicknames, which may have been one of the early reasons for their popularity. Nicknames have always been one of the unique and enduring charms about baseball, and the Dodgers always seemed to have the most colorful collection of all the teams. In the 1941 World Series, however, the Yankees gave the Dodgers a real battle in that department. It was a matchup of the team with Joltin' Joe, Flash, Scooter, King Kong, Twinkletoes, Spud, Goofy, and Tiny versus the team with Pee Wee, Cookie, Dixie, Pistol Pete, Ducky, Coonskin, Hot Potato, and Leo the Lip.

In the end, though, the 1941 World Series became one that is still talked about because of three men with more conventional nicknames—Hugh, Mickey, and Tommy.

The World Series started in the park of the American League team that year, so the Dodgers were the visiting team when the first game was played on October 1. A huge crowd filed into Yankee Stadium—68,540 fans—and it would have been even larger by one if President Roosevelt hadn't been forced to cancel his visit. He was scheduled to throw out the first ball, but he had to cancel because of the growing international crisis. Word was that he told his staff to get one of those new portable radios and put it on his desk in the Oval Office. As he wrestled with the issues of war and peace, he listened to the World Series broadcast in the background.

Even without FDR there was no shortage of celebrities in the crowd. Commissioner Landis threw out the first ball. Mayor Fiorello LaGuardia, the "Little Flower," was there and so were Roosevelt's Postmaster General, Jim Farley, and Babe Ruth. The two opponents in the heavyweight championship fight in New York four months before, Joe Louis and Billy Conn, were there too.

Louis had just defeated Lou Nova two nights before in the nineteenth defense of his heavyweight championship. He knocked out Nova in the sixth round and picked up $193,274 as his share. Louis had just been ordered to report for Army duty. He was quoted at the World Series as saying he was "looking forward to life in the Army."

The top story in the *New York Times* that morning was a report by cable from London saying, "The battle of the Atlantic is definitely swinging in Britain's favor, Prime Minister Winston Churchill indicated today in an address to the House of Commons that was optimistic in its general tone."

British bombers had reached Berlin, but the Nazis denied any damage had been inflicted and said the raid had been repulsed by antiaircraft fire. The British also bombed Hamburg and Stettin, but the German Luftwaffe bombed the northeast coast of England and caused heavy damage. In Moscow, representatives of the American and British governments were meeting with Stalin to discuss United States and English aid to Russia in its battle with the German Army while the Nazis raced to reach Moscow before the arrival of the dreaded Russian winter.

But the World Series was the big news in New York that day. John Drebinger had an article on the front page of the *Times* that made it clear that New Yorkers were excited about the events in the baseball world:

> Blasé New York, which long since had come to regard itself as fully capable of taking a World Series right in stride, found itself gripped last night in a baseball fever which threatened to reach alarming proportions.

It was the Yankees' twelfth World Series since 1921 and their fifth in six years under Joe McCarthy, but it was only the Dodgers' first since 1920 and only their third since the World Series began back in '03. Brief showers had been forecast for the morning, with temperatures in the afternoon warmer than the high of 64 the day before.

Even with their increased occupancy rates for "the subway series," the hotels were advertising the availability of rooms and suites for rent. You could live in a newly decorated "luxurious" room at the Vanderbilt Hotel on Park Avenue at 34th Street for sixty dollars a month.

Newspaper ads displayed good news for those ladies fortunate enough to be invited to the social occasions of the Series. The ads offered cocktail dresses at Lord & Taylor that had "guile, excitement, sparkle, and intrigue. And a new sort of sophistication that makes you look very worldly, very in the know . . . from our collection for spellbinders." Price: From $45.

Radio Station WOR, the Mutual station in New York, bought advertising space to tell newspaper readers that the World Series play-by-play would be "aptly, colorfully, and dramatically described for you by Red Barber and Bob Elson, two of America's great sportscasters—and the renowned Bill Corum." The broadcasts were sponsored by Gillette razors, whose "look-sharp feel-sharp be-sharp" sports events on the *Gillette Cavalcade of Sports* became a mainstay for every sports fan throughout the 1940s.

The World Series may have been the most talked about attraction in town on the morning of October 1, but it wasn't the only one. *Honky Tonk* was opening the next day at the Capitol Theater on Broadway at 51st Street. The ad in the paper said:

Clark Gable Kisses Lana Turner
and It's Screen History!

Frank Morgan, Claire Trevor, Marjorie Main, and Chill Wills
shared the billing with Gable and Turner. At the Palace there was a
double feature. *Sun Valley Serenade* was showing, featuring Glenn
Miller and his band and ice-skating star Sonja Henie, and so was
Dive Bomber, with Errol Flynn and Fred MacMurray.

There were loud complaints about ticket scalping at Yankee
Stadium, with some of the reserved seats being sold for double their
face value. That wasn't the problem for fans who were willing to
settle for unreserved grandstand seats or a spot in the bleachers.
They had to take their chances and get into a line that began
forming at 7:30 the night before the first game, hoping to get one of
those tickets and willing to put up the three dollars for an unreserved grandstand ticket and $1.50 for a bleacher seat.

Four of the first five people in line at Yankee Stadium were
Dodger fans, headed by a middle-aged woman from Yorkville. A
thirteen-year-old boy from Clifton, New Jersey, was there too,
holding his pet kitten under his jacket against the cool evening
temperatures. His kitten's name was Pete, in honor of Pete Reiser.

In Brooklyn the day before the first game, a judge presided in
a case involving a man charged with "unnecessary noise" for turning up the volume on his radio at his newsstand on Church and
Nostrand avenues on September 16, when the Dodgers were playing the Cardinals.

The defendant presented a brilliant legal defense: "Your
honor, if the Bums are playing St. Louis and Wyatt's pitching
against White, and it's a crucial game, is that unnecessary noise?"

The judge told reporters later: "I could feel for this man. I
remember that Wyatt-White game. I paid a special caddy to follow
me around the golf course that day so I could get the play-by-play
from a portable radio."

The verdict: Not guilty.

My brother Joe and Kirby Higbe of the Dodgers knew they
had nothing to worry about—they had their Camels. A large display ad showed pictures of both of them, with the ad saying: "Win

or Lose—Joe DiMaggio, Kirby Higbe, and millions of fans agree—there's nothing like a Camel."

Joe is quoted as saying, "They're a cigarette that's really fun to smoke." The ad assured the readers that Camels contained "28 percent less nicotine than the average of four other largest-selling brands tested . . . according to independent scientific tests . . ."

— 13 —

"THERE IS NO JOY IN FLATBUSH . . ."

Curt Davis of the Dodgers and Red Ruffing of the Yankees were the opposing pitchers for the first game of that memorable World Series. They were among the senior citizens on the field that day. Davis turned thirty-eight three weeks before the Series started, and Ruffing was thirty-seven that May. Davis was still only slightly more than halfway through a thirteen-year major league career in which he won 158 games. Mickey Owen remembers him as "a terrific low-ball pitcher." After pitching for the Phillies, Cubs, and Cardinals, he was in his first World Series.

Ruffing's career was a different story, a tale of achieving pitching excellence and performing with the dominant team of the time. By the start of the 1941 World Series, Red had won 254 games in a Hall of Fame career. This was going to be his sixth World Series, and his numbers were impressive for those pressure games. This was his eighth start. In his previous seven he had five wins, all of them complete games.

Mickey Owen says that as the two teams took the field to start the World Series, the Dodgers were confident of victory. "We thought we had a good chance to beat them," he says. "We knew they had a great ball club. Anytime you went into a Series against them, you knew you had to be at your best to beat them." But the Dodgers felt they were at their best, with a good chance to upset the greatest team in baseball.

There was at least one member of the Dodgers who was feeling butterflies. Pee Wee Reese had visited the World Series only four years earlier as a nineteen-year-old sandlot star after his team won a church championship.

"I was a little in awe of the Series and of Yankee Stadium," he says. "I had a fear of not getting even one base hit in the Series. But in the first game I got three hits, so things settled down a bit."

The Yankees scored the first run of the Series on a home run by Joe Gordon in the second inning. My brother Joe made a bid to get them another one in the fourth on a long drive to left, but Ducky Medwick made a leaping catch at the fence. But they got a second run anyhow, on a walk to Charlie Keller and a double by Bill Dickey.

The Dodgers picked up a run in the fifth, and the Yankees added another in their sixth, so it was a 3–1 game as the Dodgers came to bat at the beginning of the seventh inning. Brooklyn picked up another run and moved into a great position to tie the game. Reese, representing the tying run, was on second base with one out, and Durocher sent Jimmy Wasdell up to pinch-hit.

Wasdell popped out to Red Rolfe near the Brooklyn dugout on the third base side. Just after he made the catch, Reese, seeing third uncovered, bolted for third, but Rizzuto saw the same thing and broke for the bag too. Rolfe threw to Rizzuto, who tagged Reese out, and the inning was over. With the way Ruffing was pitching, the game was over too, and the Yankees got the first leg up on the World Series championship with a 3–2 win.

It was a pair of six-hitters, with Davis followed by Hugh Casey and Johnny Allen. There were some raised eyebrows when Durocher started Davis instead of Wyatt, but Davis kept Leo off the hook with a good pitching performance. Ruffing, as usual, went the full nine innings. With his victory, his sixth in World Series play, Red tied Chief Bender, Waite Hoyt, and Lefty Gomez for the most Series wins with six. He would win another one in '42 against the Cardinals. Red said he threw only one curve in the whole game, to Pete Reiser in the eighth inning. The rest were fast balls and change-ups.

For Davis it was a different story. He pitched for five more seasons, but the afternoon of October 1, 1941, was the only time he appeared in a World Series game.

In the second game the result was the opposite, with the Dodgers winning by the same score. Durocher sent one of his 22-game winners, Whitlow Wyatt, against the Yankees and Spud Chandler. Wyatt was in the same position as his teammate Davis in the first game. It was his first appearance in a World Series after twelve years in the big leagues. It was also the first for Chandler, who was in his fifth major league season, but with the Yankees in those days you had reason to expect to be in more than one World Series. Chandler appeared in three more after '41.

In this game, the Dodgers went with their best and won with their best. Dolph Camilli drove in the winning run with a single in the sixth inning that scored Dixie Walker and broke a 2–2 tie. It also broke the Yankees' streak of winning their last ten World Series games. Wyatt, after giving up a run in the New York first and another in the second, went the distance.

After a day's postponement because of rain, the Series moved to Ebbets Field for the third game. That's when fate stepped into the Series for the first time, in an incident that has since been obscured by the turmoil that erupted in the fourth game.

Unlike the first game, when both pitchers were nearing the end of their careers, the third was a duel between the young and the old, Marius Russo against Freddie Fitzsimmons. Russo was a twenty-seven-year-old left-hander, six feet one inch tall, 190 pounds, and a native of Brooklyn. He was a 14-game winner for the Yankees that season and now found himself pitching in his first World Series and in Ebbets Field, no less, the very heart and soul of the borough of his birth.

For Fitzsimmons the sands in the hourglass were mostly at the bottom now. He had been pitching in the major leagues since 1925, the same year that Lou Gehrig started his streak of playing in 2,130 consecutive games. The streak was gone now and so was Lou, but Fitzsimmons was still pitching and winning.

They called him "Fat Freddie," a nickname earned by a chunky build that spread 185 pounds over five feet eleven inches. He wasn't pitching nearly as often now as he used to. In 1927 he had pitched 260 innings for the Giants, and he topped that the next year with 264. He reached his top mark in 1932 when he pitched 287 innings for the Giants. Through the second half of the 1920s and the '30s, Freddie was consistently pitching 250 innings.

That wasn't the case anymore, though. The years were catching up with Fitzsimmons. He turned forty in July 1941, and by the end of the season he had pitched only 82⅔ innings. But he still knew how to win, and he was another of the kind of pitcher that Mickey Owen handled best—a low-ball pitcher. He started 12 games for the Dodgers that year and won 6, losing only one. He had World Series experience, too, starting one game for the Giants in 1933 against the Senators and starting twice for them in 1936 against the Yankees, but his record was no wins and three defeats.

It was an exciting day for the Flatbush Faithful as the World Series came to Brooklyn for the first time since 1920, and it was also exciting for a young man from Marcus Hook, Pennsylvania, who had driven up from Philadelphia to Brooklyn with his pals so they could stand in line all night and hope for a ticket to the bleachers in Ebbets Field.

He was Mickey Vernon, the twenty-three-year-old first baseman for the Washington Senators. He and his friends from home were rewarded when dawn came. After their all-night vigil in the ticket line, they were among the lucky ones who were sitting in the center field bleachers when Fat Freddie threw the first pitch of the third game.

Through the whole dark night Vernon never let on to the strangers around him that he was a major league player. Vernon could have told those Brooklyn fans something they might not have believed—that some of those Yankees actually were nice guys. He could testify for at least one of them, their third baseman, Red Rolfe.

Vernon was one of those combinations that managers dream about, one of the most graceful first basemen in baseball and a good hitter too. After World War II, blessed with a smooth left-handed

172

stroke, he would win two American League batting championships in a career that lasted twenty seasons, spanning four decades in the major leagues.

After two short trials in 1939 and 1940, 1941 was his first full season with the Senators. In the final weekend of the American League season he was within only a point or two of hitting .300. When the Senators' train rolled into Penn Station, Mickey was hitting .302, but after the first two games of the weekend, his average dropped to .299.

Rolfe noticed Vernon's average in the paper on the morning of the last game of the season, so he approached Vernon near the Senators' clubhouse before the game. By this time Rolfe had been a star in the American League for ten years, and he remembered how much it would mean to any rookie to be that close to the coveted .300 level in his rookie season.

He said to Vernon, "I see you need a couple of hits."

Mickey confirmed Rolfe's statement.

Then Rolfe suggested, "If you get a chance, lay down a bunt. I'll be on my heels."

Vernon didn't get the chance until his last time up. In his first three trips to the plate the Senators had runners on base and Vernon had to swing away. He had a single, a line drive to Phil Rizzuto at short, and a ground ball to Joe Gordon at second. Then, in his last trip to the plate for the 1941 season, Vernon had a chance to bunt.

He dropped one down the third base line from his spot in the left-hander's side of the batter's box, and Rolfe was true to his word. He was playing deep, and he reacted late.

But then they discovered they had a communications gap. Bill Dickey, the Yankees' Hall of Fame catcher, wasn't in on the setup, so he bolted out from behind the plate, scooped up the bunt, and threw Vernon out.

That's why Mickey Vernon finished his first full season in the American League with a batting average of .2994.

The twenty-seven-year-old and the forty-year-old battled each other on the pitcher's mound through six innings of game three with neither of them giving up a run. In the seventh inning, with Joe Gordon on second base and two outs, Russo came to bat, three decades before the American League began its system of allowing a designated hitter for the pitcher. In Russo's case it might not have been necessary. He had 18 hits that season, good enough for a .231 batting average. That's not the kind of average the rest of us would be proud of, but most pitchers would be thrilled with it.

Russo sent a blistering line drive straight at Fitzsimmons. The combination of the fierce smash, Freddie's age, and his slower reaction time made it impossible for him to field the ball or even get out of the way. Freddie had always been respected as a good fielding pitcher, but this time the ball hit him hard on the left thigh. It was coming at him with such force that it bounced off his leg and went thirty feet into the air. Pee Wee Reese caught it for the third out.

Mickey Vernon and the rest of the crowd watched as Fitzsimmons limped off the field. When the Dodgers took the field again for the start of the eighth inning, Durocher sent in a new pitcher— Hugh Casey.

Casey was becoming one of the premier relief pitchers in baseball after starting 25 games for Brooklyn in 1939 and winning 15. He pitched 227 innings that year, but in 1940 his innings were down to 154 and he started only 10 games as Durocher began using him more as a relief pitcher. In 1941 he led the relief pitchers in the National League with 8 wins.

He was no mystery to the Yankees that day. With one out in the eighth, they reached him for 4 consecutive singles by Rolfe, Henrich, my brother Joe, and Keller and won the game, 2–1.

No one knows what might have happened if Russo's line drive hadn't knocked Fitzsimmons out of the game. The Dodgers were able to score only one run anyhow, but Freddie might have pitched a shutout. As it was, speculation was useless. The Yankees had the lead in the Series, two games to one.

Freddie Fitzsimmons never played in another World Series game. Two years later his career was over.

That's the game most people have forgotten about, or if they remember it, they get confused on the details. Some will tell you it was my brother Joe who hit the line drive. Or they've forgotten that the win gave the Yankees the lead in the Series, and the teams were never tied in victories again.

But the next game is the one the people of all ages know about. It was October 5, 1941, at Ebbets Field. To this day it is known as "the Mickey Owen game."

Mickey was one of the best catchers in the business. He got his start in the minors in 1935 at Springfield, Missouri, in the Western Association and made it to the big leagues two years later as one of Johnny Mize's teammates on the St. Louis Cardinals. He was traded to the Dodgers at the end of the 1940 season.

He made the National League All-Star team four times. Over the '41 season and into '42 he set the National League record for the most consecutive chances by a catcher without an error—507. And he was deadly sure on pop-ups, a fielding chance that some catchers turn into an adventure. If you popped it up around home plate when Owen was catching, you were gone. He once caught nine of them in a single game.

In 1941 Mickey Owen was money in the bank behind the plate as the Dodgers took the field to try to square up the Series with the Yankees at two victories each. Atley Donald was the pitcher for the Yankees, a journeyman who won 9 games for them that year. His opponent was Kirby Higbe, Brooklyn's other 22-game winner.

Neither of the pitchers was around at the finish. The Yankees scored early on a single by Rolfe, a walk to my brother, and a single by Keller. They added two more runs in the fourth inning and had a 3–0 lead. The Dodgers were dangerously close to falling behind in the Series, 3 games to one.

But they rallied for two runs of their own in the fourth and two more in the fifth to take a 4–3 lead. Their big blow was a 2-run homer by their brilliant center fielder, Pete Reiser. By this time Joe McCarthy had used Donald, Marv Breuer, and Johnny Murphy. Durocher had lifted Higbe in the fourth and followed him with Larry French and Johnny Allen before bringing Hugh Casey in from the bullpen with one out in the fifth inning.

Casey pitched excellent relief ball, shutting the Yankees out into the ninth inning. Brooklyn still only had a one-run lead separating it from a 3–1 deficit and almost certain defeat in the Series, but the way Casey was pitching, one run was going to be enough. That probability grew after he routinely disposed of the first two New York hitters in the ninth, Johnny Sturm on a ground out, and Rolfe on a ball back to the mound.

Tommy Henrich, the one they called "Old Reliable" because of his knack for getting on base or making the big play in right field when the game was on the line, stepped into the batter's box. Left-handed hitter against right-handed pitcher. Henrich and Casey battled each other to 3 balls and 2 strikes. Then Owen flashed the sign. Two fingers. Curve ball.

Casey had two kinds of curve balls. One was a fast, sharp-breaking pitch, and the other came to the plate in a big, sweeping path. As a left-handed hitter facing a right-handed pitcher, Henrich knew that a Casey curve ball would be breaking into him, but he had no way of knowing which kind of a curve ball it would be, or whether it might be a fast ball. The mental confrontation between pitcher and batter was at its peak.

Casey wound up and threw. It was the big, sweeping kind of curve ball. Henrich swung and missed. Strike three. The game was over, and the Dodger fans began to scream their delight, knowing their heroes had tied the Yankees at two wins each and saved themselves from the near-certain extinction.

But the game *wasn't* over. Casey's breaking pitch eluded Mickey Owen and rolled away from home plate. Henrich, seeing Owen miss the pitch, alertly dropped his bat and darted toward first base, reaching it easily by the time Owen retrieved the ball near the Dodgers' dugout.

You don't give a good team like the 1941 Yankees a second chance in that kind of a situation. My brother was the next hitter, and Casey didn't want any .357 hitter up there in this situation. Not only that, the potential tying run was on base in Henrich, and Joe represented the winning run. You never want to see the winning run come to the plate for the other team in the late innings, and certainly not when it's someone who was having the year—and the career—that Joe was.

Joe hit a line drive single to left. Charlie Keller was up next and promptly doubled against the right field wall. Henrich scored easily, and Joe, with the exceptional speed that people didn't appreciate fully because he was so graceful, came flying home right behind Henrich. He slid in with the run that gave the Yankees the lead, 5–4.

The truth is that Keller's double did more than win the game for New York. It also won the Series. Maybe they still had to play one more game the next day, but the Dodgers weren't going to come back from that kind of defeat. Nobody could. Bill Dickey kept the inning going with a walk, and Joe Gordon hit another double to score Keller and Dickey to make the final score 7–4.

The next day the Yankees ended Brooklyn's suffering. It was the hottest October 6 on record in New York, 89 degrees. Tiny Bonham and Whitlow Wyatt both went the distance in the fifth game, but Bonham allowed only one hit after the third inning. Gordon singled in Keller with the decisive run in the second inning. Henrich—still reliable—hit a home run, and the Yankees won the game and the 1941 World Series, 3–1.

Pee Wee says today that after the final game the loss was "hard to take." But he says the Dodger players felt fortunate to be in the Series and felt "we did the best we could."

The Series didn't end without a flap involving, of all people, my brother. Joe flied out to Reiser in center in the fifth inning, and as he trotted past the mound on his way back to the Yankee dugout, he said to Wyatt, "Well, boy, this Series isn't over yet."

Wyatt misunderstood him, and they had a few words before the players from both teams started to spill out onto the field. It looked as if there might be what some writers like to call "a bench-clearing brawl," but it was over almost as soon as it started.

In the Brooklyn dressing room after the game Wyatt told the reporters: "DiMaggio mumbled something I couldn't hear. I figured he was putting up a beef about a duster ball which sent him back from the plate, so I guess I got hotheaded and hollered to him, 'If you can't take it, why the hell don't you get out of the game?'"

That's when Joe made his move toward Wyatt and things started to get interesting. It's funny to remember that episode now.

177

The whole world knows that Joe is about the last guy who would ever start a fight, especially with his team only four innings away from winning the World Series.

Joe had the satisfaction of making the last putout of the Series. He caught a fly ball by Jimmy Wasdell, who was pinch-hitting. It was Joe's nineteenth catch of the Series, and it set a record for the most catches by an outfielder in a Series of fewer than seven games. Each Yankee player received $5,917 as his winner's share of the World Series.

Gordon was unanimously selected by the writers as the "Player of the Series." The president of the City Council, Newbold Morris, presented him with his award—a hat costing $150.

If you want to go by the statistics, it was the Yankees' pitchers who beat the Dodgers. They allowed Brooklyn only eleven runs in five games. The Dodgers' best hitters were silenced by the New York pitching. Medwick hit .235, Reese and Reiser each hit .200 and Camilli hit only .167. The rest weren't any better—Walker had a .222 average, Lavagetto an even .100 and Billy Herman .125. As a team the Dodgers batted .182.

But that argument is only for the statistically inclined. The real explanation for the Dodgers' defeat was that pivotal third strike that Henrich and Owen both missed.

Red Barber remembers the feeling about the World Series after that fourth game. "Owen's play made it a three-one Series," Red says today. "Everyone knew the Series was over. MacPhail cried openly at the press club bar."

Reese points out the difference it made in the Dodger pitching rotation. "If we had won the game, the Series would have been tied at two wins each," Pee Wee remembers. "Whitlow Wyatt could have had his normal four days of rest and been ready for the sixth game. But when we lost that game, Wyatt, who was our best pitcher, had to pitch the next day with only three days' rest. With another day of rest for him, we could have won that Series."

On the day the Yankees won it, although it probably went unnoticed by most baseball fans, the Ford Motor Company announced it was laying off 20,000 workers due to a reduction in automobile production as Detroit geared up to manufacture bombers and tanks instead of roadsters and coupes. And the Nazis had three million soldiers bearing down on Moscow.

Over the years a claim has built up that Casey crossed Owen up, that he threw a spitball instead of a curve and Owen wasn't expecting it. There were only two ultimate experts on the subject, Casey and Owen, and Casey is dead.

Owen, even in the gloom of the moment on that October Sunday in 1941, stood up to the situation and shouldered the responsibility. In front of his locker in the dressing room at Ebbets Field, he told reporters: "It was all my fault. It wasn't a strike. It was a great breaking curve that I should have had. But I guess the ball hit the side of my glove. It got away from me, and by the time I got hold of it, near the corner of the Brooklyn dugout, I couldn't have thrown anybody out at first."

Then he added, "I guess you'll have to call me the goat of the game." A reporter told Mickey the official scorer had charged him with an error on the play, and he agreed without hesitation. "That's right," he said. "I should have had an error on it. I should have had the ball."

Today he speaks just as candidly about that third strike as he ever did, beginning with his description of Hugh Casey: "Hugh never threw a spitball in his life because he didn't have to. He never threw a change of pace, and he never threw a slider. He had two pitches. He had a fast ball and a curve ball. He never threw anything but the best stuff he could on them.

"He had two kinds of fast balls. He had one he'd hold off center and throw as a sinker, and it would do a kind of an in-shoot on a left-handed batter. The other one he'd hold across the seams and that would be his high, hard-rising fastball.

"For his curve ball he had a big overhand jug handle that would really break, and then he had a hard, quick curve. The quick curve wasn't a slider. It broke one time and it broke quick.

"He threw either fastball he wanted to on the fastball sign, and either curve ball he wanted to on the curve ball sign. That way, nobody could call his pitches on him. It made him furious if he thought somebody was calling his pitches, and if he really believed they were, the first thing he'd do is hit the hitter in the back or the neck or anyplace he could just to let them know they didn't do that to ol' Hugh."

Mickey is just as specific in talking about Casey's last strike to Henrich: "It was a big curve ball. It was my fault, but I'll say this —I came closer to handling it than Tommy did. He missed it by six inches.

"Hugh came in early in that game, and he tried to throw the big overhand curve ball on the first curve ball sign I gave him, and it hung outside. And on the next curve ball sign I gave him, he tried the big overhand curve ball again, and it hung again. The next curve ball sign I gave him, he tried his hard, quick curve, and it was really breaking, so he stayed with that. No one touched it, so he just stayed with that hard, quick curve for the rest of the game. So when we got two strikes on Henrich, I gave the curve ball sign. I'm the kind of a guy who gets into a rut and does things mechanically, and he reeled off that big overhand curve, and it was—'Oh, my!'—and I didn't get my mitt in the right place quick enough. One thing about it: He never threw a better curve in his life than that one.

"It was in a tough place to catch it—low and inside, on your barehand side. Even if I had called for that kind of a pitch, I would have had to be really quick to have caught it cleanly, but I should have caught it anyway." Then, in case there's any doubt about it, Mickey Owen says firmly, "That's the way it happened. That's *exactly* as it was."

Mickey laughs today and says, "If it's unusual, I'll be in the middle of it. Not by design—it just happens that way. If I hadn't missed that third strike, they'd say, 'Mickey who?' It made me famous, in a left-handed way."

Durocher had his own reaction to the most famous missed third strike in baseball history. The newspapers quoted him as saying that police officers scrambling onto the field to control the crowd got in Owen's way and prevented him from retrieving the ball in time to throw Henrich out at first.

Durocher told reporters in the dressing room: "There was one stupid sergeant, standing on home plate, and Mickey never had a chance to get the ball."

Henrich, like Owen, laughs about the play today, too, and says, "I get my picture in the paper every year—striking out." It's a famous photograph showing Henrich looking over his shoulder back at the ball as Owen is breaking to his right to retrieve it. The clenched right fist of the umpire, Larry Goetz, is still in the air, signaling the strike.

Like Mickey Owen, Tommy Henrich can tell you every detail about the pitch and the play that followed:

"It was a curve ball, and the ball broke down. Tommy Bridges of the Tigers had the greatest curve ball I ever saw, and this ball broke down, just like a curve from Bridges. As I'm swinging at that ball, I'm saying, 'You gotta be out of your mind.' I'm trying to hold up already. You can think in a hurry, and as I'm swinging the bat but trying to hold up, I'm thinking, "Maybe Mickey is having trouble too.' In that picture, I have my head turned—to see where the ball is."

The headlines the next morning told of the despair in Brooklyn:

BROOKLYN'S MILLIONS PLUNGED INTO DARKNESS BY DODGERS' COLLAPSE IN NINTH

John Drebinger wrote in disbelief in the *New York Times:*

It couldn't, perhaps, have happened anywhere else on earth. But it did happen yesterday in Brooklyn, where in the short span of twenty-one minutes, a dazed gathering of 33,813 at Ebbets Field saw a World Series game miraculously flash two finishes before its eyes.

. . . There occurred one of those harrowing events that doubtless will live through all the ages of baseball like the Fred Snodgrass muff and the failure of Fred Merkle to touch second.

Mickey Owen, topflight catcher of the Dodgers, let the ball slip away from him . . .

Shirley Povich, in his story about the game in the *Washington Post,* wrote, "Baseball fiction paled before stark ninth-inning World Series drama today . . ."

In his feature column on the same page, Povich said the incident had imposed on Casey "the cruelest martyrdom of the forty years of World Series history." He quoted Casey: "It was the best pitch I ever threw."

To which Povich added: "It's a helluva note when you lose because your best is too good."

Meyer Berger, writing in the same *New York Times* sport section, was moved to poetry:

> Oh, somewhere north of Harlem
> The sun is shining bright.
> Bands are playing in the Bronx,
> And up there hearts are light.
> In Hunt's Point men are laughing.
> On the Concourse, children shout.
> But there is no joy in Flatbush.
> Fate had knocked their Casey out.

Henrich, who played in four World Series, says today that the 1941 Series remains his favorite. "The Yankees were determined to beat the Dodgers. As far as I'm concerned, I'm glad we won that year more than any other Series. That was a tough Series. The Dodgers were good. I couldn't stand the thought of losing to Durocher or the Dodgers. Not because we didn't like Durocher. It was just that he would do anything he could to win, and he had guys on his team who played like that. That was his brand of ball. He was an aggressive guy, the kind you didn't like to lose to.

"On the Yankees we had a number one goal: 'Don't lose to Durocher.' "

No one knew it at the time, but in Los Angeles, three thousand miles from Ebbets Field, a boy who reached his fifteenth birthday only sixteen days before Owen's error felt so sorry for the Dodgers that he made a promise to himself: Someday he would grow up to be a big star for the Dodgers and beat the Yankees in the World Series.

And that's how the Dodgers were able to get Duke Snider.

Two events the next month helped to give the 1941 season its unique standing in baseball history.

On Thanksgiving Day, the Secretary of State, Cordell Hull, met in Washington with the Japanese ambassador, Admiral Kichisaburo Nomura, and handed him a document stating the United States position on relations between the two countries. The document was intended as a step toward adjusting and improving those relations. At the same time, Premier Tojo said in Tokyo that Japan remained determined to enforce her national policies.

The next day the lead item in the daily roundup in the *New York Times* column "The International Situation" on the front page of the paper, said:

"All United States efforts to solve differences with Japan appeared exhausted yesterday, and the next move—either diplomatic or military—seemed up to Tokyo."

The date was November 28.

— 14 —

THE SUPPORTING CAST

My brother Joe and Ted dominated the 1941 baseball season to a degree rarely, if ever, seen before or since. They were the headline story of the day throughout the season, to such an extent that Americans at times seemed more interested in what Joe and Ted were doing than in what the Germans and Japanese were up to.

Along with the missed third strike in the World Series, Lou Gehrig's death, and Lefty Grove's three-hundredth victory, Joe and Ted made the 1941 season what it remains today—the most historic one ever played. But others also made key contributions to 1941's stature—players like Grove, Reiser, Greenberg, Henrich, Feller, Mize, Keller, Slaughter, and Doerr, plus the World Series managers, McCarthy and Durocher. In any history of the 1941 season they must be included. Some have already been described, but the others deserve even more of a mention. And two of those who have already appeared in some detail, Grove and Reiser, are worthy of more—Grove for what he accomplished over his career and Reiser for what he achieved in 1941.

Robert Moses Grove was a coal miner's son, born in Lonaconing, Maryland, in the Allegheny Mountains, in 1900. He left school in the eighth grade and never really felt comfortable around two things: strangers and defeat.

He started his baseball life as a first baseman in Midland, three miles down Route 36 from Lonaconing, but quickly became a left-handed pitcher with overpowering speed. His first minor league contract was for $125 a month in 1920 in Martinsburg, West Virginia, a town just about as big as Lefty would prefer.

In those years, with the major league teams so rich in talent at every level of their farm systems, a ball player could spend the rest of his life in the minor leagues—even if you were Lefty Grove, future 300-game winner and member of the Hall of Fame. That's almost what Lefty did.

He moved up to the Baltimore Orioles, who were then still a minor league team in the International League, and won 109 games for them over four seasons while losing only 36. But after those four years he was still in the minors. Then Connie Mack of the Philadelphia A's paid Jack Dunn of the Orioles $100,600 for Grove, a record price at that time, and Lefty became a major leaguer. Dunn made sure the price was six hundred dollars more than the Yankees paid the Red Sox five years earlier for Babe Ruth.

Grove's greatness is shown in at least two dazzling numbers: He was the American League strikeout king seven years in a row and earned run champion nine times. Of all the great pitchers Connie Mack had, especially when his A's won the World Series three years in a row from 1929 through 1931, he said Grove was "my best one."

Joe Cronin, our manager when Lefty won his three-hundredth game at the age of forty-one, said, "He was all baseball. We all admired him and his dedication to the sport." That was a nice way of saying that whenever Lefty lost, there was hell to pay. No manager, coach, or teammate was safe. My best view of the famous Grove temper was the day in Washington when he ripped his shirt off without unbuttoning it after that 13-inning loss to the Senators.

Others, including writers, had their own evidence of Lefty's fury. Tom Meany, another winner of the J. G. Taylor Spink Award for baseball writing, wrote: "The temperament Grove brought to the majors was as remarkable as his fastball. Lefty was merely ornery. Grove wanted to win but couldn't see that it was his fault when he didn't. When his control was off or the hitters were tying into his high hard one, Grove took it as a personal insult. He couldn't wait to get the ball back from the catcher so he could fire it at the batter again."

Bobby Doerr witnessed Lefty's temper firsthand, sitting next to him after a loss in Chicago in 1941. We were leading in the ninth inning and had the game won, but with two outs, Lou Finney had a problem with the sun on a fly ball to right. The White Sox jumped on the last-minute chance, scored some runs, and won the ball game.

After we returned to the clubhouse at Comiskey Park, Lefty pulled his flannel shirt off without undoing the buttons, the same flareup he staged for me in Washington. Bobby said, "When those buttons came flying off, they sounded like a machine gun. The team was going on to St. Louis, but Joe Cronin sent Lefty back to Boston because he was so beside himself."

The testimony about Lefty's great ability was as easy to come by as the tales about his temper. Mickey Cochrane, the Hall of Fame catcher who caught Grove when they played for Philadelphia, said, "He could throw a lamb chop past a wolf." He once struck out Ruth, Gehrig, and Bob Meusel on nine pitches. Another time he fanned Ruth, Gehrig, and Tony Lazzeri on ten.

In 1930 he won 28 games for the A's while losing only 5. The next year he improved that record, believe it or not, to 31 wins and only 4 losses, giving him a two-year record of 59 victories and 9 defeats. No pitcher has ever done that.

I admired Lefty's fierce competitive drive. They say that to be a true champion, you have to have "a fire in your belly." Grove's whole body was on fire.

One other legendary display of his All-Star fury took place after he tied the record of Walter Johnson and Smoky Joe Wood with 16 straight wins only to see his streak snapped when a substitute outfielder misjudged a fly ball. Al Simmons, the star outfielder for the A's who would normally have been in left field that day, was back home in Milwaukee having some dental work done.

Grove trashed the visitors' clubhouse at Sportsman's Park—and the story was that he never forgave Simmons.

After he retired following the 1941 season, when he won 7 games but lost the same number, Lefty said, "I love baseball. If I had it to do all over, I'd do the same thing. If they said, 'Here's a steak dinner,' and I had a chance to go out and play a game of ball, I'd go out and play a game and let the steak sit there. I would."

Pete Reiser was a classic example of a young star who had it all, whose potential for greatness seemed to be without limit. He wasn't called just an outstanding prospect, or a "phee-nom" as they used to say in describing some kid in spring training. Reiser was called "a second Ty Cobb."

Durocher has said, "Reiser is the best ball player I ever saw. He had more power than Willie [Mays], both lefty and righty. He could throw as good as Willie—at least as good—and he could throw right-handed and left-handed. You think Willie Mays could run in his heyday? You think Mickey Mantle could run? Reiser was faster. He stole home for me seven times in one year."

"Pistol Pete" was a bargain-basement purchase for the Dodgers. Judge Landis released 73 minor league players, including Reiser, from the Cardinals' organization in 1938, declaring them free agents and able to sign with any team they chose. Landis declared that the 73 were not getting a fair chance to advance because the Cardinals had so many players under contract. The Dodgers signed their future star for a bonus of $100.

After his hard-to-believe rookie year in 1941, he played even better in '42. He was hitting .382 by mid-season and shocking fans, writers, and the whole National League with his performances in center field, making startling catch after startling catch. Then he tried one too many.

He was racing back for a long fly ball by Enos Slaughter of the Cards, a ball that seemed uncatchable. But Pete caught it. Then he crashed into the outfield fence and collapsed into an unconscious heap at its base.

He was hospitalized for a while, and when he returned—sooner than the doctors wanted—he became dizzy every time he looked up for a fly ball. By the end of the season, that .382 batting average was all the way down to .310. He never hit that high again, coming close only in 1947 with .309, his only .300 year after 1942.

Pete was carried off the field on a stretcher nine times in his career. In late April 1941 he was hit in the head at Ebbets Field with a fastball thrown by Ike Pearson of the Phillies and was carried from home plate. He was hospitalized for several days and out of the lineup for two weeks.

A month later, on a Sunday afternoon at Ebbets Field, the Phillies were back in town. They were leading, 4–3, in the bottom of the sixth inning when the Dodgers loaded the bases. Then Reiser came to bat. The pitcher was Ike Pearson again, the first time the two had faced each other since the beaning the month before. Everyone at Ebbets Field was curious: Would Reiser "bail out," backing away from the pitch?

Not Reiser. He hit a 3–1 pitch off the screen over the exit gate in right center field and streaked around the bases for an inside-the-park grand slam home run.

Pee Wee agrees with Durocher about Reiser's great talents. "He was a heck of an athlete," Reese says. "He wasn't the most graceful player you ever saw. All he could do was catch the ball— and hit and run. I always had a great deal of admiration for Musial, who I thought was one of the top players of my time or any time, but I think Pete would have been right there."

The two were roommates. Off the field, Reese says, Reiser was very quiet. "He smoked a lot of cigarettes—he was a chain smoker —and he drank a lot of Cokes."

On the field? "He played hard—*damn,* he played hard. If he hit the ball back to the pitcher, he'd run down the first base line just as hard as he did when he got a base hit. He ran out to center field like that, and he ran in the same way. No one hustled any more than Pete Reiser did. But he could not stay away from those walls."

People said Reiser was crazy for being so reckless with his health and safety in going after fly balls. As a center fielder myself, and an aggressive one at that, I questioned the wisdom of his style of play too. Every outfielder should be willing to risk injury to make a catch for his team, and I introduced myself to a few outfield walls myself, even at the annual Hall of Fame game in Cooperstown when I banged into the fence in my rookie season, cut up my face, and knocked myself punchy—but I made the catch.

With Reiser, though, it was far worse. He didn't just run into the outfield fences in those days before padded walls and warning tracks—he seemed to try to run *through* them. There is a limit to everything, including how much of a chance an outfielder should take, and whether it's a smart risk or a stupid one. But Pete seemed determined to prove that the limits for the rest of us outfielders didn't apply to him.

A radio announcer was interviewing several Dodgers about their prospects for the new season one year in spring training. Pee Wee Reese, Hugh Casey, and Dixie Walker all went out on the limb and predicted the Dodgers would finish in first place. Then the announcer turned to Reiser.

"How about you, Pete? Where do you think you'll finish the season?"

Reiser answered, "In Peck Memorial Hospital."

When he was asked about his daredevil style of play, he used to say, "Hell, any ball player worth his salt has run into a wall. I'm the guy who got hurt doing it, that's all."

He also got the inevitable question: How long would he have lasted and what would his batting average have been if he had played with a little less abandon? As it was, he played ten years and had a .295 lifetime average.

His answer was: "If I hadn't played that way, I may never have gotten there to begin with. It was my style of playing. I didn't know any other way to play ball."

Pete enjoyed special support in his home town of St. Louis, particularly at the Missouri School for the Blind. After speaking there for the fifth time, his curiosity got the best of him. He asked the director why he kept getting invited back to speak. He got a logical explanation.

"Our children have problems with walls," the director said,

190

"and they hear that you have the same problem. They figure you're one of them."

Hall-of-Famer Hank Greenberg was another great player from the 1930s and '40s who deserves a special mention. Until Roger Maris broke Babe Ruth's record of 60 home runs in one season in 1961, Greenberg came closer than anyone else with 58 in 1938. That's still the most home runs in one year by a major league right-handed hitter.

That was no fluke year for Greenberg. He tied Jimmie Foxx for the American League championship in 1935 and then won it in '36, '38, '40, and '46. His homers came when they would count the most too—with men on base. In 1937 he had 183 runs batted in, still the third highest season's total in history, seven RBIs behind Hack Wilson's major league record made in 1930, and only one behind Lou Gehrig's high for the American League, which he set in 1931.

In May 1941 Hank was drafted into the Army again, after being discharged the day before Pearl Harbor as one of the first men called up in 1940. In his last game before his second hitch in the service he hit two home runs off Tiny Bonham of the Yankees and led the Tigers to a 7–4 win.

In 1945, just out of the Army for the second time, his home run with the bases loaded in the ninth inning on the last day of the season won the pennant for the Tigers over the Senators.

Hank was a man of integrity in both his religion and his profession. In 1934, his second full season in the majors, he sat out the Tigers' game on Yom Kippur, the most solemn day of the year for Jews. In his conscientiousness about his faith, Greenberg anguished long and hard before telling Detroit's manager, Mickey Cochrane, that he could not bring himself to play on the Day of Atonement.

It was an extra courageous decision because his absence from the lineup broke a rare season-long streak by the entire Tigers' infield. First baseman Greenberg, second baseman Charlie Gehringer, shortstop Billy Rogell, and third baseman Marv Owen had all played every game of the season. All of them finished the season with a perfect attendance record of 154 games played, except for Hank with 153.

Greenberg explained the infield's durability by saying, "Back then you didn't come out of a game easily for fear that someone would take your job." That was something I found out myself with that sprained ankle at the start of my rookie year. When it took me until July to get back into the starting lineup, I discovered the same fact of life that Greenberg was describing.

The Tigers were not just durable in 1934, they were good too. They won the pennant.

When it came to hitting, Hank was just as honest as when he missed what people in Detroit called the "Yom Kippur game." When you talked to him about his accomplishments with a bat, Hank was willing to admit he was a guess hitter. What's more, he claimed everybody else was too.

"We're all guess hitters," he said, "if everybody would only tell the truth. They're lying, those who say they aren't guessing up there."

Greenberg was even candid about his son Steve's chances of playing in the major leagues when the Washington Senators gave him a tryout at first base: "I don't think he's good enough."

Then he added, "The boy could go to bed at night and wake up in the morning and make more money overnight while he was asleep than he could make in a year in baseball." Hank had a good reason for saying that. His wife, Steve's mother, was the former Carol Gimbel from the New York department store of the same name.

With all of his talent for hitting home runs, Hank suffered from a common problem for young power hitters in his first couple of seasons with the Tigers. He was overswinging.

It was Bill McGowan, the same umpire who reminded Ted Williams to stay loose at the plate on the last day of the '41 season, who helped Greenberg avoid the problem.

"Hank," McGowan said, "you don't have to hit the ball forty rows up into the seats." He held his thumb and forefinger an inch apart and added, "Home runs count just as much if they clear the fence by only this much."

With his home runs clearing the fences by "only this much" and sometimes by a lot more, Greenberg went on to a thirteen-year career in which he powered his way to 331 home runs and a .313 career average. Computer expert Ralph Winnie calculates that without Greenberg's four years in the Army, he would have hit 515 home runs, and his runs batted in total would jump from 1,276 to 1,883.

Of all the compliments that came his way, maybe the most significant came from Fred Haney, who managed the St. Louis Browns in Hank's early years: "Greenberg puts more thought, effort, and conscientiousness into his work than any other player in the league."

Even with Lefty Grove at his peak in those same years, both in his ability and his burning desire to compete, Haney said that Hank was "the greatest competitor in the league."

Tommy Henrich took the strongest kind of pride in being a New York Yankee: "We always knew we had a job to do. When we came up to a tough game or a tough series, we didn't walk out on the field and say, 'All right, you guys, here we are. We're the Yankees. We're going to cream you. What are you going to do about it?'

"It wasn't that way at all. Our guys would say, 'All right, we've got a tough ball club against us out there. Now, let's bear down a little harder.' And because we had that little extra when we needed it, we usually were able to pull through."

I know Joe certainly felt that way. Vince and I did too, for that matter, but the Yankees had a whole team that felt that way. It wasn't simply a case of attitude, either. I think Tommy was being modest. The truth is the Yankees really were better than the rest of us during most of those years.

But the attitude that Tommy was talking about made them that much better. They had confidence in their individual talents and in their ability as a team. They felt convinced they were going to beat you, even if it took some of their famous "five o'clock lightning" in the ninth inning.

Henrich is another player from our era who remembers what scoundrels most of the owners were. He says that when the Yankee players would ask for a raise for the coming season, the general manager, Ed Barrow, would say, "You got your raise playing in the World Series."

Charlie Keller was another Yankee with that quiet confidence of a winner. He came from Middletown, Maryland, in the Catoctin Mountains, near Camp David, about 75 miles from Lefty Grove's town. He raises horses near Middletown now on a 100-acre spread called Yankeeland Farms.

Charlie was like Lefty in his strong preference for the small-town life and never felt completely comfortable in New York. But if Charlie wasn't in love with New York, the reverse was true.

He was a star from the beginning, a .334 hitter in his rookie year in 1939 and the American League runs-batted-in champion in 1940 with 106. In 1941 he drove in another 102 runs and missed hitting .300 by two points.

The writers and broadcasters called him King Kong because of his strength and his dark, hairy arms, a nickname he never liked, and who could blame him? The King Kong movie was a smash hit of the thirties. Every time I heard that nickname used in reference to Charlie, I was delighted to settle for the "Little Professor."

Charlie is proud of outhitting Ted when they were rookies together, and like all of his teammates, he was proud of being a Yankee. "The Yankees of those years had such a big name," he says today. "I felt pride walking into the ball park."

Despite his Yankee pride and his success in compiling a life-time batting average of .286 over 13 seasons and a World Series average of .306 in four autumns, Charlie made the adjustment to life after baseball as easily as I did when I retired from the Red Sox in 1953.

"When I left baseball," he says matter-of-factly, "I left base-ball. I've always had other interests. I never was happy in the big town."

Bobby Doerr was one of the keys to our success in 1941, one of the best second baseman in baseball and one of the best clutch hitters too, all while being one of the most popular players on any team.

He was a .282 hitter for us in 1941 with 16 home runs and that great glove of his. Those numbers don't tell the whole story of his ability. Our postwar shortstop, Vern Stephens, said, "Bobby is the best second baseman I've played next to." Johnny Pesky adds to that by saying, "I never saw him misplay a ball, and he had the best backhand of any second baseman I ever saw."

In order to develop a "Fenway Park swing" for a right-handed hitter and hit home runs into the net over the "Green Monster" in left field, the Red Sox made Bobby a pull hitter when he came up in 1937. It worked, and Bobby hit 223 home runs in his fourteen years in the majors, all with the Red Sox. When we made it to the World Series in 1946, our first year back from the war, Bobby led our regulars in hitting with a .409 average.

He was just as talented with his glove. He once held the American League record for the most plays by a second baseman without an error—414. He led the league's second basemen in fielding six times, and some stats by today's computerized experts show that Bobby was the best fielding second baseman of the 1940s.

With all his ability, maybe the highest tribute to him was paid by Tommy Henrich, one of the most popular players himself in the years when all of us were playing. Tommy said, "Bobby Doerr is one of the very few who played this game hard and came out of it with no enemies."

Leo Durocher was a fiery competitor, notorious for his feuds with umpires and for baiting opposing players and ordering his pitchers to throw at the other team's hitters. He was the exact opposite of his managerial opponent in the '41 Series, Joe McCarthy. Durocher could move a dignified man like Tommy Henrich to say what he did about the Yankees' determination not to lose to the man everyone called "Leo the Lip."

Those who played for him when he managed the Dodgers and the Giants remember hearing him yell to his pitchers, "Stick it in his ear!" or "Let's see how he hits on his back!"

He was flamboyant by nature, and when fate assigned him to work under Larry MacPhail, Brooklyn's equally fiery general manager in the 1940s, the combustible combination generated enough electricity for the Dodgers to operate their own power plant. "Mac-Phail fired me sixty times, and I was still there when he left," Leo has written. "He even fired me the night we won the pennant in 1941."

That was one of their most famous episodes. The Dodgers were returning to New York after winning the pennant in Boston. MacPhail decided to get on their train at the 125th Street station so he could be part of the huge welcome home celebration waiting for the team at Grand Central Station.

Leo swears that nobody told him. So he ordered the train crew not to stop at 125th Street and proceed to the celebration at Grand Central. As MacPhail, the man running the organization, stood on the platform eager to bask in the Dodgers' first pennant in twenty-four years, the train went roaring by.

"The philosophy on the field in those years was altogether different from what it is today," Durocher says. "Today a pitcher gets fined if an umpire thinks he threw at a batter. In those days the umpire didn't have to take any course in mind-reading. The pitcher told you he was going to throw at you."

The man who handled Durocher best was Branch Rickey, who was his general manager at St. Louis when Leo was playing for the Cardinals and again in Brooklyn after MacPhail entered the Army in 1943.

Rickey was a stern man, steeped in a rigid Christian code of conduct and with a fondness for quoting the Bible. In his autobiography, *Nice Guys Finish Last,* Durocher remembers that whenever Rickey felt the need to take him to the woodshed, he would call him into his office and begin quoting from memory: "Luke, Chapter fifteen, Verse eleven: 'A certain man had two sons . . .' "

Then he would recite for Durocher—again—the parable of the prodigal son. "Through our years," Durocher says, "Mr. Rickey recited the Return of the Prodigal Son to me many, many times. . . . It got so I could almost recite it with him, right down to that most moving ending: 'It is meet that we should make merry, and be glad, for this, thy brother, was dead and is alive again; and was lost and is found.' "

Leo says he was so moved by the passage and by Rickey's

theatrical rendition of it that "I sometimes resolved to mend my ways."

Joe McCarthy was just as determined to win as Durocher, but he operated at a lower level of intensity. He was a winner with three different teams—the Yankees, Red Sox, and Cubs, which tells you something right there. He would have made a successful business executive because he was an effective supervisor of personnel. He handled personalities as different as the explosive Babe Ruth and the quiet Lou Gehrig, plus the one they called "El Goofy," Lefty Gomez, and more reserved players like my brother Joe.

"In handling ball players, you always have to remember that there are no two alike," he once said. "They come to you with different religions, different temperaments, at different salary levels and various levels of intelligence. I always believed in taking a player aside when I wanted to talk to him. And I always tried to be around the hotel lobby so the players would see me and know I was available. You might say I was a mother hen."

He had an understanding attitude toward his players about drinking, as long as they didn't overdo it. He felt that "a beer or two" after a game relaxed a player, helped him to sleep better, and therefore made him able to play better the next day. But you couldn't fool him on the subject. He was amused that players would admit to drinking beer or wine but would piously deny ever drinking "the hard stuff."

"It's an amazing thing," he said once. "I've been in baseball for twenty-nine years, and I've never had one player tell me he liked the hard stuff."

Gomez used to give McCarthy fits when he wasn't playing. Gomez would be in the dugout in the late innings, and if the opposition began a rally, Lefty would start pounding his glove and muttering something about getting loose in the bullpen. Joe said, "He kept inching toward me on the bench in those situations, and at times I thought he was going to wind up in my lap."

One of McCarthy's most famous escapades with Lefty happened during a World Series game with all the pressure that a

197

World Series game carries with it when Lefty suddenly paused between pitches so he could look at an airplane flying overhead.

When McCarthy went to the mound to ask him what the heck was going on, Lefty innocently said, "Nothing can happen, Skipper. The batters can't hit the ball as long as I have it in my hand."

Gomez never lost his baseball savvy, that strong instinct that tells a player what to do or think in a particular situation. As he lay in the hospital in the final week of his life, his doctor, testing Lefty's alertness, leaned over to him and said, "Lefty, I want to see how you're feeling today. Imagine it's the late innings of a close game and you're pitching. How would you feel about that?"

Lefty said, "Who's the hitter?"

Joe McCarthy's favorite character of all the players he ever managed wasn't Gomez or Ruth or any other major league player. He was Jay Kirke, a great hitter in the minor leagues who played as an infielder-outfielder under McCarthy at Louisville and later hit .301 in seven years in the major leagues.

Joe used to tell about the time he flashed the double-steal sign with runners on first and third in a game against Kansas City, one of the Yankees' minor league teams, when Kirke was the hitter. Kirke, who'd been stopped all day by curve balls from Red Ames, took the first pitch as ordered, but when the K.C. shortstop cut off the catcher's throw to second and fired back to the plate to get the runner coming from third, Kirke stepped into it and hit the throw against the left field fence.

McCarthy was as astonished as everyone else, knowing that Kirke could have killed the runner, the catcher, or the umpire by swinging his bat with the runner trying to score. "Kirke!" he screamed. "Are you crazy?"

"I would have been crazy if I *hadn't* hit that throw," Kirke yelled back. "It's the first fastball I've seen all day."

McCarthy's favorite Yankee player was Lou Gehrig, but he said my brother was "the most natural player I ever managed." Joe had the same amount of respect for McCarthy. He said, "Never a day went by that you didn't learn something from him."

Even the players who didn't like him, and there are always a few players on any team who don't like the manager, had great respect for McCarthy. Joe Page, the Yankees' ace relief pitcher, told Joe Durso of the *New York Times,* "I hated his guts, but there was never a better manager."

— 15 —

WHEN EVERYTHING CHANGED

In the first days after Pearl Harbor, the question wasn't whether 1941 was baseball's most historic season. Instead, the question was whether it would be the last.

There was serious doubt that baseball would be allowed to continue. Most of the players in the major leagues, and in the minors, too, for that matter, were prime candidates for the draft. Even if the owners could still find nine reasonably healthy, coordinated young men to play, there was the question of transportation.

All unnecessary travel was banned during the war. If you had to take a long trip on plane or train, you needed to have papers showing you had a government "priority," and certified you had a legitimate need to travel. A baseball team would involve moving more than thirty men, counting the players, the manager, coaches, and trainer. Would the government allow that kind of drain on the country's national wartime transportation system, with sixteen teams traveling by train from Boston to Washington, from New York as far west as St. Louis, six months a year? There was reason to doubt it.

The transportation shortage was brought home graphically in a large newspaper ad on New Year's Eve, sponsored by the Eastern

Railroad President's Conference. The ad showed a train car of soldiers being transported to an unspecified destination. The message under the photo said:

> Some morning your train may be one or two cars short. Someday, from somewhere along the line, a host of lads wearing Uncle Sam's uniforms may have crowded the train you planned to take.
>
> Army maneuvers and movements of troops, plus the everyday transportation needs of our new Army, shift hundreds of passenger cars away from their normal routes.
>
> Someday, if there isn't a seat for you, remember it is quite possible that *your* son or *your* brother or the *boy from the house next door* is sitting in it, on some distant track.
>
> If you cannot get the lower berth you want, or if you have to change your plans because everything for today is filled up —remember, too, that today the man in uniform has "priority" over all of us—and rightly so. Your railroads are cooperating to see that he gets it, and at the same time doing their utmost to take care of your civilian needs.

There was already a freeze on the sale of new automobile tires, ordered by the government four days after Pearl Harbor. Two days after Christmas, another order came out of Washington, saying that tires would now be "rationed," effective in January. The sale of new cars was halted "for the duration."

With conditions like that, no wonder there was concern that 1941 might turn out to be the last season for baseball, or any other sport, for a long time. An article in *Baseball* magazine raised that possibility. The magazine said: "No one knows even whether the 1942 season will open. No one is sure of anything. . . . Three things can happen. The 1942 season may be called off entirely. The season may be curtailed with the World Series eliminated. The season will not be interfered with in any way.

"All, of course, depends upon the progress of the war. If things go along well, the season will open as usual and continue on the even tenor of its way. If things open well and then get a bit tougher, the season will be curtailed and, if the worse comes to the worst, the campaign of 1942 will be fought only on the battlefield and not on the more peaceful diamond."

The owners of major league teams didn't agree even among themselves on the prospects or the wisest course of action. Two of them, Sam Breadon of the Cardinals and Alva Bradley of the Indians, were not convinced that baseball could make it through 1942, and Bradley wasn't even sure he wanted to, unless most of the established players were still around. He said, "It's too grand a game to be turned into a farce. If I can't present baseball of high quality, I'll close my park."

Ed Barrow, the general manager of the Yankees, was among those officials who took a different view. He said the Yankees would field a team even if he couldn't find more than sixteen players instead of the usual twenty-five.

Frankie Frisch, the "Fordham Flash," managed the Pittsburgh Pirates in 1941, and he remembered what it was like beginning in '42: "Spring training was the worst time. The uncertainty— the rumors that the owners would shut down. If we started the season, how far could we go? Were there going to be enough ball players?"

Into the uncertainty of January 1942, when the whole nation was asking the same kinds of questions about everything in our American routine, stepped Commissioner Landis, the white-haired, stern-jawed former federal judge hired by the owners after the Chicago Black Sox betting scandal to restore the integrity of the game in the 1920s.

Betting scandals were the least of the problems facing Landis now, so in the first days of 1942 he wrote to President Roosevelt, a man he disliked bitterly because of his politics, and asked for presidential guidance on what baseball should do now that America was at war.

In his letter to Roosevelt, Landis said, "Baseball is about to adopt schedules, sign players, make vast commitments, go to training camps. . . . What do you want it to do? . . . If you feel we

203

ought to continue, we would be delighted to do so. We await your order."

Roosevelt responded swiftly, on January 15:

> I honestly feel that it would be best for the country to keep baseball going. There will be fewer people unemployed and everybody will work longer hours and harder than ever before. And that means that they ought to have a chance for recreation and for taking their minds off their work even more than before.
>
> Baseball provides a recreation which does not last over two hours or two hours and a half, and which can be got for very little cost. And, incidentally, I hope that night games can be extended because it gives an opportunity to the day shift to see a game occasionally.

Baseball historians call it the "green-light letter," in which the President of the United States gave baseball permission to continue playing during the war. It made the front page of every paper in the country. The *Sporting News* said Roosevelt should be voted Player of the Year.

Shirley Povich, however, disagrees with this version of the story about the green-light letter. As the *Washington Post*'s baseball writer for so many years, he developed a close relationship with Clark Griffith. Povich says the Landis letter isn't what saved the day for baseball—it was Griffith and his strong ties to the FDR White House.

Povich remembers that Roosevelt used to describe himself as the Senators' "mascot" because he seemed to bring them good luck on his trips to the ball park. Shirley's account is that Griffith simply told FDR that baseball should be allowed to continue during the war because it would be good for America's morale, and Roosevelt agreed.

Shirley says he knows from more than one source that it was Griffith who saved baseball. Besides, he says, "Landis wasn't much more welcome at the White House than the Japanese ambassador." He was a strong opponent of America's entry into the war, a fact known to the President. Griffith once told Povich: "Landis couldn't get a cold chestnut out of Roosevelt."

Even with FDR's green light, the final decision was up to major league baseball itself. Landis was faced with the same kind of decision as the one that confronted Commissioner Fay Vincent at the time of the tragic San Francisco earthquake that struck just before the third game of the 1989 World Series was scheduled to start. As a player in 1942 and a native San Franciscan, there is no question in my mind that baseball made the right decision both times, after the commissioner in both cases made certain that the people wanted baseball to continue.

Hank Greenberg, who was drafted into the Army in May after only nineteen games of the '41 season and discharged just before Pearl Harbor, volunteered immediately and went into the Army for the second time in a year. He was gone for another three and a half years, sacrificing over four seasons at the peak of his career because of military service.

Bob Feller was driving from his home in Van Meter, Iowa, to Chicago to meet with the Indians' vice president, Cy Slapnicka, at the Palmer House before the start of the major league winter meetings so he could negotiate his contract for the 1942 season. It was a clear, cold December afternoon. As he headed his 1941 Buick Century across the Mississippi River at Davenport on the Iowa-Illinois line, the car radio jolted him out of his reverie with the bulletin about Pearl Harbor. Two days later he joined the Navy.

Hank Gowdy, the first player to enlist in World War I, resigned as a coach with Cincinnati and joined the Army again as a captain. He was fifty-three years old.

Ted Lyons, the Hall of Fame pitcher for the White Sox, didn't let his age get in the way, either. He joined the Marines late in the '42 season, just as Ted Williams, Johnny Pesky, and I were playing our last games. He was still an active player, with 259 victories and a 14–6 record that year in his twentieth season with the White Sox. He was going to turn forty-two in December.

Baseball players who were physically disqualified were sometimes criticized despite their innocence. Bill Voiselle of the Giants had a hearing defect. Snuffy Stirnweiss of the Yankees had ulcers. Nelson Potter of the Browns had undergone operations on both knees to remove cartilages. Howie Schultz was over six feet six inches tall, the Army's height limit.

Hal Newhouser of the Tigers remembers how players in that category felt. He wanted to become a pilot. Instead, the doctors giving him his physical examination discovered he had a heart problem that he never knew about.

"You got flak from people," he said. "Our friends and other people were being killed or hurt over there and here we were out playing ball."

He remembers one piece of mail in particular, a banner with letters an inch wide. The banner was yellow. The letters formed a one-word message: BASTARD.

The day after FDR delivered his "day of infamy" speech and Congress declared war on Germany, Italy, and Japan, Feller enlisted even though he could have obtained a deferment easily. His father was dying of cancer, and both of his parents and his sister Marguerite were dependent on him. But he joined up, was gone three and a half years, in his prime every bit as much as Greenberg was. After serving briefly in the Navy's physical fitness program conducted by Gene Tunney, the former heavyweight boxing champion, Feller became itchy for combat. He requested a transfer to gunnery school and went on to become one of baseball's most battle-proven stars with eight Pacific invasions to his credit as chief of an eighteen-man gunnery crew on the battleship *Alabama.*

People later asked Feller why he enlisted so quickly, especially with an open-and-shut case for deferment and while earning what may have been the highest salary in baseball. He gave an answer typical of the times: "We were losing the war. We needed heroes— right now."

For their part, the owners responded the same way everyone else did. Clark Griffith, the Senators' owner, met in Washington with Ford Frick, the National League president, Captain F. H. Weston of the Army's Morale Division, and representatives from four sporting goods manufacturers. The subject was the major leagues' new campaign to provide enough equipment to allow the GIs to play baseball in their spare time.

It was the start of the "Keep 'Em Slugging" campaign, the idea of the Baseball Writers' Association of America. The group that met in Washington committed itself to raising $42,000 at the outset to buy 1,500 baseball kits for free distribution to military bases—18,000 baseballs and 4,500 bats. Griffith became head of the Professional Baseball Equipment Fund, the goal of which was to raise money from the 1942 All-Star game and other sources.

Griffith wanted everything about the campaign to be "major league." He said the equipment would be "the best we can get—none of that cheap stuff for the soldiers and sailors. Only the best for them." For Griffith, history was repeating itself. He spearheaded the same kind of program during World War I.

Even to those of us who were not called into the service before the start of the 1942 season, there didn't seem to be an end to the different ways in which the war was beginning to affect baseball, and vice versa.

Players and officials of the major league teams took ten percent of their pay in war bonds. Servicemen and women were allowed to attend games free in most cities in the big leagues. And as hard as it is to believe in this day, when fans seem willing to kill for a foul ball, during the war they actually threw foul balls back onto the field so they could be used again or sent to military bases.

In Cincinnati the admission to a Reds' game was by cigarettes instead of by ticket at a "smokes for servicemen" game. The Louisville Colonels of the American Association collected over two thousand pounds of fat, for use in manufacturing ammunition, at a "waste-fat night."

The two biggest smash hits in baseball during the war were in Washington and New York. In Washington, Shirley Povich of the *Post* showed he could produce and promote as well as he could write. He raised enough money to build a navy cruiser for "the war effort" by staging an exhibition game between the Senators and a team of Navy All-Stars from Norfolk and Newport News in Virginia. I played in that game, and so did Bob Feller, before he was shipped out to the North Atlantic, and others like Phil Rizzuto,

Don Padgett, and Benny McCoy. We were all in the navy and training in Virginia before being shipped overseas.

Povich recruited Kate Smith to stand behind second base and sing "God Bless America." Bing Crosby performed too, and neither of them received any pay for the night.

Then, as his crowning touch, Povich pulled a beaut with Al Schacht, the baseball entertainer, who put on his famous slow-motion pantomime of pitching to an imaginary hitter. When Schacht reached the point in his act where the hitter supposedly hits a home run against him, Babe Ruth—unannounced—dramatically popped out of the dugout and circled the bases.

"I didn't know I was such a showman," Povich says, and the truth is he's not. He's a quiet, modest man who simply could outwrite and outthink almost any other member of his profession.

Shirley's showmanship attracted a capacity crowd of over 30,000 fans to Griffith Stadium and raised more than two million dollars in war bonds to build the warship. It was the second largest amount of money paid for any sports event up to that time. Only the second Dempsey-Tunney fight earned more.

In New York a unique kind of campaign to sell war bonds raised the staggering amount of well over one hundred million dollars—the exact figure was $123,850,000—through the "auctioning" of players from the Yankees, Dodgers, and Giants.

A sponsor would bid an amount in war bonds to "obtain" a certain player in the auction and would pledge to buy even more war bonds based on his player's performance—$2,500 every time the player hit a single, twice that much for a double. Triples went for $7,500, and a home run was good for $10,000, all in war bonds.

The sponsor of a pitcher was committed to buying $25,000 in bonds for every one of the pitcher's victories and $50,000 for each of his shutouts.

Americans all over the country, from school kids to grandparents, were buying twenty-five-cent war-bond stamps and pasting them in books until they added up to $18.75. Then they could turn them in for a bond that would bring them $25.00 on maturity ten years later.

But the New York auction of baseball players was a bond

bonanza. Dixie Walker of the Dodgers lived up to his nickname, the "Peepul's Cherce." He brought the most money of all the players, with one organization bidding $11,250,000 for Walker's performances. A group from the Esso Corporation put up $11 million for Arky Vaughan.

The baseball season itself unfolded with surprises almost every day. We expected the unexpected, with each new day holding the sobering possibility that either you'd get your draft notice in the mail or your roommate might or the guy whose locker was next to yours.

There were 61 major league players in the armed forces when the 1942 season began, 41 from the American League and 20 from the National. The Senators, who finished in seventh place 31 games behind the Yankees in '41, were the hardest hit of all teams in '42. They lost 13 players, including their two greatest stars—Cecil Travis and Buddy Lewis.

Elmer Gedeon, a Senators outfielder, was also in the service in '42. He had only one year in the major leagues and was still trying to make the grade when the war came. He never got the chance. He was killed in France on his twenty-seventh birthday in 1944, the only major league player to be killed in action in World War II.

Feller and Greenberg were two of the biggest stars who were gone then, but many established players were also having their careers interrupted for three years or more because they "answered the call to the colors" in 1942. They included Cookie Lavagetto, Hugh Mulcahy, Billy Cox, Fred Hutchinson, Mickey Harris, and Johnny Berardino.

Maybe the most dramatic scene of them all involved Buddy Lewis. Buddy was a consistent .300 hitter with the Senators who came up to Washington in 1935 as a third baseman and moved to the outfield in 1940. He hit over .300 in three of his first five seasons, lost three years because of service as an Air Corps pilot flying supplies over the Hump in the Himalayas in a C-47 transport plane, and finished his career in 1949 with a .297 lifetime average.

Lewis entered pilot training early in 1942, and when he got his wings at Lawson Field in Georgia and shipped out, he flew his plane into Washington for a final visit with his old team before

209

heading for the China-Burma-India theater. After visiting his teammates at Griffith Stadium, Lewis told his pal, Walt Masterson, to keep his eye toward the sky.

Masterson, who left for the Navy not long after, remembers well what happened next. In the middle of their afternoon game Masterson looked up and saw an Air Force C-47 cargo plane headed toward Griffith Stadium. By Lewis's own admission, he broke every rule in the book. He nosed his plane down and made a dive over the stadium, contrary to all flying safety regulations. "I was down low enough so I could almost read the letters on the uniforms," he said later.

Lewis circled his plane once, then dipped its wing in a farewell salute to his teammates. George Case, a Lewis friend and teammate for five years, was at bat. He looked up at the plane and threw his bat high into the air in a salute of his own.

And then Lieutenant Lewis flew off to war.

Even before the season started, we could see that things were changing. For one of our exhibition games in Tampa against the Reds, the crowd included 2,000 GIs, most of them from McDill Field. At any ball game, there seemed to be more fans in uniform than in civilian clothes. One of the men in training at Tampa to be a bombardier was Sergeant Hank Greenberg.

Even though the draft and enlistments were making a shambles out of every team's roster of players, no team ever filed an appeal or yelled foul about the players it was losing. And not all the players were being drafted, not by a long shot. Although we knew our careers lasted only a few years and that we were in the middle of those years, many of us enlisted. We went voluntarily, without Uncle Sam having to send anybody to come after us.

Every team in organized baseball, including the minor leagues, contributed the proceeds from at least one game to the Army-Navy Relief Fund, which aided widows and orphans of servicemen.

We played two All-Star games in '42, another change from the way things used to be, with each fan buying a one-dollar war-bond stamp. Major league baseball was donating all that baseball equipment under Clark Griffith's program, funded by $100,000 from the All-Star games.

Servicemen and servicewomen, in addition to getting into the wartime games free, also got reduced rates at the concession stands. The Giants and Cubs even made sure those fans who were lucky enough to get passes into the games did their part. They made them buy a twenty-five-cent war-bond stamp. With over 77 home games and all your free admissions, that added up to a pile of stamps for the war effort.

The teams had special arrangements for the fans to take shelter under the stands in the event of an air raid, and right at the end of the first All-Star game, at the Polo Grounds in New York, an air raid drill provided an eerie finish and a picture of the way life in America was changing.

The drill was scheduled for 9:30, so the All-Star game was scheduled as a twilight event, to start at 6:30 and end by 9:10, Eastern War Time. You might not cut it that close today, but in 1941 two hours and forty minutes seemed ample time to play a nine-inning game in the major leagues.

Air raid drills were serious business. Every city conducted them from time to time as practice against the possibility that Germany's or Japan's long-range bombers might try to sneak to our shores under cover of darkness and attack our major cities. Government officials and the general population alike wanted strict compliance. Windows were covered every night during the war with "blackout curtains," the top halves of automobile headlights were painted black, and even the tiny light from a radio dial in a living room could produce a loud knock on the door from a stern air raid warden wearing a white helmet.

The drill this night was going to be practice for all that, plus darkening a lighted stadium. But Mother Nature, showing no favorites in the war, delayed the start of the game with a brief shower, so permission was granted to play until 9:30, the moment the air raid drill was to begin.

The Polo Grounds sat like a giant docked showboat ablaze in its own new lights on the edge of the Harlem River as Ernie Lombardi of the Braves hit a fly ball to Tommy Henrich in right field

211

for the final out. Two minutes later everything went black. The fans were advised to remain in their seats. The American Leaguers, 3–1 victors, couldn't celebrate in the dark. Some players stayed in the dugout. Others were able to make it to the clubhouse beyond the center field fence before the lights went out.

Joe McCarthy, the winning manager, gave an interview in the dark. In the National League clubhouse someone lit a cigarette, immediately followed by the inevitable result—a shout from an air raid warden outside the clubhouse to douse it. Twenty minutes later the lights went on again, life in New York returned to normal, and the usual postgame celebrations and post mortems began.

The American League victory came on three runs off Mort Cooper of the Cardinals in the top half of the first inning—a home run by Rudy York after Henrich doubled, and a bases-empty homer by Lou Boudreau. Mickey Owen got some measure of revenge for the World Series defeat the year before by spoiling our shutout with a homer of his own as a pinch hitter.

Mickey likes to claim that his homer tied him with Babe Ruth in one home run category. "Ruth was the first player to hit a home run in an All-Star game, and I was the first to hit a pinch-hit homer. That ties me with Ruth."

Mickey would be the first to admit that in that other important home run category—home runs in a career—Ruth's total of 714 is 700 more than Mickey had.

The next day we played another All-Star game, this one in Cleveland. This time it was the American Leaguers, as the winners the night before, playing a team of "service All-Stars" managed by Mickey Cochrane, another winning idea from the Baseball Writers' Association.

The city fathers of Cleveland put on a parade and declared the occasion a holiday. Cochrane's team was loaded with ex-major leaguers, but we won the game anyhow, 5–0, over stars like Feller, Greenberg, Berardino, Travis, and Lewis.

The pregame show was just as good as the game, maybe better. In a star-spangled production, tanks and jeeps were on display, a precision drill team of Marines showed its skills, and sailors and Coast Guardsmen formed a huge white "V for victory" at home plate. Governor John Bricker and Mayor Frank Lausche were there, along with 62,092 other fans.

Wartime emotions were at one of their first peaks in those early months of America's involvement in the war, and they showed up on our sports pages as well as everywhere else. In his story about the show in the *Sporting News,* Fred Lieb wrote: "One could feel the patriotic fervor. . . . It sent needles shooting down one's spine. . . . It started honest tears trickling down the cheeks and made one murmur to oneself, 'Thank God I am an American.' "

The two All-Star games in 1942 raised $100,000 for baseballs and bats for our servicemen, an enormous sum then, plus $60,000 for Army and Navy welfare agencies to help America's war widows and orphans.

There was another special event, this one at Yankee Stadium on August 23. Babe Ruth was facing Walter Johnson in an exhibition of baseball immortals as an added attraction before a doubleheader between the Yankees and the Senators, with the money going to Army and Navy relief. There were 69,136 fans in the "house that Ruth built," and every one of them had to pay to get in, including the players.

The catcher was Benny Bengough, one of Babe's teammates on the Yankees in the 1920s and a coach with the Senators during the war. The umpire was Billy Evans, who was behind the plate for Johnson's first major league game in 1907 and again in 1927 when Ruth hit hits sixtieth home run.

Ruth delighted the fans with a "home run" into the lower right field seats during their battle, the last time the two men faced each other on a diamond. After the game someone asked Johnson, then the major league all-time strikeout king and the mildest and most modest man ever to walk the face of the earth, why he hadn't thrown more hard stuff to Ruth in an attempt to strike him out.

Johnson, the man they called "The Big Train" because his fastball seemed to be as fast as a runaway freight, seemed surprised by the question. "The fans didn't come to see me strike anybody out," he said. "They came to see Babe hit a home run."

213

James Dawson wrote in the *New York Times* the next day: "Babe Ruth hit one of his greatest home runs yesterday at the stadium, a typical Ruthian wallop in the interests of freedom and the democratic way of living."

16

ROOKIES AND VICTORY GARDENS

The rosters were taking on a different look already. Almost one-fourth of all the players in the major leagues in 1942—nearly 100 out of 400—were rookies, the most ever. The year's crop included Johnny Pesky, Stan Musial, Hank Borowy, and Willard Marshall.

Pesky was a talented addition to our club. He was twenty-one years old at the start of the season, and we'd heard plenty about him. Playing for the Red Sox farm team in Louisville—and making $350 a month—he was the Most Valuable Player of the American Association in 1941. He grew up in Portland, Oregon, and was the clubhouse boy for Portland when Bobby Doerr made trips there as the second baseman for the Hollywood Stars and I played there with the Seals. In that job he used to shine our shoes.

Johnny became one of the outstanding contact hitters in baseball, after being smart enough to take the advice of Heinie Manush, his manager when he was breaking into the minors at Rocky Mount, North Carolina, in the Piedmont League.

If there was one thing Heinie Manush knew how to do, it was hit a baseball. He enjoyed an extremely successful career for seventeen years in the major leagues as an outfielder. He achieved a .330 lifetime batting average, hit .300 eleven times, and led the league in

1926 with Detroit, hitting .378. That wasn't the only time he hit .378. He did it again in 1928 with the Browns, but he lost the batting championship by a single percentage point to Goose Goslin of the Senators.

When Pesky was breaking in, Manush advised him to be a singles hitter "instead of hitting fly balls to the other team's outfielders."

Johnny reached the rare level of 200 hits in each of his first three seasons in the major leagues, and he wasn't hitting wartime pitching. In his first year up with us there were still a lot of quality pitchers in the American League. Then he went into the Navy, at the same time Ted and I did, and when he came back for his second and third 200-hit seasons, it was after the war and all the star pitchers were back, plus some new ones.

Pesky was an immediate success in '42, hitting .331 and playing 147 games at shortstop. Cronin's playing career was approaching its final years, and he began devoting more time to his duties as our manager. Besides, Joe had a third job. He was an aircraft observer in Boston at an airplane-spotting observation tower as a member of the aircraft warning service.

Some of the rest of us also volunteered for this job. In those less complicated days, aircraft observers stood in high wooden towers and scanned the sky for enemy aircraft. Radar was still in the developmental stage and we were decades away from spy satellites, so the observers used binoculars. There was always a nagging thought at the back of my mind that by the time I saw an enemy airplane through a pair of binoculars, it would be too late anyhow. But in World War II you did what you could.

After getting to play in that many games as a rookie and then surviving the challenges of the war, Pesky came back to hit .335 in our pennant-winning season of '46 and compiled a total of six .300-plus seasons in a ten-year career. His lifetime average was .307. But he didn't look that promising when he broke in. We used to play the Braves for the "city championship" in Boston on the final weekend before the start of the season, and in '42, as a rookie trying to make "the big club," Johnny made four errors in one game.

"I was sure I was headed back to Louisville," he says, "so I went to Mass the next morning. I didn't make an error for another eighteen games."

Pesky's most vivid memory of his rookie year was a game late in the season when he was facing Spud Chandler of the Yankees. He was hitting .340 and tearing up the league, but he was 0 for 14 against Chandler when he found himself the hitter with our catcher, Bill Conroy, and me on base.

"Williams was telling me to stop trying to pull the ball against Chandler," Johnny remembers. "He said, 'I'm a foot taller than you are and forty pounds heavier and *I* can't even pull it, so how the hell can you expect to? You're hitting those weak little ground balls to Gordon at second. It's got to be up the middle or to left. That's your stroke anyway.' Then, for good measure, as he always did in case you missed his point, he said, 'Don't be so damned *dumb.*'

"Just as I step into the batter's box, Ted yells, 'Besides, you *know* they're not going to walk you and have to pitch to me.' " Johnny says he was embarrassed beyond words. "Well, I damn near died. I looked up and said a silent prayer: 'Dear God—'

"I was looking for Chandler's hard slider, and I got it. I managed to hit it into left field, a little humpbacked line drive, but it scored both runners. Now Chandler is stalking around the mound and calling me every name in the book. Finally, the first base umpire, Bill McGowan, says to Chandler, 'C'mon, let's go. You made a lousy pitch and the kid got a base hit.'

"I felt insulted all over again. 'Jeez, Bill,' I said, 'it was on the black.' And of course Chandler is madder than ever and gives me another blast from his mouth.

"Before Ted steps in, he looks down at me and points his finger to his chest as if to say, 'See? Listen to me, dummy.' Then he hits the first pitch thirty rows into the bleachers.

"I was so pumped up I hustled around the bases and was in the far end of the dugout sitting next to Bobby Doerr when Ted is still between second and third. All the guys are jumping up and down and screaming about Ted's home run, and I say to Bobby,

217

'Nobody's saying anything about my hit. It was the big blow of the inning.'

"By now Ted has circled the bases and he's trotting back to our dugout and saying, 'Where's that horn-nosed little shortstop of ours?'

"I waved my hand from the opposite corner of the dugout, like a kid in class, and he comes over and says, 'Didn't I tell you how to hit Chandler?'

"I said, 'Let me tell you something, Ted—Chandler was so damn mad at me for getting that dinky little single that he forgot you were the next hitter.'

"Ted looks at me for a moment and says, 'You know, you might have something there.' "

Joe, Ted and I were among the lucky ones after the 1941 season. It wouldn't be our last one for the duration of the war, just our next to last. All three of us went into the service after the '42 season. Joe joined the Army, Ted signed up with the Navy and later became a Marine fighter pilot, and I enlisted in the Navy. We didn't make it back until most of the rest of the guys did, in time for the 1946 season.

Military service dealt a blow to the Yankees. Tommy Henrich signed up early in the season, like most of us, and then waited to be called to duty. He was called into the Coast Guard in August, and the Yankees were left to repeat as American League champions and prepare for their World Series against the Cardinals without their starting right fielder.

Tommy also remembers that he took some ribbing from his teammates in '42 because of his German ancestry. There was sort of a "virus" going around the country then, kind of a low-grade fever infecting some Americans. It wasn't a great time to be German or Japanese, or Italian either for that matter. Some people— not many, but a few—who were cheerful friends and neighbors before the war began putting some distance between you and them. Tommy says today he "got nicked a little bit by my teammates." But, being a class guy, he knew his teammates were kidding, so he accepted their needling in that manner.

Henrich's departure for military service in the middle of the Yankees' stretch drive for the American League pennant was typical of how the war was beginning to affect many major league teams. Enos Slaughter of the Cards was luckier. He enlisted on August 27 but wasn't called to active duty until January. "That's the only reason I got to play in the '42 Series," he says.

Country made the most of his chance while he was waiting for his call into the service. He hit .318, his fourth straight .300 season after beginning his major league career five years earlier, led the National League in hits and triples, scored 100 runs, batted in 98, and got some big hits in the series, including a home run, as the Cardinals upset the Yankees in five games.

Then, like so many of us—boom!—he was off to war, and left to wonder if he'd ever play baseball again. His one consolation was that he had played so well in his five seasons and had starred in the World Series.

Even the Series was a bittersweet experience because he knew service in the war was in the immediate future. He remembers that the World Series triumph "was a happy moment, but a sad one." Regardless of whatever success ball players were having that year, almost all of us knew that our days on a baseball diamond were numbered.

At the end of the '42 season we were still wondering what it would take to beat New York. Ted won the Triple Crown that year—a .356 batting average, 36 home runs, and 137 runs batted in. I hit .286 and led the American League's center fielders in putouts, assists, double plays, and chances per game. Pesky had his rookie average of .331, Doerr hit .290 and had 15 homers, and Tex Hughson led the league's pitchers with 22 wins.

But we still didn't beat out those Yankees. Gordon hit .322, my brother Joe was second on the team with .305 including 21 homers, and Keller hit .292 with 26 homers. Tiny Bonham had a sensational year with 21 victories and only 5 defeats to lead the league in won-lost percentage.

In the National League, Mickey Owen had been impressed with the attendance in Brooklyn, war or no war, and never mind that the stars were disappearing. "In 1942," he says, "we filled the ball park every day. On Sundays the sidewalks near Ebbets Field would be filled with people for several blocks, walking away because they couldn't get in—and the ball park hadn't even opened yet."

In the minor leagues some things never changed. Eddie Lopat was pitching for Oklahoma City in 1942, and the booming wartime economy wasn't helping at all. "The owners had to sell a player every month to meet their expenses, and we always got paid eight to ten days late."

As most of us either left for the war or prepared to, things began changing for every American. "Victory gardens" began sprouting up in backyards and on downtown squares, wherever there was a vacant plot of ground. The idea was suggested by Roosevelt's Secretary of Agriculture, Claude Wickard, who encouraged Americans to grow their own vegetables so the yield from America's farms could feed the military population.

Victory gardens could be found in places like the Portland [Oregon] zoo, Arlington Park, a racetrack in Chicago, and the Cook County jail. By 1943, there were twenty million victory gardens across the country that produced forty percent of all the vegetables grown in the United States.

Civilians turned in scrap iron, flattened tin cans, silk and nylon stockings, waste paper, tires and toothpaste tubes—all of it for recycling into war materials.

In Boston during the 1942 season there was a black-tie scrap-iron party to which various guests brought a horse-drawn buggy, a Gatling gun from the Civil War, and the personal rowing machine of Massachusetts Governor Leverett Saltonstall.

A Seattle shoemaker donated six tons of rubber heels to the war effort, and the people of Los Angeles collected 5,000 tons of car tires. The Boy Scouts produced 150,000 tons of waste paper by June 1942, and their drive had to be temporarily halted so the paper mills could catch up with the overflow of paper being recycled.

The most severe adjustment was caused by rationing. The War

Production Board issued a directive restricting the sale of gasoline, and the kind of gas ration card you had determined how much gas you could get. Most of us had an "A" card, which meant you could buy three gallons a week. You couldn't very well drive to spring training on that. Even before the rationing was ordered, the Secretary of the Interior, Harold Ickes, urged the public to reduce its driving as much as possible to save gasoline. He asked gas stations to close early, but the New Jersey legislature passed a resolution condemning the idea as harmful to its tourist industry.

Those of us employed in the eastern states felt the gasoline pinch first largely because German U-boats were sinking the oil tankers supplying the East Coast. Gas rationing in seventeen eastern states was ordered, effective May 15, and it was extended to the rest of the nation in December. A national speed limit was put into effect—forty miles an hour. It was further reduced to a "victory speed" of thirty-five by the end of 1942.

Food was rationed, too, and you needed stamps with point values to buy almost every kind of food. Ham was fifty-one cents a pound—plus seven points. Pineapple juice was twenty-two points for a 46-ounce can. Hamburger was seven points, but if you wanted to put tomato catsup on it, that would cost fifteen additional points.

Rationing made sense, and we didn't protest. At least the ball players who couldn't get any more steaks for breakfast weren't griping. But rationing also created a monster bureaucracy. No wonder that eventually twenty-five percent of all retail business in the country would be done on the "black market," where people either bought stolen goods or got them without surrendering the necessary rationing points. The biggest black market business was in cigarettes, meat, canned food, and shoes.

Money took on a different look too. Pennies weren't made out of copper, a much-needed metal for the war effort. They were made from zinc-coated steel instead and had a silvery look.

America began singing songs like "I Left My Heart at the Stage-Door Canteen" and "We Did It Before and We Can Do It Again." One of the most popular melodies was only four notes, the opening of Beethoven's Fifth Symphony. They became the musical

221

version of the three dots and the dash in Morse code that represent the letter *V.* Beethoven's "da-da-da-dum" helped to create a new slogan:

. . . —

V FOR VICTORY

It was played on the radio, and shown in movie theaters as part of the drive to encourage Americans to buy war bonds and quickly became one of the best known "melodies" in the country.

On our road trips, when we went to the movies to see *Yankee Doodle Dandy* with Jimmy Cagney or *See Here, Private Hargrove* or *Mrs. Miniver, Bambi,* or *Holiday Inn,* we also saw Bugs Bunny singing "Any Bonds Today?" as he and Mel Blanc did their part for the war effort. And you could buy war bonds in the lobby on your way out.

Things were changing in the baseball broadcast booth too. Radio announcers were warned not to say anything that might accidentally provide aid and comfort to the enemy. The weather was an example. Information on meteorological conditions might help the enemy in making decisions about possible bombing raids.

Dizzy Dean heard from his bosses after telling his listeners in St. Louis that it was raining at the ball park. The next time a game was called because of rain, Ol' Diz told his listeners, "Well, folks, they ain't gonna play anymore today. I can't tell you the reason, but if you'll just stick your head out the window, I think you'll be able to figure it out for yourself."

Baseball wasn't the only sport being affected. The 1942 Army-Navy football game, traditionally played in Philadelphia, was moved to Annapolis. Tickets were sold only to people who lived within a ten-mile radius of the Naval Academy stadium.

Our days as civilians grew shorter in number as the war grew hotter. The Japanese captured Bataan, Corregidor, and the Philippines, but our planes defeated the Japanese in the Battle of the Coral Sea and halted Japan's advance. In April, just as our season was starting, Jimmy Doolittle led his gutsy squadron of B-25 bombers over Tokyo, sending the government and the people of Japan a message that we could reach them when we felt so inclined.

The Marines invaded Guadalcanal as the armed forces began the strategy of "island-hopping," winning strategic islands from the Japanese in a campaign to retake our position in the Pacific one key island at a time. Across the Atlantic, the first B-17s, or "Flying Fortresses," made bombing raids over Nazi-occupied Europe.

The draft age was lowered to eighteen, another sign that we were as good as gone. The Women's Auxiliary Corps was established for each branch of the armed forces. Satin flags of white with a red border and gold trim began appearing in the windows of homes all over America to signify that a son, brother, or husband was serving in uniform, or a daughter, sister, or wife. Each man or woman in uniform was represented by a blue star on the white background. A gold star meant the family's GI wouldn't be coming home.

All around us we saw government posters boosting the war effort:

WHEN YOU RIDE ALONE,
YOU RIDE WITH HITLER!
—JOIN A CAR-SHARING CLUB TODAY!

IS THIS TRIP NECESSARY?

A SLIP OF THE LIP
CAN SINK A SHIP!

SWAP RIDES TO WORK,
SAVE YOUR CAR
FOR THE LONG PULL!

Rationing and car-pooling began to work. Gasoline consumption dropped twenty percent in 1942 and another twenty percent in '43.

●

When Ted and I signed up for the Navy early in the '42 season, we were assigned to the reserves and allowed to continue playing baseball until we were called to active duty. On September 27, Tex Hughson won his twenty-second game of the year as we defeated the Yankees in Fenway Park, 7–6, on the last day of the season.

The Navy was about to order Ted, Johnny Pesky, and me to report for duty. World War II was starting for all three of us. Hughson's victory was more than just the last game of the season for us. It was our last game period, until Johnny and the rest of us came marching home again.

— 17 —

"THEY'RE EITHER TOO YOUNG OR TOO OLD"

Toward the end of 1942, the manpower shortage was handicapping every business on the "home front," including baseball, and it kept getting worse. By the end of 1944, 470 major league players had "answered the call to the colors." That was seventy more than the number of active players on major league rosters in both leagues. The figure exceeded 500 before the end of the war. Johnny Mize tried to reduce the number by one. He was in the Navy during the 1943–44–45 seasons. While he was stationed in the Pacific, he told his commanding officer, "If you let me go back to civilian life, I'll send you a check every month for the same amount you're paying me."

His skipper said no.

By 1944 more than sixty percent of those of us who were in the starting lineup on opening day of the 1941 season were in the service. More than 4,000 players in the minor leagues were also called to military duty.

But baseball endured. The 1945 All-Star game was canceled, but that was the only casualty. Both leagues played their usual 154-game schedule every season, and the World Series was held every year.

There was one noticeable difference—the players. Women filled in for men in the civilian jobs, building the ships, tanks, and planes for "our fighting men," and one of the most popular songs was "Rosie, the Riveter." But women couldn't relieve the manpower problem in baseball. Another hit song of the day voiced the complaint many girls had about the men who were left at home: "They're Either Too Young or Too Old." Baseball fans could have sung the same song.

The pitchers ranged in age from fifteen-year-old Joe Nuxhall of the Reds to forty-two-year-old Johnny Niggeling of the Senators. In 1944, the Senators tried to relieve their manpower problems with two imports from New York, a seventeen-year-old third baseman named Eddie Yost, straight from the sandlots of Queens, and thirty-six-year-old Eddie Boland, who was discovered playing right field for the New York City Sanitation Department. Because teams were prohibited from traveling to Florida, Connie Mack's Philadelphia A's opened spring training at Frederick, Maryland, with players that included a pitcher with heart trouble and an outfielder with three toes.

Bob Feller was asked how the players in the armed forces, the *real* major leaguers, felt about the ragtag collection of kids, old men, and 4-Fs who were masquerading as big league baseball players. He said, "There are some things at home that we griped about, but a few hundred 4-Fs and overage men playing baseball wasn't one of them."

Fresco Thompson of the Dodgers remembered that Branch Rickey made sure Brooklyn continued a full-scale scouting effort during the war even though most of the other teams had cut back these operations—or maybe *because* they had. "The other clubs dropped all but about five of their scouts," he said. "They figured there wasn't any sense in signing young players who would soon be drafted."

Rickey, however, never let up. "Mr. Rickey said, 'We'll gamble. We'll sign every good young player we can get our hands on.' We had no competition. We picked up Duke Snider, Carl Erskine, Clem Labine, Gil Hodges, Rex Barney, Carl Furillo, and dozens of others."

The Dodgers trained at Bear Mountain, New York, in 1944. While other teams were struggling to put nine men on the field, 200 players were in the Dodgers' camp, most of them peach-fuzzed kids waiting to be drafted into the army. The inn at Bear Mountain was called "the day nursery." In the evenings, instead of the players heading for the bars like some of their prewar counterparts, they were taken to the movies on a team bus. Brooklyn's traveling secretary, Harold Parrott, said, "I was used to players coming to me for advances on their salaries, but Duke Snider was the first player who ever asked me for candy money."

The teams that escaped serious damage were the teams to beat, but that varied from one season to the next. Teams that were out of the pennant race one year were contenders the next if they were able to avoid losing too many players while other teams had their ranks depleted.

The Washington Senators were an example—second in 1943, last in '44, and second in '45. The Browns finished sixth in 1943, 8 games below .500. The next year they were 24 games over .500 and won the pennant. The Cubs went from 75–79 in '44 to 98–56 and the World Series in '45, all because of the way the draft was reshaping the rosters from one year to the next.

The shortage of prewar players was enough of a burden for the fans, but they had to suffer through a shortage of prewar writers too. The sportswriters had gone off to war with the rest of us, as war correspondents in Europe and the South Pacific. There were so many of them in the Pacific they could have formed their own chapter of the Baseball Writers' Association of America.

Gordon Cobbledick of the *Cleveland Plain Dealer,* Don Donaghee of the *Philadelphia Bulletin,* Shirley Povich of the *Washington Post,* John Lardner—who once wrote: "While Jones is not a very good fielder, neither can he hit"—Bob Sherrod of *The Saturday Evening Post* and Bob Ruark of Scripps-Howard all left the press boxes of the major league ball parks to cover the war in the Pacific.

The few major leaguers from the prewar era who had not been called in 1942 were gone sooner or later. Bobby Doerr, married and a father, was drafted into the infantry, served for a year and a half, missed the Battle of the Bulge in Europe by a week, and was in training in the South Pacific for the invasion of Japan when the war ended.

Johnny Vander Meer went into the service in 1944 and missed that season and '45. For Vandie, the war was a doubly disappointing development in his career. In 1939, after pitching his back-to-back no-hitters the season before, Johnny hurt his pitching arm. The injury cost him most of the 1939 season and almost all of 1940. He made a comeback late that year and even got to pitch three shutout innings in the World Series for Cincinnati when the Reds defeated the Detroit Tigers in seven games.

He continued his comeback with sensational success by leading the league in strikeouts for the next three seasons, only to have his career interrupted again, this time by a world war. He was thirty years old when he entered the service, which gave him an uncertain future in baseball, to say the least. But he made it through the war and returned to pitch in the major leagues for six more years, finishing his bright career with 119 victories.

Two of the most publicized players to make it to the big leagues during the war were Pete Gray and Bert Shepard. What Shepard accomplished was remarkable, although Gray is probably better remembered.

Gray lost his right arm just above the elbow in a childhood accident, but he didn't let that stop him from playing baseball. By the time the war came along, he was playing professionally in the low minors, a left-handed hitter and an outfielder who would catch a fly ball, stuff his glove under his stump, roll the ball onto his chest, and then throw it back to the infield, all quickly enough to keep base runners from getting any ideas.

In 1944 Gray had an outstanding season with the Memphis Chicks of the Southern Association. He hit .333, stole 68 bases, and was voted the league's Most Valuable Player. The War Department made movies of him in action and showed them to wounded GIs in our military hospitals.

In '45 he played major league baseball with the St. Louis Browns, the previous year's pennant winners, appearing in 77 games, hitting .218, and making 162 catches in the outfield. He threw out three base runners. He encountered one serious problem that he simply was unable to overcome, and Walt Masterson remembers what it was: "He couldn't adjust to the curve ball."

Gray could hit the fastball, but every hitter knows you have to be ready for the fastball but be able to check your swing and wait that extra split second longer if it's a curve. But Gray, holding the bat with only one hand, wasn't able to do that. As a result, he was swinging early at the curve, out in front of the pitch, and when the American League pitchers found this out, Gray's days in the majors were numbered.

At that level, even with wartime players, Gray was also deprived of one of his greatest offensive weapons, the bunt. In the minors he could lay one down the third base line or drag one past the pitcher and leg it out. In the majors he couldn't get away with that as often as he did in the minors. The third basemen began playing in on him, knowing he wasn't a threat to hit the ball past them because he simply didn't have the power.

Gray's manager, Luke Sewell, was candid on the subject: "The Browns bought him partly as a gate attraction. He didn't belong in the major leagues, and he knew he was being exploited."

Gray himself admitted that his major league horizon was limited. "I knew I couldn't stay up too long," he said. "I didn't have the power. It seemed I hit a lot of line drives that they'd catch ten or fifteen feet from the fence. Far, but just not quite far enough."

Bert Shepard's story was different. He was a minor league pitcher before the war who enlisted in the Air Force and was shot down over Germany in his P-38 Thunderbolt fighter plane. He crash-landed at 380 miles an hour, and was wounded in his right leg below the knee. He had been shot in the chin too, and also suffered a fractured skull.

The German doctors saved his life by amputating his leg. While a prisoner of war, he began practicing baseball on a crude artificial leg made by a fellow POW. He fielded ground balls, took batting practice, worked on his pitching motion as a left-hander—and made sure he could field bunts.

229

After his liberation from prison camp as the Allies closed in on the Nazi army, Shepard was a patient at Walter Reed Army Medical Center in Washington. Clark Griffith heard about him, gave him a tryout, and signed him to a contract as a player-coach in March 1945.

He pitched against the Dodgers in an exhibition game and was the starting and winning pitcher. Later that season, in a game against the Red Sox in a season when every game was crucial because the Senators were battling the Tigers for the pennant, Bert Shepard became a major league baseball player.

Before 13,000 fans at Griffith Stadium, Shepard entered the game as a relief pitcher in the fourth inning with the bases loaded and two out. Pitching on a new artificial leg, he struck out George "Catfish" Metkovich and received a standing ovation as he walked toward the Senators' dugout on the first base side of the field.

Shepard finished the game for the Senators, pitching 5⅓ innings and giving up only 3 hits and one run. He struck out 3, walked one and threw out 2 hitters on ground balls.

It would be nice to say that Bert went on to pitch for years in the major leagues, but he never played in another big league game. He had to undergo five more operations in the next three years, spending his time in hospital beds instead of on major league baseball diamonds.

He did pitch for the American League All-Stars on postseason barnstorming trips. He twice faced Bob Feller's All-Stars and once struck out Stan Musial.

He played in the minors after his operations, and with success. Amazingly, he stole 5 bases one season. In one game, when the hitters on the other team weren't able to do anything against his pitches, they laid down 9 bunts against him. He threw them all out.

His attitude on the subject of bunts tells you why he was able to make it to the big leagues—"If they had done that all game long, I would have had a perfect game."

On June 10, 1944, Joe Nuxhall of the Cincinnati Reds achieved his distinction of being the youngest player in the history of major league baseball. At Crosley Field his manager, Bill McKechnie, sent him in to pitch against the Cardinals in relief.

Nuxhall admits he was throwing the ball "all over the damn place" while warming up in the bullpen with catcher Al Lakeman, and he became even more nervous after being signaled into the game to start the ninth inning.

After getting two outs, "I started realizing what was going on. Here I am pitching against a junior high school two weeks before and now I'm pitching against the potential world champions. After that, all hell broke loose."

Five walks and two hits later, a compassionate McKechnie walked to the mound and told the teenager: "Son, I think you've had enough."

The record shows Nuxhall pitched two-thirds of an inning in 1944, with an earned run average for the season of 67.50. He did better after that. He was back in the big leagues with the Reds in 1952 and enjoyed a highly successful career, pitching for 16 seasons and winning 135 games.

How did Nuxhall as a kid feel on that shell-shocked day in '44 when McKechnie finally took him out of the game? "I tended to agree with him."

— 18 —

THE GROWING GLORY

When we came marching home after V-J Day, it was to be the happiest kind of return for the Red Sox—we finally beat the Yankees and won the 1946 American League pennant. We buried them by 17 games. They weren't even second. The Tigers were, 12 games behind us. At one point our record was 55 wins and only 10 losses.

We put it together right from the beginning. Williams hit the first pitch of spring training over the fence and had a .342 season. Pesky came back to hit .335, and I hit .316. Of the top five hitters in the American League, we were three of them.

Johnny and I became the Red Sox "table setters"—setting the table for Ted. When he came up, you could expect one or both of us to be on base ready for him to drive us in. Teddy drove in 123 runs that year. In addition to his high average and RBI total, he hit 38 home runs. Bobby Doerr chipped in with 18 and Rudy York with 17.

One reason for our American League championship was that most of the Red Sox players were lucky enough to be able to resume playing at our prewar level of performance. The Yankees, on the other hand, experienced problems.

Tommy Henrich says: "I had a lousy season. I was champing

at the bit to get out and play. My number one concern was how well am I going to play? How much do I have left? I found out I had a lot of rust to chip off."

Charlie Keller hit .275 with 30 home runs and 101 runs batted in, but he says most of his success came in the first half of the season. He never had any doubt in spring training about his ability to play up to his 1941 standard. One reason for his confidence was that he was married and had a family. On the possibility that he might not be up to his prewar levels of playing, he says: "I just couldn't afford to have that happen. I had a good half year, but then I ran out of gas. I still had my sea legs."

There wasn't a .300 hitter on the Yankee team in that first year back from the war. Joe was New York's leading hitter with .290. Joe Gordon, the star of the 1941 World Series, hit .210. Phil Rizzuto dropped to .257, 27 points below his last season in '42 and 50 points from his rookie average in '41. Tommy Henrich and Snuffy Stirnweiss both hit .251, but that was a drop of 58 points for Stirnweiss from the year before, when he won the 1945 league batting championship with .309.

Spud Chandler was a 20-game winner for the Yankees that year, but Bill Bevens, with 16 wins, was the only other pitcher on their staff who won more than 11 games. The first casualty of all this was Joe McCarthy, who was replaced as the Yankees' manager after 35 games. Bill Dickey took over for the next 105 games, and then he was succeeded by Johnny Neun, who managed the team for the final 14 games of the year.

With their players still working to reach prewar levels, and with three managers in one season, it's small wonder the Yankees finished so far back. The next year they reached their usual level of excellence, and Bucky Harris managed them to the pennant and victory in the World Series—over the Dodgers again.

Enos Slaughter's 1946 season was more like those of us on the Red Sox, so it probably should have been no surprise that our teams won the pennants and met in the World Series.

Slaughter returned from the service by leading both leagues in runs batted in with 130 and hitting .300 right on the button with 18 home runs. He was second behind Stan Musial in the National League in runs scored and second to Stan in total bases. Then he capped off his outstanding year by dashing home in the seventh game of the Series to win baseball's championship for his team.

Bob Feller was another one who didn't miss a beat. He was discharged from the Navy late in the '45 season after three years and eight months in the service. He struck out the first batter he faced, and in 1946 he was just as invincible as he was in '41. The former schoolboy from Iowa was approaching his twenty-eighth birthday by the time the '46 season ended. He won 26 games for the Indians and led the American League's pitchers in games, games started, complete games, innings pitched, and strikeouts. He tied Hal Newhouser of the Tigers for the most wins in either league and led both leagues in shutouts and strikeouts.

I always admired that about Feller, Slaughter, Williams, Mickey Vernon, Pesky, and the rest of the returning GIs who were able to perform so well after being gone so long. We had added pressure on us, because we knew that those war years were lost forever. Lawyers and accountants coming home from the war would be able to pursue their careers for another thirty years, but the limited number of years available to us in our chosen profession had been reduced to an even lower number.

We never knew what that number was because it was going to be a different one for each of us, but we knew that what was going to be a short career anyhow was going to be even shorter now. We couldn't afford to spend a couple of years getting our sharpness back. A ten-year career in the major leagues is far above the average length, and if a player lost three of those ten years because of military service, that's thirty percent of his career.

The most surprising news in baseball in 1946 occurred off the field. That was when Brooklyn's Branch Rickey announced the Dodgers had signed baseball's first black player—Jackie Robinson —and assigned him to their Triple-A farm team in Montreal. But there was another surprise too—and this one was on the field— when Mickey Vernon of the Senators beat out Ted, my brother, and everybody else to win the American League batting championship with a .353 average. While everyone was having fun speculating on which one of the prewar stars would win the title, along came Mickey. To prove it wasn't a fluke, he did it again in 1953. In the National League, Stan Musial won the 1946 title with .365, but that wasn't any surprise. It was already Stan's second championship, and he won five more after that.

The postwar changes in baseball continued, but for us, one of the changes was strictly temporary. The Red Sox traveled by plane on our first western swing of the '46 season, but from the second trip on, all of our travel was by train again. One of the reporters covering us, Jack Malaney, wrote that the Sox were "putting too many eggs in one basket. Too many of the players, which includes some who did plenty of flying during the war, were far from comfortable flying." Tom Yawkey, our owner, decided there would be no more flying that year.

Joe and I picked up right where we left off in our brotherly competition. We were playing a three-game series against each other in New York in mid-May when Joe leaped against the wall in Yankee Stadium and robbed me of a triple. As I trotted out to center field at the end of the inning and he trotted in, he called over to me, "It's 32-21." We had kept score of the number of times we took hits away from each other, going back to 1940. In '46 we resumed the counting.

I was winning, but there was a good reason for that. Joe used to hit more long fly balls than I did, so I had more chances. But I felt compelled to point out to one of the Boston writers, Bill Fay, "in the last Series, I sent him back farther than he sent me."

Pesky, the one we called "Needle Nose," and I were having a high old time together. He's still a good-looking guy today, but we always called him by that nickname because of his sharp nose, and that was fine with Johnny. He still calls me on the phone and identifies himself by saying in his cheerful voice, "This is Needles."

After playing together for a while, Johnny and I could manufacture a run in various ways. One of our favorite tricks, if I was on first, was for Johnny to bunt down the third base line. He was as skilled at bunting as he was at hitting, and had the ability to "kill" the ball on a bunt, bouncing it to the turf with no spin on it so it wouldn't roll. Defending players had to run in for it, and by that time we'd both be safe.

Sometimes when I was on first and Johnny dropped one down the third base line, forcing the third baseman to come in to field it, I'd keep going around second and make third because the third baseman hadn't gotten back to the bag yet. But Bill Dickey got wise eventually. One day we tried the same stunt, and as soon as Snuffy Stirnweiss, the Yankees' third baseman, came in to field the ball, I continued streaking around second—but when I came steaming into third, there was Dickey with the ball, waiting to tag me out. He had run down to third from behind the plate as Stirnweiss came in for the ball and had taken the throw across the diamond from first base in plenty of time to nail me.

When I slid into third, I was the most surprised person in the ball park. I said, "What the hell are you doing here?"

He was laughing as he put the tag on me and said, "Gotcha this time."

In the summer of '46 we had every reason to believe that things were going to be just the way they were in 1941. The world had been made safe for democracy again, we were back in our civilian jobs, and the fans were flocking to the ball parks in happy numbers. Those of us who were lucky enough to be major league baseball players were picking up a bat to challenge Bob Feller again, feeling the therapeutic sunshine of spring training in Florida and enduring —even enjoying—those thirty-six-hour train trips from Boston to St. Louis and the sweaty, steamy fun of a doubleheader on the Fourth of July. America, including baseball, was picking up where it left off.

It seemed like 1941 all over again, but it wasn't. The changes in baseball set into motion by the war were still coming. At times they seemed to come in tidal waves—more and more night games, airplanes, TV, integration, teams moving to other cities.

Even with the changes from their world of 1941, the men who made baseball history in that historical year continued their success in the postwar years and then gradually began to fade from the player ranks. Of the five men who played pivotal roles in that historic season—Joe, Ted, Hugh Casey, Mickey Owen, and Tommy Henrich—Ted outlasted all of them. He maintained his unique skills until he was forty-two years old, retiring after the 1960 season with a .344 lifetime average, the sixth highest in history. He continued to coach the Red Sox hitters in spring training, later became manager of the Washington Senators and Texas Rangers, and also became one of the world's great authorities on fishing. Today he makes personal appearances and divides his spare time, what little he has, and his lures, which he has plenty of, between Florida and Canada.

My brother Joe completed his career in 1951, a major league star for thirteen seasons who led his team to ten American League pennants. It is a great tribute to his ability as a player and his success as a leader that those pennant winners won nine of their ten World Series. Since his Hall of Fame career, Joe has traveled around the world and has won recognition as baseball's most prominent goodwill ambassador.

Joe and I enjoyed six more parallel years as American League center fielders after the war until his retirement. When he played his last game in a Yankee uniform, except for a few old-timers' games, I was with him. We were on an All-Star team playing exhibition games in Japan following the 1951 season. It was the ninth inning of our last game, and I got a base hit. Joe hit a home run behind me in his last time at bat. When he returned to our dugout, Joe said, "That's it, boys. I'm taking off the uniform for the last time."

I played for two more seasons and then retired after being able to play in only three games of the 1953 season because of an eye problem. I started a business career immediately, opening a textile manufacturing company specializing in making carpeting for automobile floors. Emily and I were blessed with three children, and we now divide our time between our home on Buzzards Bay in Massachusetts and our winter home in Florida.

Tommy Henrich continued to perform as "Old Reliable" for

five seasons after the war, retiring in 1950 after eleven seasons. He reached the majors in 1937, one year after Joe, played his entire career with the Yankees, and retired one year before Joe, making him Joe's teammate longer than any other man. He went into the beer business back home in Columbus, Ohio, became successful in that business and in public relations, and now enjoys golf in the Arizona sun with his wife, Eileen.

Hugh Casey, whose curve ball Tommy couldn't reach in the 1941 World Series, was the only tragic figure of those who played key roles in 1941. Ten years later, upset over the apparent breakup of his marriage and the target of a paternity suit, Casey took his life with a shotgun while his estranged wife pleaded frantically over the phone. She told police, "He was just as calm about it as if he was about to walk out on the ball field and pitch a game."

Mickey Owen played in the short-lived Mexican League after the war, missing the 1946, '47, and '48 seasons, but he still compiled a major league career that lasted through 1954. The 1941 season was his only World Series appearance. After baseball he returned to his native Missouri, where he operated a baseball school and was elected sheriff of Greene County four times.

At age seventy-four, he's two pounds under his playing weight thanks to a strict routine of walking twenty-five miles a week and doing exercises. He remains a student of our sport, poring over *The Baseball Encyclopedia* every evening to compile charts showing trends, tendencies, and evaluations of players and teams, past and present.

Today the changes in baseball go on—covered stadiums with fake grass, million-dollar salaries, player strikes, designated hitters, playoffs before the World Series. Even the uniforms are different, with names on the back and numbers on the front. It's still baseball, and God bless it. But it's not the way it used to be, and it's not the way we were—any of us.

That's why the 1941 season has grown across the years and the decades into something special—historic yet legendary, so long ago yet so recent, so hazy in our memories yet so clear, so distant from us yet to close to us, something we miss yet something that has never left us.

Nineteen forty-one has become a baseball monument, the season of unmatched glory that shines still brighter with the coming of each spring, like the men who were its heroes.